CW01213166

Finding Freedom

Finding Freedom

Texts from the Theravadin, Mahayana
and Dzogchen Buddhist traditions

introduced and translated by
James Low

Wandel Verlag berlin 2019

Khordong Commentary Series XIV

Thangka painting on p.185 with friendly permission: Yama Dharmaraja, Tibet; 19th century, Pigments on cloth, Rubin Museum of Art, Gift of Shelley & Donald Rubin Foundation F1997.31.7 (HAR 404). The line drawings included in this book are taken with friendly permission of Robert Beer from his book "The Encyclopedia of Tibetan Symbols and Motifs" published by Serindia Publications, London. Frontispiece by Eberhard Grossgasteiger, twitter.com/eberhardgross

ISBN: 978-3-942380-27-0

© 2019 James Low
published by edition khordong at **WANDEL VERLAG** berlin

First edition, 2019

All rights reserved. No part of this book may be reproduced in any form without prior written permission of the publisher.

Printed by SDL in Berlin, EU on FSC certified 100% acid-, wood- & chlorine-free, biodegradable, recyclable, long-lasting paper, conforming to ANSI standard.
We are supporting NatureFund for planting trees: Blue Planet Certificate 105WN

Cover design and layout by Andreas Ruft, Berlin.

edition khordong is the publication series established by the german non-profit Khordong e.V., inspired by the late Kyabjé Chimed Rigdzin Rinpoche (1922-2002), published by **WANDEL VERLAG** berlin.

Please visit our websites:
Web: khordong.net   tsagli.de   wandel-verlag.de   simplybeing.co.uk
Contact: edition@khordong.net   mail@wandel-verlag.de

Wandel Verlag berlin 2019

CONTENTS

Preface	7
General Introduction	9

SECTION 1 FIGHT THE GOOD FIGHT

Introduction to The Dhammapada	19
The Dhammapada	27
Notes	87

SECTION 2 MISTAKEN IDENTITIES

Introduction to Sharp Weapon Wheel	117
Foreword by C R Lama to Sharp Weapon Wheel	139
Sharp Weapon Wheel – *in format for recitation*	143

SECTION 3 SWEET SIMPLICITY

Introduction to Sweet Simplicity	239
Lamp Clarifying the Essentials *by Tulku Tsultrim Zangpo*	
Tibetan text and English translation	245
The Evocation of Samantabhadra aka Kunzang Monlam	
Tibetan and English text in format for recitation	251
Uncovering the Presence of the Mother of all the Buddhas	
by Gonpo Wangyal – Tibetan text and English translation	279
The Record of the Heart-felt Advice of the Dakini,	
Indestructible Glorious Lamp *by Ayu Khandro*	
Tibetan text and English translation	283
Links to the original texts and teachings on them	288

PREFACE

THE OCEAN OF BUDDHADHARMA, the Buddha's teaching and practice, is vast. So many views and paths, such richness and variety of styles and methods – yet they all focus on the task of helping us awaken from the sleep of our assumptions. We are not who we think we are. The true depth and wonder of our potential is hidden from us by our own busy activity through which we seek to maintain the illusions we believe in.

This book offers three approaches to awakening. The first section, *Fighting the Good Fight*, is concerned with how we can commit ourselves to the mindful activity of renouncing our familiar and often comforting limiting habits. Here the orientation is towards leaving our familiar ego-home and going on a journey to seek something which seems only to be available elsewhere. By renouncing samsara we hope to gain entry into nirvana and enjoy the happiness which is free of all suffering.

The second section, *Mistaken Identities*, is concerned with how we can commit ourselves to developing the honesty and courage necessary for facing the karmic consequences of previous actions arising from our limiting habits and the many transient mistaken identities which we have adopted. Here the orientation is towards recognising how our self-centredness has harmed others and made us blind to our interdependency. By accepting that we have been the cause of so much suffering we see that we must turn to face every difficult situation without self-pity or blame.

For this we need the courage of the transcendent qualities of generosity, morality, patience, diligence, concentration and wisdom and especially the mental clarity necessary for maintaining the view of the emptiness of all phenomena.

The third section, *Sweet Simplicity*, is concerned with how we can relax and release ourselves from all limiting habits and thus effortlessly abide in our limitless intrinsic freedom. Here the orientation is towards awakening to the actuality of our mind as it is. For this to occur we need to receive the transmission which is grounded in non-conceptual clarity. We cannot think our way out of samsara since samsara is itself constructed out of thought. We seek only 'early retirement' from the burden of the ceaseless activity of maintaining delusion. By letting go of our central role as the indispensable master of ceremonies of our life drama we find ourselves in the intrinsic freedom of our true home, our unborn mind which cannot be found by seeking yet is always freely available.

These three sections are quite different in tone yet are harmonious and compatible in their underlying message of freedom. The Buddha offered all he was to help us and if we offer ourselves fully to the path then we will awaken with the same smile he offers us.

The texts were translated from Tibetan by me with the guidance of C R Lama. They have recently been revised for this book. Barbara Terris typed many revisions. Without her collaboration, support and untiring efforts this book would have remained asleep in the bundles of my aging papers.

May we all find the path we seek!

James Low, 2019

GENERAL INTRODUCTION

THE ROOT OF SUFFERING is alienation from our source and this suffering is maintained by non-attention to how our mind actually is. The fact of this non-attention is obscured by our ongoing activity of imagining how we are in ways that conceal rather than reveal what is simply present. When we do not awaken to our own mind as it is but rely on beliefs that we have inherited from our families and cultures we continue in the delusions these beliefs generate. If we can catch a glimpse of how erroneous our common beliefs are then two paths open up. The first indicates that there is a lot to be done and therefore we should strive. The second indicates that we suffer due to succumbing to the illusion of lacking the direct non-dual presence of our own awareness and therefore we should relax. When we seem to only have concepts to rely on in order to work out how we are, we can either avoid the issue altogether, which leaves us in delusion, or we can seek information. However the accumulation of such information presented as 'knowledge' offers us only concepts about our idea of our mind. This indirect, mediated relationship generates cover-up rather than revelation.

In daily life the mind itself seems invisible and somewhat irrelevant and so is easily taken for granted. We have a mind – of course we do. And that is that. For most of us most of the time our concern is more with our personality and our experience of ourselves as we change and develop with the world around us. What is happening for me, to me, as me, seems to be who I am. And since these happenings are ever-changing there is always something new to identify with, reflect on, or respond to.

From the Buddhist point of view this way of experiencing life is unlikely to generate much happiness since it is inseparable from our sense that our personal identity is not as stable as we would like it to be. Insecurity, anxiety, and uncertainty feed both our sense of alienation and our longing for a reliable sense of belonging. The Buddha's teaching points the way to a different sense of oneself, one that is less dependent on happenstance and reactivity.

The Buddhas' illuminating insight is liberating if it is lived. It provides a path to liberation if understood and aligned with. But someone hearing his teaching for the first time may find it radical and shocking. We all have good days and bad, yet if we are lucky then life seems basically okay. However the Buddha indicates that we feel this because at the moment we have a comfortable cell in the prison of samsara.

Causal factors lead us to be born in different realms with different kinds of bodies and different abilities and qualities. As specific causal factors are exhausted new ones arise through which we find ourselves in a new form with no recollection of what went before. When we see our existence in terms of transience and limitation then the ideas of liberation, freedom and enlightenment become much more meaningful. Buddhism is not an add-on to the life we have but offers an awakening to a new vision of our potential.

This book has three sections, each addressing the question of what our mind is and how it functions. The Buddha taught many different views or re-orientations to help us loosen up from our habitual fixations. He was very aware of the rich diversity of beliefs and temperaments that sentient beings manifest through variations in interest in and access to their environment, levels of volatility and impulsivity, degrees of finesse in embodied motility and so on. To simply present one 'truth' and hope that everyone would find it meaningful was not the Buddha's way. Uniting wisdom and compassion he revealed many thousands of pathways towards calmness and clarity, relaxation and creativity, profundity and connectivity. A short book like this can only touch on some key themes. However, if we let them, they can act as a mirror, allowing us see more clearly who and how we actually are, free of the disguising identities we habitually adopt.

The first section, *Fight the Good Fight*, contains a key text belonging to the Theravadan tradition of Buddhism. Here the mind as we ordinarily experience it is understood as a tendency to believe in the inherent existence, or individual reality, of ourselves and all other sentient beings. Holding on to the idea that I am someone and you are someone else, I have to work out if I like you (as I take you to be) or do not like you. Our mind, seemingly organised by and around our ego self, is concerned with winning and losing, with getting more of the pleasant and less of the unpleasant. This entails a Sisyphus-like effort since all situations, as complex, compounded events, are unstable and impermanent and therefore have to be repaired and recreated again and again. Sometimes impulses arise in us which undermine all that we have established and sometimes it is outer events which hurl us into unpredictable states of becoming.

The text presented in this first section is THE DHAMMAPADA which sets out clearly the importance of ethics as the necessary frame of reference if we wish our experience to be fulfilling. Negative actions lead to negative consequences and positive actions lead to positive consequences. This may seem over-simplistic and even naïve but such a sense of the determinism inherent in the unfolding of cause and effect provides a perspective, a distance from enmeshment, that allows us to review our intentions in the light of both their short and long-term outcomes. Activity of body, voice, and mind generates its own outcomes and consequences. No other, no god or devil, is rewarding or punishing us. It is the logic of intention and enactment that drives the multiplicity of possible resultant experiences.

Who am I in this situation? What am I up to? How do I think about you? Who do I take you to be? Who do you seem to take yourself to be? If we are able to pose such questions so that they let us see our habitual identifications in a new way then more options become available. We gain a meta-vision that offers some protection against the vexations, provocations and seductions of the engulfing moment. The Buddha pointed out that suffering, limitation, disappointment and so on arise from causes and if these causes are no longer activated then suffering will end. The two key causes of suffering are i) ignoring the actuality, the how-it-is-ness, of each situation and ii) imagining that our interpretation is the simple truth. Believing what we imagine, our assumptions seem self-valid while our ego-self's craving for something real to hang on to is pacified by being fed intense illusions.

Our minds are busy. In order to slow them down we need to cut back on our aroused involvement since desire and aversion distort and obscure the actual situation. The main Theravadan methods for such slowing are: meditation to develop undistracted focus; ethical restraint of impulses and increased attention to others as other; and engagement in analysis of our assumptions and beliefs so that we can see the deluding quality of our comforting complacency. As long as my mind seems to be simply its current content of thoughts, feelings, memories, sensations and so on there is little reflective space. Therefore these three methods of slowing are mobilised together to illuminate the possibility of letting go, of disengaging, so that new options are revealed along with a new sense of the one who may choose or not. This leads to calmness and clarity and to a fresh, mindful ease that is no longer driven by unconsidered mental events.

The second section, *Mistaken Identities*, belongs to the Mahayana tradition of Buddhism and focuses on the famous text, THE SHARP WEAPON WHEEL. This beautiful and moving text highlights the power of karma and the terrible fact that we cannot evade the consequences of our actions except by awakening from our own dualistic delusions. We have mistaken the rich display of emptiness for endless real entities and this mistaken identification will have ever-multiplying consequences if we do not recognise what has happened. When we separate self and other and act as if we were more important than others, this self-cherishing hides our own potential and blinds us to the potential of others.

Our Buddha potential, the capacity for awakening which is always already present in all beings, is our true identity. All the constructs that we hold about ourselves and others actually do the opposite of what we believe them to do. We rely on our thoughts, feelings, and sensations to show us ourselves and the world. We act on the basis that they tell us something true and dependable. But in fact they are empty constructs, delusions, obscurations, misleading fantasies which take us ever further from the simple truth of how it is. We impute a real existence to ourselves and others and also to all that we encounter. We see people, dogs, trees and so on as distinct separate entities each having their own inherent existence. This is the primary delusion of reification which arises in the absence of clarity about emptiness, the absence of inherent existence. There is no essence or substance to anything we encounter since all phenomena are dependently arising and have no individual existence of their own.

The great scholar sage Nagarjuna sets this out clearly in chapter 18 of his Root Verses of the Middle Way. Verses 2 and 3 address the absence of inherent existence or 'self' in sentient beings. Verse 9 addresses the absence of inherent existence in all phenomena.

> v. 2   *If there is no 'me' to be had*
> *How could there be anything 'mine'?*
> *With this pacification of 'me' and 'mine'*
> *There is no clinging to 'me' and 'mine'.*
>
> v. 3   *Those who do not cling to 'me' and 'mine'*
> *Are also without existence.*
> *Those who do not cling to 'me' and 'mine'*
> *See clearly and therefore do not see existents.*
>
> v. 9   *Unknowable by anything other; peace;*
> *Not propounded by any propositions;*
> *Free of thoughts; free of distinctions –*
> *Such are the characteristics of the ungraspable.*

The sense of self, I, me, myself, the inner sense of who I am, is not our friend but our enemy. This may seem alarming. If I am not who I think I am, then who am I? Well, this might seem like a reasonable question but the very way it is framed points to our key problem. If I am not this, then I must be that. I am here, I exist, so I must be someone. If I let go of one identity, say being a child, then I have a new one, being an adult. But from the Mahayana point of view all such identities are delusions, mistakes which lead us astray, seeking to turn shadows and echoes into reliable substantial entities. Exchanging one mistake for another is no liberation from the land where mistakes are normal.

Analysis of the structure of limitation reveals that the key to freedom is to cut off all identities. Actually such identities are just identifications. They have never been real 'things' but are conventions whose status is established by shared consensus. My identity is a mental event not a material one. When this fact becomes clear, all identities, that is to say all my beliefs and concepts about illusory appearances that I take to be real 'things', are seen to dissolve by themselves. Now I have nothing and am nothing – yet here I am! Who am I? I can't say, nor can all the Buddhas. I am nothing and yet I appear. This is the non-duality of form and emptiness which has been set out so clearly in the Heart Sutra. This is a mystery to be lived. It is not a problem to be solved. But if you take it up as a problem you can spend/waste your whole life coming up with solutions. All such solutions are composed of thoughts, memories and so on, and when seen clearly rather than merely believed in, are revealed to be mere gossamer.

The midsection of the text invokes the powerful activity of Yamantaka, a fierce form of the Buddha. This marks the transition from the general Mahayana focused on analysis to a more dynamic Tantric mode in which the powerful presence of enlightened energy manifesting many symbols provides a new dimension free of the duality of samsara. This is appearance and emptiness redolent with the wisdom of the Buddha – a method of transformation that turns poison into enlightening elixir and limitation into the radiance of the Buddha's mind. In an instant I drop my habitual identity and become this fierce Buddha. My ordinary self and my Buddha self are both without real existence so it is not that I stop being my usual 'me' and become someone 'else'. Both are illusions like a mirage or a rainbow. The past is gone – this is a new moment, open, fresh, undeniable and yet ungraspable.

The third section, *Sweet Simplicity*, presents four short texts. The first by Tsultrim Zangpo, also known as Tulku Tsulo, offers an account of emptiness that opens the way to the Dzogchen tradition of Buddhism, the central focus of the other three texts. Tulku Tsulo highlights the importance of the ground or source. If you know where things come from then you have more sense of what they are. An orange is not an orange all by itself. Its 'orange-ness' arises from its having grown on an orange tree. When we look at our mind there is a lot going on – the arising of experience is unceasing. Yet these arisings come and go, self-arising and self-vanishing. This is not a dogma – you can look for yourself and directly gain this clarity. There is always movement, movement showing itself as object and as subject. "This is what is happening to me." That is a thought with both object and subject aspects. If we take it at face value it may seem to be a definitive statement of something real yet it also expresses the mutually influencing coming into manifestation of an arising object-formation and a corresponding arising subject-formation. The subject is not a fixed identity or even a fixed reference point. It is part of the dialogic flow within which the notion of 'objects' and 'subjects' is merely conventional.

Yet there is presence, awareness, a lucidity within which all arisings are revealed. If we look for this presence we find nothing – the looker is empty and ungraspable, and so is all that is looked at. This reveals the lucidity of the mind as non-dual seeing, the all-revealing clarity of ungraspable awareness. Empty awareness, empty clarity, empty appearance, empty relaxed open contentment: this is the whole, the undivided, unfragmented, integral great completion. Everything is as it is. When we do not enter into duality we do not enter into judgment. When awareness shines forth free of reification it is uncontaminated by bias, by comparing and contrasting, and so the intrinsic perfection, the perfect this-ness of everything is bright and clear.

The next text is *The Evocation of Samantabhadra* which is believed to be the actual statement of the primordial Buddha. It shows clearly and in detail how the infinite dramas of the six realms of samsara are enacted within the theatre or sphere of the unborn mind. This sets the frame for Gonpo Wangyal's brief introduction to the mind as it is. This is a practice text and each sentence can be activated by sitting with it in opening presence. The concluding text by Ayu Khandro is also a brief Dzogchen practice text. It is an excellent reminder for those who have received many teachings and also functions well as a first taste of how to become aware as awareness. Here we are at the limits of language. The meaning is disclosed through participation alone. Texts such as these are often described as being 'self-secret'. Their meaning is not something that can be grasped and no amount of conceptual study can prise open the seemingly hidden, but actually evident, truth. The texts and what they point to have the indestructible vajra seal – they cannot be opened by dualising curiosity. The meaning is open and it opens to us if we open to it as it is by dropping our habit of incorporating all we find into our pre-established body of knowledge.

These three sections are not presented as items for intellectual speculation but as methods to end suffering. The first section highlights the need for calm clear consistent effort mobilised by the stick of the dangers of karma and the carrot of the hope of peace.

The second section presents similar areas of experience but in a more personal and provocative way. Feelings are now part of the path rather than merely an impediment. The vitality of the text catches us – this is about me! This is what I do and how I get lost! Passionate liberation achieved by utilising all the potential of our situation is the path set out here. The orientation has moved from the relative clarity of discerning the difference between good and bad to seeing that all that arises is empty and therefore liberating and simultaneously full of our projections and identifications and therefore imprisoning. It is not that we have to let go of these limitations in order to find freedom, for freedom does not lie somewhere else. It is by seeing the emptiness of limitation that we are free wherever we are. Emptiness is the golden key to unlock this door to nonduality. It is available everywhere yet remains hidden from the elective blind.

The third section highlights the fact that the ground and source of everything is not a god or a conceptual factory but is an empty ungraspability. This would suggest that we might simply stop grasping. Relax and release. I tie myself in knots by identifying with the idea of a self which can be tied in knots. Relax and release. Open to what is occurring. Stay open whatever is occurring. No limits. No beginning or end. Open, clear, responsive – these three inseparable modes of the mind as it is and as it always has been are the fruit we find at the end of our journey from here to Here.

Section One

FIGHT THE GOOD FIGHT

INTRODUCTION TO THE DHAMMAPADA

THE DHAMMAPADA (Sanskrit Dharmapada) is a collection in 423 verses of short teachings by Buddha Shakyamuni 563-483 BCE. Maintained at first solely in oral tradition it seems to have been written down in the 3rd century BCE. What seems to be the original version is in the Khuddaka Nikaya belonging to the Sutta Pitaka of the Pali canon. Many different versions and recensions arose through time including the Udanavarga compiled by Dharmatrata which was translated into Tibetan at the time of King Ralpachen and can be found in the Kangyur collection of the Buddha's speech.

Buddhaghosa, in the 4th or 5th centuries AD, prepared an edition, THE DHAMMAPADA ATTHAKATHA, in which each verse is supported by a story of how it came to be said. An edited version in English of this very lengthy text is available online as a PDF and people have permission to access and print copies for their own use. *The Dhammapada and its Commentary, edited by Bhikkhu Pesala, Association for Insight Meditation, January 2018.*

The translation offered here is based largely on the 20th century translation into Tibetan by Gendun Chophel, a Gelugpa monk who spent many years in India. The translation was done in 1980 by CR Lama and James Low for inclusion in a volume containing Pali, Sanskrit, Tibetan and English versions. This is now freely available online at the website simplybeing.co.uk/dhammapada/. See also wandel-verlag.de/finding-freedom-dlds.

The term 'Dhammapada' indicates the footprint or impression of the Dharma, the truth about existence revealed by the Buddha, and this short text is an accessible presentation of the key points of Buddha Shakyamuni's teaching. Although grouped in chapters it can be opened at any page since each verse has its own specific point to make.

The background is the teaching given by Buddha Shakyamuni on the Four Noble Truths: suffering, the cause of suffering, the ending of suffering, and the way to end suffering. These set the frame for all subsequent Buddhist practice.

Suffering is a fact, the truth of which is a call to abandon complacency. We will all become old, sick, and then die. This is what happens. Even if our lives are easy, war and famine, flood and fire, unemployment, enforced refugee existence, and many, many problems are present in the world around us. This suffering has a cause which, due to the kindness of the Buddha, is now known. Ignorance or inattention to the actual truth of experience leads to the delusion that self and others have real, inherent existence. I am someone. I am me. This belief becomes an object of clinging and is often lived as an irreducible fact. The unstable, ungrounded ego has a thirst for the pleasure that arises through contact between our sense consciousnesses and the appearances of the world.

On the basis of the seeming givenness of me as me and you as the you I take you to be, liking and disliking arises followed by actions of desireful involvement or aversive discarding. Due to this we act to increase our benefit and to avoid pain. This intentional activity has a causal force which gives rise to karmic consequences manifesting long after the initial event. As a result of these propulsive tendencies we find ourselves wandering in samsara, the endless cycle of birth and death, moving to the upper realms when good actions ripen and to the lower realms and hells when bad actions ripen. This is our actual situation. We will soon die. Yet we have a brief window of opportunity to a) mobilise ethics and so diminish bad action and increase good action b) learn to calm the mind, diminishing involvement in whatever occurs and c) through this non-involvement learn to see the confusion that arises from taking the transient content of our experience as a support for our deluded belief in our 'real' existence.

The third truth is that of the ending of suffering. This cessation is available to all sentient beings. Our mind, the centre and basis of everything we do and are, is not to be found in its content, neither as the objects that appear to be outside nor as the subject that seems to be the experiencer within. Subject and object are transient but the mind is not. When this misleading fusion is disidentified from, the mind's own clarity is revealed as deathless liberation.

Fourthly, there is a path to gain the cessation of suffering. This is the Noble Eightfold Path: right knowledge or vision, seeing the fact of impermanence and the absence of inherent existence; right intention, deciding to follow the path; right speech, clear and undeceiving; right action, behaviour guided by the teachings; right livelihood, supporting yourself with work that is ethical and helpful and not harmful; right effort, focusing on developing virtue and diminishing evil and harm; right mindfulness, undistracted attention to all details of what is occurring; right meditation, concentrating on the practice so that the misleading refuge of thoughts, feelings and sensations can be dispensed with. This eightfold path is not a set of options – all eight aspects need to be practised.

This is the basic reorientation offered by the Buddha. He offers two maps, a map of the prison and a map of the way out of the prison. We are trapped though we hardly even know it. When we see that we are on the way to death and to the loss of all that we know and moreover, that this process will be repeated again and again and again in life after life until we put a stop to it, we have the first breath of freedom. Avoiding the bad, developing the good, and cutting off craving so that the mind can taste true contentment, form the heart of the practice. The mind is chief – not our feelings, not the shiny objects and people of this world. This is the basis of the turn towards renunciation which helps to separate us from involvement in samsara.

In a busy life with many demands, the outer renunciation of living in a forest is rarely feasible. Yet the renunciation of non-involvement is always possible in any situation. The text talks a lot about taints. This refers to the mark or stain that occurs when we leak out into the world with our aroused emotions and when the world leaks into us so that we feel invaded and overwhelmed. To avoid this we must be attentive, heedful, and careful. The intoxication of the moment is our greatest danger for then we are carried away by aspects of self and environment that are privileged causing everything else to be relegated to the background. It is as if 'this is all there is' and 'this is all I am'. Blind passion catches us and only later do we become conscious of even the immediate outcome of our actions while we remain oblivious to the future karmic consequences.

We have to choose between the intoxicating excitement of heedless involvement or the calm spaciousness of clarity. This clarity is neither cut off and avoidant nor self-abandoning into fusion. The middle way avoiding the extremes is the true path to freedom. To stay surefootedly on this path requires us to develop life-affirming qualities such as diligence, patience, commitment, and courage.

The Buddhist view very clearly sets out that life has a purpose. We are not mere puppets of fate thrown about in the pinball machine of happenstance. We sentient beings, each and everyone of us, no matter how limited our current situation, can gain unchanging freedom through liberation from all that limits us.

The MAHAMANGALA SUTTA says

> *To live in the world*
> *With your heart undisturbed by the world,*
> *With all sorrows ended, dwelling in peace –*
> *This is the greatest happiness.*

The ANGUTTARA NIKAYA says

> *Loss and gain, disrepute and fame,*
> *Praise and blame, pleasure and pain –*
> *These things are transient in human life,*
> *Inconstant and bound to change.*
> *The mindful wise one discerns them well,*
> *Observant of their alterations.*
> *Pleasant things do not excite his mind*
> *Nor do the unpleasant annoy him.*
> *All likes and dislikes are dispelled by him,*
> *Eliminated and abolished.*
> *Aware now of the stainless, griefless state,*
> *He fully knows, having gone beyond.*

Seeing the suffering around us it is important to bring the relief of Dharma to others according to our capacity. In fact being aware of the needs of others can spur us on to deepen our study and practice:

The Vinaya Pitaka (1, 20-21) says

> *Therefore go forth brethren on your journey, for the joy of the many, for the happiness of the many, out of compassion for the world. Teach the dharma which is beautiful in the beginning, beautiful in the middle, and beautiful at the end.*

Freedom from suffering is the goal and all the methods and encouragements in this text have that as their focus. But we must choose and if we choose freedom we have to struggle with our own habits of adopting small identities. Letting go of attachment means that we go from the definite knowledge of who we think we are to an experience of openness, indefinability, and potential. When we give up clinging our view widens and we can start to see the world as it is and allow the impact of others' suffering to awaken our love and compassion. Many verses in this text praise the solitary life, a life which is not resting on cultural assumptions about what is important. In western societies virgin marriage was important in the past, but no longer. Now it is tattoos that give one a stylish identity. All such signs are transient. To find what is stable and enduring we have to let go of fads and the wish to be approved of by those around us.

Of course Buddhism as a social formation manifesting under specific cultural conditions carries with it, along with the unchanging value of Dharma, certain cultural attitudes which are less and less valid in the modern world. The text is very strongly focused on men as the sole beings who can study and practice Dharma. There is a lot about being a good monk and avoiding 'ordinary life' or a 'worldly existence'. But deep Dharma is for all, since all beings have a mind, the one necessity for awakening. The mind is necessary but not sufficient since effort is required to engage in study and practice. Now in the west such study and practice is freely available for all so we should be like the great goose in Indian mythology which can drink the milk and leave the water it was mixed with. Go for the nectar and leave the dross.

Freedom is clean, fresh, bright, alive – and it rests on nothing. In order to let go of what we know and value, we rely on the teachings as a transitional support. We have to trust them more than our own moods, memories, impulses, and desires. As the text says, fools trust themselves and so sign up for suffering.

Getting lost is easy – our habits and tendencies will effortlessly lead us astray. And of course if the goal of liberation is not guiding us then we will not even notice that we have gone astray. To stay on the path we must become immune to the enticements of the passing show. Liberation is the goal. Study gives us a map. Meditation practice gives us a method. But we have to do the work. We have the necessary foundation, our own mind. So now we have to choose, freedom or captivity! As the Buddha said at the end of his life, "All compounded things are subject to vanishing. Strive with earnestness!"

James Low

REFUGE PRAYER

རྐང་གཉིས་རྣམས་ཀྱི་མཆོག་སངས་རྒྱས་ལ་སྐྱབས་སུ་མཆི་འོ།

KANG	NYI	NAM	KYI	CHO	SANG GYE	LA	KYAB	SU	CHI O
feet	two	all	of	best	Buddha	to, in	refuge	for	go
(humans)									

I take refuge in the Buddha, the best of all humans

ཞི་བ་འདོད་ཆགས་དང་བྲལ་བ་ཆོས་ལ་སྐྱབས་སུ་མཆི་འོ།

ZHI WA	DOE CHAG	DANG	DRAL WA	CHO	LA	KYAB	SU	CHI O
peaceful	desire	and	free of	dharma	to, in	refuge	for	go

I take refuge in the Dharma, peaceful and free of desire.

ཚོགས་རྣམས་ཀྱི་མཆོག་འཕགས་པའི་དགེ་འདུན་ལ་སྐྱབས་སུ་མཆི་འོ།

TSHOG	NAM	KYI	CHO	PHAG PAI	GEN DUN	LA	KYAB	SU	CHI O
assemblies*	all	of	best	pure	monks	in, to	refuge	for	go
(* of knowledge and virtue)									

I take refuge in the renunciate Sangha who have the best assemblage.

I take refuge in the Buddha, the best of all humans.
I take refuge in the Dharma, peaceful and free of desire.
I take refuge in the renunciate Sangha who have the best assemblage.

THE DHAMMAPADA

Walking in the Dharma

CHAPTER 1 | THE PAIRS

1. Mind[1] is the forerunner of all experience. Mind is their chief and they are mind-made. If with an impure mind one speaks or acts then misery follows just as the cartwheel follows the hoof of the ox.

2. Mind is the forerunner of all experience. Mind is their chief and they are mind-made. If with a pure mind one speaks and acts then happiness follows one like an inseparable shadow.

3. "He abused me, he beat me, he defeated me, he robbed me." The anger of those who harbour such thoughts is not appeased.

4. "He abused me, he beat me, he defeated me, he robbed me." The anger of those who do not harbour such thoughts is appeased.

5. In this world hatred is never pacified by hatred. It is by the absence of hatred that hatred is pacified. This is the ancient truth.

6. Some people do not know that we are all guests in this world.² Those who recollect this let their quarrels settle.

7. Whoever is preoccupied by pleasure, with senses unrestrained, immoderate with food, lazy and lacking diligence is overpowered by Mara³ like a weak tree in a storm.

8. Whoever contemplates the impurities⁴, restrains their senses, is moderate in food, confident and diligent cannot be overpowered by Mara, like a mountain in a storm.

9. He who wears the monk's yellow robe without being cleansed of defilements, and who lacks self-control and truthfulness, is not worthy of that robe.

10. He who has cleansed his defilements, who cherishes pure morality and is endowed with self-control and truthfulness, is a person worthy of the yellow robe.

11. Mistakenly taking the unessential⁵ to be essential and the essential to be unessential, those who inhabit the realm of misleading thoughts never arrive at the essential.

12. Those who clearly see the essential to be essential and the inessential to be inessential, those inhabitants of the realm of undeceiving discernment arrive at the essential.

13. Just as rain penetrates a badly thatched house, so desire penetrates a mind which does not meditate.

14. Just as rain cannot penetrate a well-thatched house, so desire does not penetrate a mind which meditates well.

15. Suffering in this life and suffering in the hereafter, the harmful⁶ person suffers in both situations. Seeing the actions which have arisen from his own afflictions he suffers and is tormented.

16. Rejoicing in this life and rejoicing in the hereafter, the virtuous person rejoices in both situations. Seeing his own very pure actions he rejoices and is happy.

17. Tormented in this life and in the hereafter, the harmful person is tormented in both situations. He is tormented by the fact that he has done harm and he is tormented even more when he has to go to the realms of woe[7].

18. Happy in this life and in the hereafter, the virtuous person is happy in both situations. He is happy with the fact that he has been virtuous and he is happier still when he goes to the realms of joy[8].

19. If a person recites many Dharma texts yet heedlessly does not put them into practice, then, like a cowherd counting the cows of others, he cannot be counted among the righteous.

20. If a person hardly recites Dharma texts yet acts in accordance with the Dharma, then, rejecting desire, aversion and opacity, and with pure insight[9] and a liberated[10] mind, he will be counted among the righteous.

CHAPTER 2 | HEEDFULNESS

21. Heedfulness[11] is the site of the deathless. Heedlessness is the site of death. The headful do not die while the heedless are already dead.

22. The wise are awake to this distinction and so are heedful. Enjoying being heedful they are happy in the sphere of the noble ones[12].

23. Always meditating and maintaining stable perseverance they reach the unsurpassed happiness of liberation[13].

24. One who is diligent, mindful, pure in conduct, discerning, disciplined, right living and heedful will increase in glory.

25. By diligence, heedfulness, discipline and self-control, the wise one makes an island which is safe in any flood.

26. The childish and ignorant indulge in heedlessness, but the wise protect heedfulness as if it were their greatest treasure.

27. Do not indulge in heedlessness. Do not depend on sensual pleasures. By heedful meditation great happiness will be gained.

28. When the wise use heedfulness to discard heedlessness, as if looking down from a mountain peak, free of regret they ride on their shining insight and observe the foolish ones immersed in sorrow.

29. Heedful among the heedless, alert among the dozy, the wise advance like a swift horse leaving the weak horses behind.

30. Heedfulness is praised while heedlessness is disparaged. Heedfulness made Indra the chief of the gods.

31. The monk who delights in heedfulness and looks with fear on heedlessness is like fire burning up all attachments large and small.

32. The monk who delights in heedfulness and looks with fear on heedlessness will not be corrupted but will remain close to nirvana.

CHAPTER 3 | THE MIND

33. This mind, so elusive and unreliable, is difficult to watch over and difficult to pacify. Just as an arrow maker straightens his arrow so the discerning person straightens his mind.

34. Like a fish thrown onto dry land so the mind flutters in agitation on leaving the arena of Mara.[14]

35. The mind is difficult to restrain as it chases everywhere seeking what it likes. It is good to control the mind. A controlled mind leads to happiness.

36. The mind is extremely subtle and difficult to perceive as it chases everywhere seeking what it likes. The discerning person watches over it. A mind that is watched over leads to happiness.

37. The formless mind remains hidden as it wanders alone, travelling far. Those who restrain it are freed from the fetters of Mara.

38. If the mind is unstable, without knowledge of the holy Dharma, and wavering in faith, then clear knowing will not be fully achieved.

39. One whose mind is invulnerable[15] and unwavering, who has fully discarded merit and demerit is awakened and free of fear.

40. Being aware that this body is like a clay pot[16] and making the mind as secure as a walled city, with the weapon of clear knowing one should triumph over Mara and keep watch over that rival without relaxing.

41. How sad! Before long this body will separate from consciousness and be discarded in the cemetery to lie upon the earth like a useless lump.

42. Whatever a rival may do to a rival or an enemy to an enemy, even more harm will arise from a mind directed towards the wrong way.

43. Neither mother nor father nor any other relative can bring as much good as a well directed mind.

CHAPTER 4 | FLOWERS

44. Who wishes to conquer this earth, this realm of Yama[17] and the gods? Who will truly study the virtuous dharma instructions just as a garland maker seeks out the best flowers?

45. A true student will conquer this earth, this realm of Yama and the gods. A true student will study the virtuous Dharma instructions just as a garland maker seeks out the best flowers.

46. Knowing this body to be like a bubble and seeing precisely that all phenomena are like a mirage, one should cut off the flowering darts of Mara and go to where you cannot be seen by the king of death.

47. The person whose mentation is desireful and who collects desires as if they were flowers, will be carried off by the lord of death the way a sleeping village is swept away by a flood.

48. With desireful mentation, collecting desires as if they were flowers, the insatiably desiring go under the power of the lord of death.

49. Just as the bee collects pollen and departs without injuring the colour or scent of the flower, so the sage should move through the town.[18]

50. Not identifying the faults of others and the things they have done or not done, one should instead identify what one has oneself done or not done.

51. Like a beautiful flower full of colour yet without scent, are the well-spoken but fruitless words of one who does not act on them.

52. Like an attractive flower that is beautiful in colour and well scented, well-spoken words that are acted upon will be fruitful.

53. Just as many garlands can be made from many different flowers so many virtuous deeds should be performed by all mortals.

54. The perfume of flowers, even that of sandalwood, tagara and jasmine, cannot spread against the direction of the wind. However the fragrance of the virtuous spreads even against the wind. The virtue of beings spreads in all directions.

55. There are many fragrances such as sandalwood, tagara, lotus and jasmine, but the best scent arises from moral discipline.

56. The pleasing fragrances of tagara and sandalwood are meagre compared with the scent of one with moral discipline, for this scent wafts up to the gods.

57. The path of those with pure moral discipline, who abide in heedfulness and are freed by pure knowing cannot be found by Mara.

58. On a heap of bad-smelling rubbish discarded at the side of the road charming fragrant lotuses may blossom.

59. Similarly on the rubbish heap of blind mortals a disciple of the fully enlightened Buddha shines with the clarity of true knowing.

CHAPTER 5 | THE IMMATURE

60. For those who cannot sleep, the night is long. For those who are weary, the road is long. For those who are foolish and do not know the holy Dharma, cyclical existence is long.

61. While on one's way, if one does not meet one's better or an equal then one should be steadfast in travelling alone. There is no fellowship with a fool.

62. The fool thinks, "I have children, I have wealth" and so he excites himself. Yet he does not even have a self, so how could he have children or wealth?

63. The fool who recognises that he is foolish is wise to that extent but the fool who believes he is wise deserves to be called a fool.

64. Even if a fool lived with a wise person all his life he would gain no knowledge of Dharma, just as a ladle gains no knowledge of soup.

65. If a person with insight spends only a moment with a wise person he quickly gains knowledge of Dharma just as the tongue knows the flavour of soup.

66. The fool with little insight acts as an enemy to himself by performing evil acts whose result is bitter.

67. If one experiences regret on completion of an action then it was not a good action to have done and its ripening consequences will later bring tears to one's face.

68. If one experiences no regrets[19] on completion of an action then it was a good action to have done and its later consequence will be joyful and happy.

69. As long as the evil deed does not ripen the fool thinks that it is sweet. But when the evil ripens then the mind is sorrowful.

70. If a fool were to eat his food with the tip of the blade of *kusa* grass[20] for month after month he would still not be worth a sixteenth of the value of those who comprehend the Dharma.

71. An evil deed does not ripen immediately, just as fresh milk does not curdle at once. It follows the fool, smouldering beneath the surface like ash-covered embers.

72. Knowledge gained by the fool becomes the cause of ruin. It darkens his simple goodness and spoils his head.[21]

73. The fool desires undeserved reputation and precedence over monks. He is envious of those with high station and wishes to receive offerings from others.

74. "Laymen and monks should both think that this was all done by me. They should accept my authority in all matters, both great and small." This is how the fool thinks and so his pride and desire increase.

75. The methods that bring worldly gain and the causes that bring one to nirvana are not the same. Seeing that this is so and taking no delight in being respected by others, the monk, as a disciple of the Buddha, should gradually develop in solitude.

CHAPTER 6 | THE WISE ONE

76. If you find a wise one who can point out your faults and challenge you on them you should follow him like one pointing out hidden treasure. You will be better off and not worse off for cultivating such a wise one.

77. The one who advises, instructs and removes obstacles is a joy to the good but disliked by the bad.

78. Do not cultivate the evil as friends nor those of low character. Rather, cultivate spiritual friends and those of good character.

79. Those who drink deep of the Dharma with a clear mind live happily. The wise ones delight in the Dharma spoken by the ever-pure[22].

80. Peasants channel the water, fletchers fashion the arrows, carpenters shape the wood and the wise discipline themselves.

81. Hills and rocks are not disturbed by the movement of the wind. Similarly the wise are unmoved by praise or blame.

82. Just as a deep lake is clear and undisturbed, so the wise are clear when they hear the Dharma.

83. The Holy Ones are uninvolved whatever the circumstances. The sages do not indulge in desire. Whether touched by happiness or suffering the wise are neither elated nor cast down.

84. Not wishing sons, wealth or territory for themselves or others, nor self-advantage by unvirtuous means, such a person is ethical, wise and aligned with Dharma.

85. Among all humans few are those who cross over to the far side[23]; the rest run about on this side.

86. Those who follow the well-spoken[24] Dharma will cross to the far side beyond the domain of death, so difficult to traverse.

87. Fully abandoning black[25] beliefs and practices the wise cultivate the white[26]. Leaving home they become homeless and solitary with a joy that is hard to find.

88. Abandoning every desire for something, and wishing only for true happiness[27], the wise fully control the troublesome afflictions[28] of the mind.

89. Those whose minds contemplate well the seven branches of awakening[29], those who find no pleasure in taking things and fully abandon acquisitiveness, who have put an end to corruption and are clear of all faults, have attained nirvana while in this world.

CHAPTER 7 | THE ARAHAT

90. With movement finished and free from sorrow, completely liberated from everything and with all binding attachments cut, now there is final freedom from longing.

91. The mindful ones renounce worldliness and are not attached to any place. Like swans leaving a lake, they leave one habitation after another.

92. Those you have given up acquisition, who know what food is for[30], who abide in emptiness, signlessness and aloneness[31] – the way of such people is difficult to follow, like the path of birds in the sky.

93. Those who have brought an end to corruption[32], who are free of desire for food, whose abode is emptiness and the signless liberation – the way of such people is difficult to follow, like the path of birds in the sky.

94. With senses peaceful like a horse well controlled by its trainer, and with pride discarded and all corruption ended – even the gods wish to emulate such a person.

95. Imperturbable like the earth, firm and steady like Indra's weapon[33], clear like a lake – this is the way to end rebirth.

96. Peaceful in mind, speech and action, achieving complete liberation with clear knowing, such is one who is at peace.

97. Free of credulity, knowing the uncreated[34], establishing boundaries[35], abandoning reliance, and free of longing – this is the noblest of beings.

98. Whether in a village or a forest, by a lake or on the open plain, wherever an arahat dwells becomes delightful.

99. The isolated forests where worldly people find no joy are delightful for those who do not go seeking after objects of desire. Being free of desire and attachment they are truly happy.

CHAPTER 8 | THE THOUSANDS

100. Better than a thousand meaningless words is to hear one meaningful word and become peaceful.

101. Better than a thousand verses of meaningless words is to hear just one line of a verse which brings peace.

102. Better than reciting a hundred verses full of meaningless words is to recite one verse of Dharma which brings peace upon hearing.

103. In a battle a thousand thousand men may be defeated yet that victory is less than one person defeating[36] himself.

104. Sentient beings who discipline themselves and are always controlled have the cause of defeating themselves – and this is superior to defeating others.

105. Gods, gandharva spirits, mara demons and even Brahma himself – none of them can defeat the being who has gained victory over himself.

106. Though month after month for one hundred years one were to make sacrifices with a thousand offerings, this century of sacrifice is surpassed by just one moment of offering made to a true meditator[37].

107. Though for a century a man might tend the sacrificial fire in the forest, this century of sacrifice is surpassed by just one moment of offering to honour a true meditator.

108. Whatever sacrifices and offerings might be made in a year by one seeking merit, the value of this has not even a quarter of the worth of paying homage to the righteous.

109. Those ever inclined to honour and respect the elders will increase in lifespan, beauty, happiness, and power.

110. Though one were to live for a hundred years, if immoral and without meditative composure, it would be better to live for just one day disciplined and settled in meditation.

111. Though one were to live for a hundred years, if confused and disturbed, it would be better to live for just one day with clear knowing and meditative stability.

112. Though one were to live for a hundred years, if lazy and without diligence, it would be better to live for just one day with resolute diligence.

113. Though one were to live for a hundred years, if this was without seeing the arising and passing[38], it would be better to live for just one day in which one saw the arising and passing.

114. Though one were to live for a hundred years, if the deathless stage[39] is not seen, it would be better to live for just one day in which one saw the deathless stage.

115. Though one were to live for a hundred years, if the supreme Dharma[40] is not seen, it would be better to live for just one day in which one saw the supreme Dharma.

CHAPTER 9 | EVIL

116. Hurry in the direction of virtue and reject any evil[41] that arises in your mind. Those who are slow to make merit will find their mind delighting in evil.

117. If a person commits much evil they should not continue to repeat this. They should not develop a longing for evil since the accumulation of evil leads to sorrow.

118. If a person creates merit they should continue to repeat this. They should develop a longing for virtue since the accumulation of virtue leads to happiness.

119. For as long as their evil has not ripened the evil person can still encounter good events. But when their evil ripens, the evil that was done becomes visible.[42]

120. For as long as their virtue has not ripened that person can still encounter evil. But when their virtue ripens, the good that was done becomes visible.

121. Do not think lightly of evil believing that its consequences will not come to you. Just as a water jug is filled up drop by drop so a foolish person gathers evil bit by bit until they are full.

122. Do not think lightly of virtue believing that its consequences will not come to you. Just as a water jug is filled up drop by drop so a virtuous person gathers virtue bit by bit until they are full.

123. A merchant with valuable goods and only a small escort avoids dangerous paths, and a person who loves life avoids poison. Likewise one should avoid evil.

124. If your hand is free of wounds you can carry poison in it. Poison has no effect if there is no entry wound. Those who do no evil are untouched by evil.

125. The fool who harms an innocent, pure and faultless person finds that their evil rebounds on them, just like fine dust thrown into the wind.

126. Some beings are born in the womb, while the evil go to the hells and the virtuous to the highest realms – but those free of corrupting taints pass into nirvana.

127. There is nowhere on earth, not in the sky or in the ocean or in clefts in the rocks where one can escape the results of one's evil deeds.

128. There is nowhere on earth, not in the sky or in the ocean or in clefts in the rocks where one can evade death.

CHAPTER 10 | VIOLENCE

129. All beings fear violence, all are afraid of death. Knowing this to be true of oneself one should neither beat nor kill others.

130. Life is dear to all beings and all are afraid of death. Seeing that others are like oneself one should neither beat nor kill them.

131. A person who seeks happiness for themselves yet acts violently towards other happiness-seeking beings, will not find happiness after death.

132. A person who seeks happiness for themselves and who does not act violently towards other happiness-seeking beings, will find happiness after death.

133. Do not speak harshly to anyone. If you do, people will speak back to you as you have spoken to them. Harsh words are painful and their retaliation will hurt you.

134. If you silence yourself like a broken gong no strife will arise for you and you will gain access to nirvana.

135. Using his staff the cowherd drives the cattle to pasture. Likewise those who are attached to this life are herded towards its end and face old age and death.

136. The fool does not recognise that his activities are evil. The idiot is tormented by his own deeds as if burned by fire.

137. Those who are violent without reason, harming those who offer no provocation, will soon encounter one of the ten results:

138. Intense pain, disaster, physical injury, severe illness, mental troubles,

139. Trouble from the king, grave accusations, bereavement, loss of wealth, or

140. Property destroyed by fire. With the death of the body those without clarity go to the hell realms.

141. Wandering as a naked ascetic with matted hair, covering oneself in filth, fasting, lying on the ground, smearing on dust and ashes, prolonged sitting on one's heels – none of these can purify a person who is not free of desire, longing and doubt.

142. Even if well attired, if someone lives according to Dharma, calm and controlled, chaste, and careful not to harm any being, then they are a brahmin, a Holy One, a monk.

143. Like an excellent horse avoiding the whip, is there anyone in this world who, restrained by shame, practises faith, morality, contemplation, stability in Dharma, awareness and mindfulness?

144. Be fearless and determined like a thoroughbred horse touched by the whip. With faith, virtue, effort, concentration, investigation of Dharma, knowledge, ethics and mindfulness, free yourself from the great suffering of samsara.

145. Peasants channel irrigation water, fletchers fashion arrows, carpenters shape wood and the good discipline themselves.

CHAPTER 11 | OLD AGE

146. Everything is a blazing inferno! So why this laughter, this delight? Enveloped in darkness[43], will you not seek a lamp?

147. Look at this beautified form, covered in sores, full of disease and a source of anxiety. There is nothing stable about it.

148. This body is worn out by time. It is a nest of disease and very frail. This putrid heap will disintegrate for life ends in death.

149. Like gourds discarded in the autumn these dove-coloured bones are scattered. What joy can come from seeing them?

150. In this city constructed of bones and plastered with flesh and blood reside old-age and death, pride and self-deception.

151. The splendid royal chariot will wear out and this body is definitely ageing. But the Dharma followed by the Holy Ones does not age. The true teaching of the Holy Ones is how to know satisfaction.

152. A person who has studied little grows old like an ox. His bulk increases but his wisdom does not.

153. In many births in samsara I have searched without rest or pause for the maker of this house. To take birth after birth is only sorrow.

154. House-builder, you are seen! You will not build me a house again. All your rafters are broken and your ridgepole is shattered. My mind is freed from the conditioned and craving is ended.[44]

155. Those who have not lived with pure conduct have not gained the wealth of youth[45]. They die like old cranes by a lake without fish.

156. Those who have not lived with pure conduct have not gained the wealth of youth. Thinking of the past, they are full of regret as if regarding a worthless broken bow.

CHAPTER 12 | SELF

157. If you know that you hold yourself[46] dear you should carefully protect yourself. The wise person is like a watchman during the three periods of the night.

158. At first one should harmoniously engage oneself in ethical behaviour. If a wise one then instructs others in this, they will not err.

159. One should oneself act as one instructs others to do. If one is controlled then one can control others[47]. It is control of oneself that is difficult.

160. One is one's own guard. Who else could be such a guard? If one is well-controlled then one has found a rare and precious guard.

161. The evil that one does is born from oneself and arises from oneself. Evil grinds down the unwise as the diamond grinds a pearl.

162. Just as a creeper can kill a tree so those with very poor morals do to themselves what an enemy would wish to do to them.

163. It is easy to act in ways that are bad and so harm oneself. It is truly difficult to do what is good and beneficial.

164. Foolish people follow wrong views and scorn the teaching of the pure and virtuous ones. Like the *khattaka* reed, they ripen only for self-destruction[48].

165. It is by oneself that one does this evil. It is by oneself that one is afflicted. It is by oneself that one can desist from evil. It is only by oneself that one can become pure. No one can purify another. Purity and impurity depend on oneself alone.

166. One should not neglect one's own welfare[49] for the welfare, however great, of someone else. If one has understood how to increase one's own welfare then that welfare will be the supreme concern.

CHAPTER 13 | THE WORLD

167. Don't follow a debased way of life. Don't settle into heedlessness. Don't embrace wrong views. Don't increase your worldly tendencies.

168. Wake up! Avoid carelessness! Act well according to the Dharma. Those who practice Dharma are happily at ease in this world and the next.

169. Act well according to the Dharma and avoid debased conduct. Those who practise Dharma are happily at ease in this world and the next.

170. See the world as a bubble, see it as a mirage. Those who see the world in this way cannot be seen by the king of death.

171. Look at the world as if it were a gilded royal carriage. The foolish become involved but the acute are free of attachment.

172. When one who was formerly heedless becomes heedful they illuminate the world like the moon freed from clouds.

173. When those who have done evil cover[50] it over with virtue then they illuminate the world like the moon freed from clouds.

174. This world is enveloped in darkness. Few indeed are those who see this. Those who ascend to the upper realms are as few as the birds who can escape a trap.

175. Wild swans take the path of the sun and those with magic powers fly in the sky. But the unwavering[51] transcend this world having defeated Mara and his followers.

176. One who abandons the sole true Dharma, who lies, and gives no thought to future lives will find no evil that they are incapable of.

177. Misers do not ascend to the upper realms of samsara. The foolish do not praise the benefits of generosity. Those who rejoice in the teachings on generosity will be happy in the future.

178. Better than being the ruler of the earth, better than ascending to the upper realms, better than having the entire world under your power – better than all this is to gain fruition as a Stream Enterer.[52]

CHAPTER 14 | THE BUDDHA

179. No one has the power to defeat the Victorious One or to diminish his victory over the world. There is no limit to the sphere of activity of the Buddha. Free of fixed abode, free of travel – by whom could he be led?

180. He cannot be led by the entangling poisonous net of craving. There is no limit to the sphere of activity of the Buddha. Free of fixed abode, free of travel – by whom could he be led?

181. The gods aspire to be like those dedicated to meditation, free of activity and enjoying peace – the mindful perfect Buddhas.

182. It is hard to gain a human birth. It is hard to live knowing that you are mortal. It is hard to gain the opportunity to hear the holy Dharma. It is hard to emerge as a Buddha.[53]

183. To do no evil whatsoever, to do all that is good and virtuous, to fully control one's own mind – this is the teaching of the Buddha.

184. The patience of asceticism is holy patience[54]; the Buddha called it 'the Supreme nirvana'. The renunciate who harms or troubles others is not a true monk.

185. Not demeaning, not harming, practising self-restraint according to one's vows, eating in moderation, dwelling in seclusion, cultivating the highest potential of the mind – this is the teaching of the Buddha.

186. Desires cannot be satisfied, even with a shower of gold. The wise know that desire means little pleasure and much suffering.

187. Seeing that the desires of the gods bring them no true happiness, the disciples of the Buddha take delight only in the ending of craving.

188. Driven by fear people seek refuge in hills and forests, in gardens, graves and shrines,

189. But these places offer no secure refuge for they are not the ultimate refuge. By going to such sites of refuge you will not be free from all sorrow.

190. However those who have gone for refuge to the Buddha, Dharma and Sangha see suffering, the origin of suffering, the ending of suffering, and

191. The Noble Eightfold Path[55] leading to the complete cessation of suffering. With pure discerning wisdom they see the Four Noble Truths.

192. These are the virtuous refuge, the ultimate refuge. Having taken them as one's refuge one is freed from all sorrow.

193. It is hard to find an omniscient person for they are not born everywhere. Happiness increases in the family where such a person is born.

194. Joyful is the occurrence of a Buddha. Joyful is their teaching, the holy Dharma. Joyful is harmony in the Sangha. Joyful is the Dharma practice of those who live in harmony.

195. Having fully transcended all conceptual elaboration, and completely terminated all craving and sorrow, the Buddhas are worthy of homage as are their close disciples.

196. Venerating those great beings who are fearless and beyond suffering generates such merit that no one can measure it.

CHAPTER 15 | HAPPINESS

197. Living without enmity amongst those who hate we live very happily free of this sickness amongst those who hate.

198. Living without sickness[56] amongst those who endure sickness we live very happily free of sickness amongst those who are sick.

199. Living without longing[57] amongst those who experience longing we live very happily free of longing amongst those who long.

200. Having nothing at all we live happily; like the radiant gods our food is happiness.

201. Victory creates enemies. Defeat makes people miserable. Dispensing with both victory and defeat we will live happily in peace.

202. There is no fire like desire. There is no disturbance between people like fierce anger. There is no suffering like that of the aggregates[58]. There is no bliss higher than the peace of nirvana.

203. Hunger is the worst disease. Propensities[59] are the greatest sorrow. If one sees that this is truly how it is, nirvana is the supreme happiness.

204. Health is the most precious possession. Contentment is true wealth. A reliable friend is the best relation. Nirvana is the highest bliss.

205. Having tasted the flavour of complete solitude and the flavour of peace, one imbibes the flavour of the bliss of Dharma and becomes free of fear and sin.

206. It is good to see the Holy Ones for their pure friendliness is always a source of bliss. If one can avoid seeing fools then one will always be blissful.

207. If one keeps the company of fools one will suffer for a long time. Foolish people are like the enemy and so making friends with them will bring only sorrow. The steadfast are like close relatives, meeting with them is pleasurable.

208. Thus, those who are heedful, wise, learned, stable in morality, diligent and noble should follow the intelligent Holy Ones just as the moon follows the path of the stars.

CHAPTER 16 | PREFERENCE

209. By applying oneself to things best left alone[60] and avoiding applying oneself to that which is worthy, one abandons true value. One who seeks pleasure will apply themselves to whatever attachment they are currently drawn to.

210. Not to see what you like is suffering as is seeing what you don't like. Therefore do not get involved with ideas of what you like and what you do not like.

211. Therefore do not rely on anything as a source of happiness.[61] If the object of happiness is lost one will feel hurt. Those who do not seek happiness from anything are unfettered.

212. All that we like gives rise to misery. All that we like gives rise to fear. If we can discard[62] all that is liked then there is neither misery nor fear.

213. All that we cherish gives rise to misery. All that we cherish gives rise to fear. If we can discard all that is cherished then there is neither misery nor fear.

214. All that we are attached to gives rise to misery. All that we are attached to gives rise to fear. If we can discard all that we are attached to then there is neither misery nor fear.

215. All that is desired gives rise to misery. All that is desired gives rise to fear. If we can discard all that is desired then there is neither misery nor fear.

216. All that one craves for gives rise to misery. All that one craves for gives rise to fear. If we can discard all that is craved for then there is neither misery nor fear.

217. Those who are perfect in morality and in view, abiding in Dharma, speaking truthfully, and performing the tasks ascribed to them – such beings make others happy.

218. One in whom a longing for the ineffable has arisen, whose mind is clear and turned away from involvement in desire, is known as One Bound Upstream.[63]

219. When one who has been travelling for a long time returns home they are greeted with happiness by their family and intimate friends who rejoice to see them.

220. Similarly, when someone who has generated merit goes from this world to the next, their merit will be waiting to welcome them just as relatives welcome home a loved one.

CHAPTER 17 | ANGER

221. Renouncing anger and renouncing pride one should free oneself completely from all that one is caught up in. Suffering does not befall one who does not cling to name and form[64] and who has no longing for anything at all.

222. I say that someone who can check their rising anger just as a charioteer checks a runway chariot is a true charioteer. The rest are just holding the reins.

223. The absence of anger will overcome fury. Goodness will overcome evil. Generosity will overcome meanness. Truth will overcome lies.

224. Speak the truth and don't get angry. Even if one has very little one should give something whenever asked. With these three one will enter the presence of the gods.

225. The sages cause no harm to others and are always restrained in body. They go to the changeless[65] state where there is no misery.

226. Awake both day and night, continuously training and fully committed to nirvana, they bring an end to all defiling taints.

227. Atula,[66] the following is true not only for today, it was also true in the past. Those who are silent are criticised for this. Those who speak much are criticised for this. Those who speak little are criticised for this. There is no one in this world who is not criticised.

228. There never was, there never will be, and nor is there now, a person who is only blamed or only praised.

229. Those whose faith, morality and undiminished intelligence have been observed and appreciated on a daily basis are praised by the wise.

230. Who could find fault with such a person? They are like a coin of refined gold. They are praised by the gods and even Brahma, the chief of the gods, offers praise.

231. Guard against anger[67] in the body. The body should be restrained. Abandoning causing harm with one's body one should use it to do good.

232. Guard against anger in one's speech. One's speech should be restrained. Abandoning causing harm with one's speech one should use it to do good.

233. Guard against anger in one's mind. One's mind should be restrained. Abandoning causing harm with one's mind one should use it to do good.

234. The steadfast are restrained in body and also in speech. The steadfast are restrained in mind. They are perfectly restrained.

CHAPTER 18 | FAULTS

235. Now you are like a withered leaf and death's messengers await you. You are at the threshold of death yet you have no provisions for your journey!

236. So strive quickly and wisely to make yourself an island[68]. Purify your faults till you are stainless, then you can arrive at the level of the Holy Ones in the upper realms.

237. The end of your life has come. You have arrived close to the king of death. There is no interruption to this journey and you have no provisions to take.

238. So strive quickly and wisely to make yourself an island. Purify your faults till you are stainless, then you will not experience birth and death again.

239. Step-by-step, little by little, moment by moment, the wise person removes his stains until clear just as a silversmith removes impurities from silver.

240. Just as rust emerges from iron and then eats away at its source, so it is for those with bad conduct, as the deeds arising from themselves lead them down to the lower realms.

241. Non-performance brings faults to recitation. Lack of repairs brings faults to houses. Laziness brings faults to healthy appearance. Carelessness is a fault in watchmen.

242. Bad behaviour is the taint of women. Meanness is the taint of benefactors. In this world and in the next all kinds of harm arise from taints.

243. Worse than all other taints is the taint of ignorance[69]. Monks, completely abandon this taint! Be free of all taints!

244. Life is easy for the shameless, for those who are impudent like a crow, offensive and depraved.

245. Life is hard[70] for the modest, for those who seek purity, and are detached and unassuming, pure and discerning.

246. Those who destroy life, tell lies, take what they are not entitled to in this world, use the wife of another, and

247. Habitually drink alcohol until they are drunk – such beings in this very world are cutting their own root.[71]

248. In this way you should know that evil habits are difficult to restrain. Do not let desire and non-Dharma pull you into protracted misery.

249. People give alms according to their faith. If you become upset by the food and drink prepared by others then in neither day nor night will you be able to settle into concentration and meditation.

250. But those who cut their hopes[72], root them out and cast them away, will enter still absorption.

251. There is no fire like intense desire. Nothing grips us like fury. There is no net like opacity.[73] There is no torrent like craving.

252. Other people's faults are easy to see. We can winnow out their faults like chaff from grain. Yet we hide our own faults like a dishonest gambler hiding an unlucky throw.

253. If one looks for other people's faults with a permanently heightened perception, then one's own taints will increase. In this way one is far from exhausting one's own taints.

254. There is no path in the sky.[74] The practice of virtue is not to be found outside oneself. Some find pleasure in the proliferations of the world but the Buddhas are free of such conceptual elaborations.

255. There is no path in the sky. The practice of virtue is not to be found outside oneself. All compounded[75] things are impermanent. The Buddhas are unwavering.

CHAPTER 19 | THE RIGHTEOUS

256. To make decisions without due consideration is to act without Dharma. The wise ones investigate both the seemingly valid and the invalid.

257. Non-impulsively leading others according to Dharma, that intelligent practitioner of Dharma is said to be imbued with Dharma.

258. One does not become wise from speaking a lot. Those who are patient, friendly and fearless are said to be wise.

259. One is not a bearer of the Dharma on the basis of speaking a lot. Even those who have but a little learning, if they look at the Dharma through their body[76] and are not heedless towards the Dharma are said to be imbued with Dharma.

260. A monk is not an Elder simply because of having grey hair. He may be advanced in years yet still be called 'grown-old-in-vain'.

261. When a monk is truthful, virtuous, harmless, restrained, controlled and steadfastly free of stain, that person is to be called an Elder.

262. Even if one has a fine complexion and great beauty, along with flowing eloquence, as long as one is jealous, rough and deceitful one will not be an inspiring presence.

263. But if these bad qualities are cut down, uprooted and discarded, that intelligent person free of faults, will be known as an inspiring presence.

264. An undisciplined liar is not made virtuous by their shaved head. How will someone who values desire and grasping become virtuous?

265. He who pacifies his evil tendencies both great and small is entitled to be known as a righteous peaceful person due to their pacification of evil.

266. One is not a monk simply because one begs. One is a Buddhist monk only if one has fully adopted the Dharma.

267. Discarding both merit and evil[77], leading a pure life, and behaving with a clear understanding of the world, this person is truly worthy of being called a Buddhist monk (*bhikshu*).

268. If one is stupid and ignorant, merely keeping silent will not make one a sage. As if they were evaluating possibilities by weighing them on scales, the wise sages choose the best, and

269. Discard evil. On the basis of this one is a sage. It is through being familiar with the two worlds[78] that one is called a sage.

270. One does not become noble by taking life. Those who cause no harm to all who value their lives are called noble.

271. Not by morality, not by committed endeavours, nor by great learning, nor by maintaining absorbed contemplation, nor by living in isolation,

272. Did I reach the bliss free of dualistic activity which is not gained by ordinary people. Monks, do not relax and rest until you have attained the extinction of all taints.

CHAPTER 20 | THE PATH

273. The best of all paths is the Eightfold Path[79]. The best of truths is the Fourfold Truth. The best of Dharmas is nonattachment. The best of humans is the seer.[80]

274. There is no other path that leads to seeing clearly.[81] You must follow this path which completely stupefies Mara.[82]

275. By keeping to this path you will bring an end to suffering. I teach this path with the full knowledge of the ground[83] of thorns.

276. Teaching is given by the Thus Gone Buddhas. You yourself must strive to apply it. Those who meditate and abide in profound equanimity are completely freed from Mara's binding.

277. "All that is compounded is impermanent." When this is seen with true discernment one will not be afflicted by suffering. This is the pure path.

278. "All that is compounded is suffering." When this is seen with true discernment one will not be afflicted by suffering. This is the pure path.

279. "All phenomena are without inherent existence." When this is seen with true discernment one will not be afflicted by suffering. This is the pure path.

280. When it is time to get up and act they do not get up. Though young and strong they are lazy. Their mind is feeble in its attempts to gain clarity. Such a lazy person will not find the path of clear knowing.

281. With the purity of these three paths of activity – being careful in speech, well restrained in mental activity and doing nothing unvirtuous with the body – may we be stable on the path taught by the sage (Buddha)!

282. Flourishing arises from yoga.[84] Without yoga flourishing declines. Knowing these two paths of progress and decline, in as much as flourishing increases, to that extent is one firmly established in the right way.

283. Cut down the whole forest,[85] not just a single tree. Fear arises from the forest. If you cut down the forest and all the undergrowth, monk, you will be in nirvana!

284. For as long as the man has even the slightest desire for a woman, to that extent binding is in place just as a suckling calf is bound to its mother.

285. Just as one pulls up an autumn lily by hand so one should cut off all self-cherishing. As the Happily Gone Buddha has said, "Cultivate the peaceful path that leads to nirvana."

286. "I will live here during the rainy season and also during winter and spring." The fool imagines his future in this way, unaware of what may interrupt[86] his plan.

287. As a great flood carries away a sleeping village, death carries off one whose mind is deeply attached to children and cattle.

288. When death puts us under its power we find no refuge in our family – sons, fathers, relatives, none can provide the protection we need.

289. Seeing the power of this fact, the wise person, contained and moral, quickly clears the path that leads to nirvana.

CHAPTER 21 | MISCELLANEOUS

290. If one would be willing to let go of a small[87] pleasure in order to experience a greater one, then you can see why the steadfast renounce small pleasures in order to experience great happiness.

291. If you create suffering for others while wishing happiness for yourself, you will have created a lot of enemies.[88] Moreover, you will not be able to free yourself from them.

292. Those who ignore what needs to be done yet are active towards what should not be done are fault-ridden and careless and increase their taints.

293. Earnestly and continuously practising mindfulness of the body they do not attend to what is not their concern but promptly do what is required: such mindful and appropriate people find their taints dying away.

294. Having killed mother[89], father, and the two warrior kings, and destroyed the country together with its inhabitants, the brahmin becomes free of faults.

295. Having killed mother, father, the two holy kings[90], and destroying the fifth one, the tiger, the brahmin becomes free of all sins.

296. Fully awake and always aware are the disciples of Gautama. By day and night they are ceaselessly mindful of the Buddha.

297. Fully awake and always aware are the disciples of Gautama. By day and night they are ceaselessly mindful of the Dharma.

298. Fully awake and always aware are the disciples of Gautama. By day and night they are ceaselessly mindful of the Sangha.

299. Fully awake and always aware are the disciples of Gautama. By day and night they are ceaselessly mindful of the body.

300. Fully awake and always aware are the disciples of Gautama. By day and night their minds delight in being harmless.

301. Fully awake and always aware are the disciples of Gautama. By day and night their minds delight in ceaseless meditation.

302. The life of a renunciate[91] is difficult. It is difficult to delight in it. Living with others is difficult. There is suffering in the household life. There is suffering in living with difference. Suffering comes with the wandering life. Therefore do not take up the wandering life, do not chase after suffering.

303. With faith, morality, qualities, good repute and wealth one is respected wherever one goes.

304. The good are bright and visible from a distance, like snowy mountains. But the wicked are not seen even when they are near, like arrows shot at night.

305. Those who can live alone, sleep alone and travel alone without wavering, and who can maintain self-discipline when they are alone, will enjoy the furthest reaches of the forest[92].

CHAPTER 22 | THE LOWER REALMS[93]

306. Those who speak untruths go to hell, as do those who deny that they have done what they did. At death they become equal in the other world since both are performers of ignoble activity.

307. Many sinful people, evil and unrestrained, wear the yellow robe.[94] Due to their sinful actions they will be born in hell.

308. It would be better for an immoral, uncontrolled person to eat a ball of iron that is red hot with tongues of flame than to eat alms[95] gathered in the countryside.

309. Four situations arise for the heedless man who seduces another man's wife: accumulation of demerit, sleeplessness, disgrace, and hell.

310. This accumulation of demerit leads to more sin and sorrow in future lives. The pleasure of the illicit encounter is brief and both parties are frightened of discovery. Moreover the king will impose a heavy punishment. Therefore no man should become intimate with another man's wife.

311. Just as wrongly handled *kusa* grass can cut the hand, a tainted approach to the spiritual life will drag one down to hell.

312. Lax behaviour, perversity in religious practice, spoiled purity of vows – no great benefit will arise from these.

313. If something has to be done then do it diligently and completely. Slackness in a renunciate scatters even more dust[96].

314. It is better not to engage in bad activity for such tainted actions will lead to later torment. It is virtuous to engage in good deeds for such actions never lead to torment.

315. Towns on the frontier are guarded inside and out. This is how you should protect yourself. Do not let even a moment go by unutilised. Those who are careless with the moments of their life will regret it when they arrive in hell.

316. Being ashamed of what is not shameful, and unashamed of what is shameful – with such deceitful ways of viewing the world sentient beings go to the woe of the lower realms.

317. Being afraid of what is not fearful and unafraid of what is fearful, with such deceitful ways of viewing the world sentient beings go to the woe of the lower realms.

318. Imagining fault where there is none and not seeing fault where it is present, with such deceitful ways of viewing the world sentient beings go to the woe of the lower realms.

319. Knowing what is wrong to be wrong and what is not wrong to be not wrong, sentient beings who maintain this pure accurate view go to a happy rebirth.

CHAPTER 23 | THE ELEPHANT

320. In battle elephants can bear many arrows shot from a bow. I also will patiently endure abuse. People are often ill natured.

321. A trained elephant can manage in a crowd and kings ride on such elephants. Those disciplined ones who have the power to patiently endure abuse are the best of men.

322. Trained mules are excellent, as are thoroughbred horses from Sindh and the great elephants who lead the herd. But more excellent than these is a person who has trained themselves.

323. These animals cannot take you to the never-reached land[97] which is only accessible to those who are self disciplined and well controlled by themselves.

324. During rut the elephant[98] called Dhanapalak cannot be controlled. When tied up he will not eat for he recalls the elephant forest.

325. The sluggish and gluttonous, dozy whether sleeping or walking, are like a great overfed pig. These foolish ones will be born again and again.

326. In the past my mind would wander off whenever and wherever it pleased. But now I will control it properly and carefully, like a mahout with a rutting elephant.

327. Take pleasure in being careful. Guard your mind well. Pull yourself back from bad tendencies as an elephant pulls himself out of the mud.

328. If you find a mature, stable, well-behaved friend who does the same practices as yourself, then overcoming all difficulties together, happily and mindfully keep company with them.

329. But if you cannot find a mature, stable, well-behaved friend who does the same practices as yourself, then, like a king leaving his conquered kingdom, or a lone elephant in the elephant forest, you should go your way alone.

330. It is better to be on one's own. There is no companionship with a fool. Like a great elephant in the elephant forest, be solitary, harmless and with few desires.

331. It is a joy to have friends when troubles occur. It is a joy to be contented with whatever occurs. It is a joy to have merit at the end of life. It is a joy to free oneself from all sorrow.

332. It is a joy in this world to serve one's mother. It is also a joy to serve one's father. It is a joy to practice virtue in this world. It is a joy to be a sage.

333. It is a joy to practice virtue into old-age. It is a joy to be steadfast in one's faith. It is a joy to retain true discernment. It is a joy to refrain from all evil.

CHAPTER 24 | CRAVING

334. For those who behave carelessly craving develops like a creeper. Like a monkey searching for fruit in the forest they spend each day rushing about.

335. Due to this craving which is the essence of poison, one is tormented by diseases in this world and one's misery grows like wild grass after a rainfall.

336. Whoever abandons this sticky craving which is hard to discard in this world will repel all misery like drops of water running off a lotus leaf.

337. This is the good advice I give you. I wish all of you here good fortune! You should dig up the root of craving as one digs up the *birana* grass to find the fragrant *ushi* root.

338. Just as a tree which is been cut down will grow again if the root is firm and embedded, if the latent tendencies to craving are not extirpated then suffering will continue to occur.

339. Due to thoughts invested with longing, the wrong views of the thirty-six[99] streams will flow continuously in one's mind.

340. Due to the flow of these streams the creeper of craving is fed and climbs up. If you see that creeper growing then cut its root with the clarity of true discernment.

341. Beings who seek happiness are moistened by craving. Those who seek a continuous stream of happiness will find themselves subject to old-age and death.

342. Those strung along by craving go round and round like a hare in a trap. Fixated by attachment they experience protracted suffering again and again.

343. Those strung along by craving go round and round like a hare in a trap. A bhikshu monk who wishes to be free of his own attachment should stop giving rise to craving.

344. When those who seek nirvana leave the forest[100] and then scurry back into the same forest even though they had found no freedom there, they have in fact rushed back into bondage. Look at that person and learn!

345. The wise do not say that iron, wood or hemp make strong fetters. The powerful fetter is attachment to jewels and ornaments, children and wives.

346. These fetters are deemed strong by the wise for they bind easily and, although they feel loose, are difficult to break free from. So cut yourself free from these bindings, renounce the world and without regret abandon the pleasure of worldly desires.

347. Those who fall into the stream of attachment and longing are like a spider bound inside the web it has made itself. The wise cut themselves free from these bindings, renounce the world and, without regret, discard all sorrow.

348. Let go of the past, let go the future, let go the present, and pass beyond becoming.[101] Free your mind from everything and you will not be led to birth and death in the future.

349. The person who is agitated by their own thoughts, and whose intense attachments cause them to seek out the pleasurable, will experience a consequent increase in craving. Their tight binding of themselves is quickly completed.

350. Those who delight in stilling their thoughts, contemplate all that is unpleasant and are ever mindful, they will totally reject craving and cut free of Mara's bonds.

351. Such a person has left behind all limitation. Abandoning craving they are free of fault. Drawing out the thorns of becoming this is their last birth.

352. With craving cast away there is no wish to take up anything. Knowledgeable about words and expressions, one understands how to order letters and their sequences. Such a person is in their final body and are renowned for their great wisdom.

353. I subdue[102] all and I know all. I have no attachment to any phenomena whatsoever. Having renounced all and put an end to craving I am completely liberated. Awakening to complete clarity by myself, who is my teacher?

354. The gift of the Dharma exceeds all other gifts. The taste of the Dharma exceeds all other tastes. The joy of the Dharma exceeds all other joys. The cessation of craving conquers all sorrow.

355. The foolish do not search. Those of weak understanding are killed by wealth. By their craving for wealth those of weak understanding kill themselves as if they were being killed by another.

356. Weeds blight the fields and desire blights beings. For that reason offerings made to those free of desire bring abundant fruit.

357. Weeds blight the fields and anger blights beings. For that reason offerings made to those free of anger bring abundant fruit.

358. Weeds blight the fields and delusion blights beings. For that reason offerings made to those free of delusion bring abundant fruit.

359. Weeds blight the fields and craving blights beings. For that reason offerings made to those free of craving bring abundant fruit.

CHAPTER 25 | THE MONK

360. Good is restraint of the eye, good is restraint of the ear, good is restraint of the nose and good is restraint of the tongue.

361. Good is restraint of the body, good is restraint of speech, good is restraint of mental activity. It is good to be restrained in all areas. The monk restrained in all areas is completely freed from all suffering.

362. Restrained in hand, restrained in foot, restrained in speech, and with higher mental restraint, delighting in inner development, settled in meditation, solitary and contented – such are the qualities of a bhikshu monk.

363. When a monk controls his tongue, speaks appropriately and without pride, and elucidates the meaning and structure of the Dharma, then his speech is pleasing.

364. Dwelling in the Dharma, delighting in the Dharma, contemplating the Dharma, mindful of the Dharma – such a monk will not fall away from the holy Dharma.

365. Do not be proud of what you receive and be without desire for whatever others receive. The monk who desires what others receive will not attain meditative absorption.

366. If a monk is content with whatever he receives no matter how little, and is diligent and pure in his way of living, he will be praised by the gods.

367. Not imputing inherent existence to anything and everything identified by name and form[103], and untroubled by that ab-

sence of inherent existence – with such conduct one is worthy to be called a monk.

368. The monk who dwells in loving kindness with clear faith in the Buddha's teaching will still their associative activity[104] and attain the stage of peace and happiness.

369. Monk, empty this boat![105] When it is empty it will carry you swiftly. Discarding attachment and aversion you will gain nirvana.

370. Cut off five[106], discard five, then cultivate five. The monk who frees himself from the Five Impediments is called 'One who has Crossed the Flood'.

371. Monk, do not be heedless! Meditate. Do not bewilder your mind with what is taken to be desirable. Do not swallow the hot iron ball of heedlessness or you will cry out, "I am suffering!"

372. There is no mental stability[107] without clear knowing and no clear knowing without mental stability. Those who have both mental stability and clear knowing are close to nirvana.

373. Living in an empty house[108] the monk with a peaceful mind truly sees the pure Dharma and by this experiences a joy beyond ordinary human joy.

374. Carefully examining, both this way and that, the arising and passing of the aggregates[109] one experiences joyful happiness. To the wise this is the ambrosia of deathlessness.

375. The necessary bases for the life of a wise monk are: control of the senses, contentment, discipline in accordance with monastic vows, keeping the company of virtuous friends and a pure life free of laziness.

376. By being open and friendly to all and virtuous in all his conduct, the monk will experience much joy and make an end to suffering.

377. Just as jasmine drops its withered flowers, monks should discard attachment and aversion.

378. Peaceful in body, peaceful in speech and peaceful in mind, evenly abiding and without concern for the things of the world, a monk like this is said to be peaceful.

379. You yourself should rouse yourself. You yourself should examine yourself. Guarding[110] yourself as a mindful monk you will live happily.

380. I am my own protector. My refuge[111] is myself. Therefore I must discipline myself the way a merchant trains a fine horse.

381. Full of joy and with clear faith in the teachings of the Buddha, with the peace that comes from stilling the associative activity of the mind, a monk attains the stage of happiness.

382. If a monk applies himself diligently to the teachings of the Buddha when he is young, he will illuminate the world like the moon free of clouds.

CHAPTER 26 | THE BRAHMIN

383. Brahmin[112] cut off the flow! Defeat desire with your awesome presence. Knowing that all compounded things are finished[113], Brahmin, you will know the uncompounded.

384. When the Holy One has gone to the other shore by means of the practices of calmness[114] and clarity then with that knowledge he has power over all involvement.

385. Free of this shore[115] and the far shore, and free of both of them, fearless and free of all involvement is the man I call a Holy One.

386. Stable in contemplation, free of faults, completely settled, free of activity[116] and without stain, he has attained the highest value. Such a man I call a Holy One.

387. The sun shines in the day. The moon shines in the night. The warrior shines in his armour. The Holy One shines in his meditation. But the perfect Buddha shines with brilliance by day and by night.

388. A person who discards evil is called a Holy One. A person of pure conduct is called a practitioner of virtue. A person who has discarded all his stains is thereby called a renunciate.

389. One should not strike a Holy One and Holy Ones should not respond with anger. It is bad to strike a Holy One but it is worse for a Holy One to respond with anger.

390. By abandoning a preoccupation with pleasure the Holy One gains a not inconsiderable benefit. To the extent that harmful

intentions are stilled in his mind, his suffering is stilled to the same extent.

391. Whoever does no harm through body, speech or mind and is restrained in these three pathways, I call a Holy One.

392. Just as a Brahmin priest reveres his sacrificial fire, so one should offer homage and respect to those who have enabled you to learn the Dharma teachings of the perfect Buddha.

393. One does not become a Holy One by means of matted hair, family, or birth. It is the pure person who lives by truth and Dharma who is a Holy One.

394. Foolish man, what is the benefit of your matted hair and antelope skin? You wash[117] your outside yet within you are full of filth.

395. Wearing dust-stained rags over their emaciated vein-covered body and meditating alone in the forest is the man I call a Holy One.

396. I do not call a person a Brahmin Holy One on account of the mother he was born from, nor because of his reputation or wealth. But he who has cast off everything and holds onto nothing is the one I call a Brahmin Holy One.

397. Having cut off all involvement he is completely without fear. Having left attachment behind he is uninvolved. I call that man a Holy One.

398. He who has cut the tie of hatred, the thong of craving and the fetters of doubt along with all the tendencies that support them, and who has cleared the obscuring[118] obstacles and is enlightened, that is the man I call a Holy One.

399. Not irritated by enemies and troublemakers, but free of anger and most patient, having the strength of an army of patience – such is the man I call a Holy One.

400. Free of anger, determined, ethical, much studied, disciplined and in his final body – such is the man I call a Holy One.

401. Like water on a lotus leaf, like a mustard seed on a pin, whoever desire cannot touch – such is the man I call a Holy One.

402. Whoever by himself fully knows the end[119] of suffering, and has cast off all burdens and is free of involvement – such is the man I call a Holy One.

403. The wise one with profound clear knowing can well distinguish the true path from non-paths[120] and so gain the highest value – such is the man I call a Holy One.

404. He does not mix with householders or renunciates, wandering aimlessly[121] with few desires – such is the man I call a Holy One.

405. Abandoning violence towards all creatures whether moving or stationary, he neither kills nor beats – such is the man I call a Holy One.

406. Friendly amongst the abusive, peaceful amongst those who threaten with clubs, ungrasping amongst those who grasp – such is the man I call a Holy One.

407. Desire, anger, pride and jealousy fall from him like a mustard seed from the point of a pin. I call that man a Holy One.

408. One who speaks truthfully, gently, helpfully, causing offence to none – I call that man a Holy One.

409. Whether it be long or short, small or great, good or bad, the person who takes nothing in this world that is not given to them, I call a Holy One.

410. In this world and the next whoever is free of the basis[122] for desire, who is without the basis of desire, and is free of involvement, I call that man a Holy One.

411. Knowing all by knowing that everything is without foundation[123], free of the stain of doubts and with full appreciation of the deathless ambrosia is the man I call a Holy One.

412. Whoever has stopped supporting[124] both merit and sin is without misery and is free and pure. I call that man a Holy One.

413. Stainless and pure like the moon, clear and without fault, and completely free of craving for worldly pleasure – I call that man a Holy One.

414. Abandoning the bewilderment of samsara's paths that are so difficult to traverse[125], having transcended conflict and entered unwavering stable contemplation free of doubts, all grasping is stilled. I call such a man a Holy One.

415. Whoever gives up desire and becomes a homeless renunciate completely ending all objects[126] of desire – I call that man a Holy One.

416. Who ever gives up craving and becomes a homeless renunciate completely ending all objects of craving – I call that man a Holy One.

417. Abandoning all human involvement, dispensing with involvement with the gods and becoming free of all involvement[127] – I call that man a Holy One.

418. Having given up all likes and dislikes, cool and without attachment, the hero conquers the entire world. I call that man a Holy One.

419. The person who comprehends all the ways in which sentient beings die and take birth, and is free of attachment to any such possibility, is a Happily Gone Buddha. I call that man a Holy One.

420. Whoever's path is unknown to gods, gandharvas and humans, having ended all taints, is an arahat – I call that man a Holy One.

421. He who takes possession of nothing in the past, present or future, who has nothing and takes nothing – I call that man a Holy One.

422. The chief, the leader, the hero, the great sage, the conqueror of all, unwavering, purified and enlightened – I call that man a Holy One.

423. Who ever knows the location of his former lives, who can see heaven and hell, who has attained the ending of birth, gained the perfection of prescience, and done all that had to be done – I call that man a Holy One.

Translated by C R Lama and James Low in 1982.
Revised by James Low in 2018.

May all sentient beings have happiness and the cause of happiness.
May all sentient beings be free of suffering and the cause of suffering.
May all sentient beings never be separated from happiness free of suffering.
May all sentient beings abide in the great equanimity free of both attachment to those held close to them and aversion to those kept at a distance.

NOTES

1) The term 'mind' translates the Sanskrit *manas* which indicates mind as a mental function, the activity of mental consciousness as it formulates the identity of what it is experiencing. It is the mentation or mental activity which organizes information, draws conclusions and plans actions. Because it is largely intentional it can be controlled in ways that stray thoughts and random impulses cannot. This mental activity takes what it experiences to be either 'in here' as my experience or 'out there' as all that we encounter in the environment. All the things or dharmas that can ever be encountered are encountered by the mind. Things, entities, objects that appear to have their own existence, are all the result of misunderstanding our own experience.

2) As guests we are just passing through and so there is no need to get involved in others' quarrels. This world is not our true home and we only borrow what we temporarily have – and so what is there to fight over?

3) Mara is the name given to the forces which trouble us. Sometimes they are taken to be demons, malevolent creatures who wish to cause trouble primarily by erotic attractiveness or disturbing aggression. Maras are also understood to be our own negative patterns which deflect us from the right path and bring us to grief. Maras can also be placed in

for classes: i) the demon of misperception, ii) the demon of imagination, iii) the demon of egoic pride, iv) the demon of excitement.

4) These are the thirty-two unpleasant aspects of the body, contemplation of which diminishes attachment and desire. It also refers more generally to those aspects of the world that bring grief. By contemplating them one loses desire for anything to be found in the cyclical existence of samsara.

5) The unessential refers to the transient factors of existence, food, clothing, status and so on, while the essential refers to the aspects of mental discipline that free one from further immersion in samsara.

6) Although there are no really existing sentient beings, when the pattern of the five compositional factors of form, feeling, perception, association and consciousness are under the power of the afflictions of opacity, desire and aversion many actions occur which are harmful to self and others.

7) The realms of woe are the three lower realms of samsara, the realms of the animals, hungry ghosts and hells, where suffering is the dominant experience.

8) These are the three upper realms in samsara, occupied by humans, jealous gods and gods in which there is more pleasure than in the lower realms.

9) Pure insight or clear seeing is the discerning clarity, (*prajna* in Sanskrit) which sees the precise details of every situation without imputing the least inherent existence to what is seen.

10) A liberated mind is one which does not look to the past or future and is unattached to whatever is occurring in the present. Free from involvement there is equanimity and openness.

11) To be heedful or careful means to be attentive to whatever is arising within body, voice and mind, and to be attentive to the senses and

all that they reveal. This fresh attention, free of judgement and involvement, is uninfluenced by what arises and so is not fused with any of the transient events that are born and quickly die. This mental clarity or attention does not die. However egoic identification with selected aspects of events binds the sense of self to the ephemeral and so keeps one subject to death.

12) The noble ones are those who never stray from the Dharma or truth of how experience actually is. They are noble because they are not contaminated by the temptations that are all around.

13) Liberation or nirvana is the extinction of all the tendencies and beliefs which bind one to samsara. It is the ending of suffering since it is the ending of attachment to the delusion of the reality of inherent existence which is the root cause of suffering.

14) The mind gradually takes on a limited form through how it perceives options, makes choices, and sustains habits and tendencies. These limiting patterns come to be experienced as our identity and so although they generate much sorrow, because they 'feel like me', it is difficult to part from them. We are so used to swimming in Mara's small pond that when we step out of it in order to fulfil our aspiration for awakening we find that we are agitated and restless like a fish out of water. This is the new level of disturbance that meditators encounter when they make progress.

15) The invulnerable mind is neither flooded by experiences nor does it leak out into events. Balanced, stable and uninvolved, all that occurs is met with equanimity. When this equanimity is profound then even a virtuous meditator is no longer privileging merit and avoiding demerit. Seeing that the mind itself is free and uncompounded, and thereby not improved by what is conventionally taken to be good and not undermined by what is conventionally taken to be bad, all polarities can be let go of.

16) The health of the mind and its ethical integrity is often sacrificed for the sake of the body. Yet this body, so pampered and cherished,

is heading for destruction since it is vulnerable and breakable like a clay pot. Old-age, sickness, accidents and finally death hover around the body like flies around a corpse. Therefore it is better to focus one's attention, care and concern on the balanced stability and clarity of the mind.

17) Yama is the god-demon who stands at the gate of death ready to weigh up the sins and virtues of those who have left their body and all that was familiar far behind. Yama's henchmen are ready to drag the unvirtuous down to the lower realms where they will painfully encounter the fruits of their negative actions. Yama is implacable and ferocious and only purity of heart and calmness of mind allow us to slip past him.

18) The bee focuses only on the pollen it seeks; everything else is irrelevant. Hence it is careful not to get involved with what is unnecessary. Likewise the sage is focused on calm clarity and equanimity and so moves through the town undisturbed and without causing disturbance to others.

19) This verse highlights the experience of one who has a finely-tuned sensitivity to their own ethical or unethical behaviour. If one is aware of what one is doing and is committed to practising virtuous activity then there would be no basis for having regrets on completion of an action. It is for this reason that all religions encourage us to practise virtue so that life becomes easier and we are freed from the shadow of guilt and shame.

20) *Kusa* grass is the fine-tipped grass that Siddhartha Gautama sat on under the bodhi tree when he became enlightened. One would require great patience and diligence to use the fine tip of the grass to bring food, perhaps a single grain of rice, to one's mouth.

21) The top of the head is the highest opening in the body and the one through which the subtle consciousness of the virtuous person will exit at death. When this is spoiled or obscured one's consciousness is directed towards the realms of samsara.

22) The ever-pure, the *aryas*, are those who are free of defilements and limitation. They are beyond being contaminated by the obscuring forces of samsara and none of their activity brings contamination to others.

23) The 'far side' is nirvana, peaceful and free from the constraints and sufferings of samsara. 'This side' is samsara within which we are generally blind to the fact that there is another side.

24) 'Well-spoken' indicates that the speaker is the Buddha. Being established in the truth of how things are, he has a pure vision which is conveyed by his speech. It is because of this that his words can be tested and trusted.

25) 'Black' or dark beliefs are those that arise from not seeing how things are. Moreover, they generate further obscuration which hides how things are.

26) 'White' or bright beliefs are those expressing the truth of how things are. They are taught by the Buddha from his enlightened clarity. Relying on them will bring all beings to enlightenment.

27) True happiness is that which arises from liberation from delusion. It is not dependent on subjective mood nor on the qualities of people, objects or situations.

28) The afflictions are the orientations of body, voice and mind which generate suffering for self and others. The principle afflictions are opacity or assumption, desire, aversion, pride and jealousy. When they arise in the mind they suffuse it so that there is little conflict or resistance. In this way they are experienced as valid and necessary, which leads them to be acted on leading to consequent accrual of negative karma.

29) The seven branches are mindfulness, wisdom or clear knowing, energy, joyousness, serenity, focussed meditation, and equanimity. These are the attitudes and experiences to be cultivated under all circumstances.

30) From this perspective the function of food is simply to maintain health and energy so that one can progress on the Dharma path.

31) Emptiness is the actuality of the absence of inherent existence in sentient beings and in all phenomena. Due to this there is nothing to grasp at and so the grasping tendency of the mind is calmed. Signlessness means that the qualities we see as present in self, in others, and in phenomena are not actually there. They are signs projected by our mind onto ungraspable appearance. Appearance itself is not actually touched or defined by these signs. 'Aloneness' points to the mind's freedom from relativity. It is beyond comparing and contrasting, beyond dependent origination, and so is free of reliance on appearances.

32) 'Corruption', *asava*, refers to the factors which cause an outflow of virtue and an influx of confusion and non-virtue. There are said to be four principal corruptions: desire, craving for existence, ignorance, and wrong views about how things are and how the mind is.

33) Indra's weapon is the *kila* or nail that fixes itself firmly in its target and cannot be moved. Indra is the chief of the gods and his power is beyond contestation.

34) 'The uncreated' is nirvana. Everything else is compounded, created, artificial, and with both beginning and end. Nirvana is entered by the wise, not made by them. It is always present as an option and we all have the potential to turn towards it and find ourselves within it.

35) 'Establishing boundaries' means separating the far shore, nirvana, from the near shore, samsara. Attachments, habits, and the longing for pleasure dependent on objects, all create links back into confusion. All such tendencies need to be cut by maintaining the imperturbable calm of settling into the uncreated.

36) To defeat yourself is to overcome and tame the tendencies which create trouble and suffering for self and others. When these urges

are disempowered the mind is untroubled and one gains true peace, the greatest victory.

37) The true meditator focuses on the following three marks of conditioned existence. Seeing that suffering is pervasive they release their desire. Seeing that all phenomena are impermanent they release their habits of constructing inner and outer forms. Seeing the absence of inherent existence in everything, they relax all their many habits of arousal and grasping.

38) Due to complacency and drifting along in the dreams of our assumptions, we imagine that we are stable, enduring people living in a world of stable, enduring entities. Although we note that 'things change' and 'the years go by', this knowledge is non-transformational. To see the arising and passing is to see directly that all conditioned phenomena, including the five component skandhas (form, feeling, perception, association, consciousness), are impermanent and devoid of any enduring essence or substance. The world and we are not what we think they are.

39) The deathless stage is the stage or state or level in which all the factors of death have been let go. All compounded phenomena are impermanent and since the ego self has no other ingredients but these it starts to loosen up and dissolve. By disidentifying with the transient and seeing how one has maintained the deluded belief that the transient is reliable, one is freed from involvement with all that arises and passes. With this the deathless is revealed.

40) The supreme Dharma is the peace revealed by seeing the absence of inherent existence in all compounded phenomena. This is the great door to liberation.

41) The word 'evil' is used here to translate the Tibetan term *digpa*, which indicates something toxic and poisonous. Sin or evil is poisonous for it arises from the five afflictions or poisons. Good intentions, if weak in commitment, easily fall prey to evil. The good that I would do I do not do while the ill that I would not do, I do. The need

for mindfulness, heedfulness, and discernment is emphasised again and again in this text. Getting lost in the polarities is easy. Staying on the middle way is hard.

42) All sentient beings have accumulated negative karma yet the consequence of this activity is invisible to us until it ripens. When ripe the consequences of evil deeds are manifest and one can no longer pretend that one is simply a nice person.

43) Chaos and confusion are everywhere. Hopes and dreams go up in flames. Cities and children go up in flames. Your past has already vanished into the flames of time. What is there to be truly happy about in samsara? The darkness of ignorance surrounds us and the only illumination we have is from the fire of dualistic imagination fuelled by the five afflictions. What we see is revealed by the misleading light of death and not by the true light of undying life.

44) 'House-builder' refers to attachment to phenomena which are taken to have inherent existence. When the fact that they are empty of imagined essence and substance becomes clear to us then the mind is free of the conditioned entities it has 'created' by its own involvement. Conditioning mental activity is impermanent and its product, conditioned phenomena, is also impermanent. Seeing this, the builder of the house is made redundant.

45) If the energy of youth can be turned towards the practice of a pure holy life then great spiritual wealth will accrue. But if we wait till we are old and tired we will find that the opportunities for practice are much diminished as is our strength and focus.

46) Although there is an absence of inherent existence to the 'self', as a sentient being wandering in the duality of samsara, there are many events which can lead us astray. If our goal is nirvana, peace and freedom from reactivity, then we have to find out how not to sink in the swamp of duality. This self influences the other and the other influences the self. Instability and impermanence are ongoing factors that call us to mindfulness. If the sense of self is stable then it can be

examined and its actuality revealed. But if we are endlessly reacting to circumstances then our clarity will diminish and our impulsivity will increase.

47) Control requires discernment and effort. To follow a discipline such as playing the violin one has to learn to control one's tendencies to avoid, to be distracted, to be uncommitted. The teacher can help by being boundaried and reliable. They can teach self-control but the student has to learn self-control. This means to accept that one is a divided or fragmented being, harbouring many conflicting habits and tendencies. One has to restrain the tendencies that some parts of oneself would love to indulge. Through sustained effective inner struggle in this conflict which is already in place, one can free oneself from entanglement and so settle into undistracted clarity and focus.

48) All the effort that one makes in following wrong views – such as disbelieving in karma and believing that phenomena really exist – brings no positive gain but ripens as the destruction of one's clarity and ethics. This is like the *khattaka* reed that dies as soon as it flowers.

49) The verse might appear to advocate a selfish attitude but it does not. If you sacrifice your time and energy for the worldly benefit of others (looking after children and other loved ones, feeding the poor and so on) to the degree that you have no time for your own spiritual practice you will have made the worldly more important than the holy. Whereas to focus on removing one's faults and increasing one's virtues will bring one to liberation with the capacity to help others in a profound way that leads them to the uncompounded deathless.

50) One's evil deeds are like dark clouds obscuring the clarity of the mind. When one ceases from evil and practises virtue instead then the former dark covering is replaced by light. The light covers the dark and renders it impotent. The practice of virtue displaces evil and its traces so that they cease to impinge and cause trouble.

51) There are many ways to pass a life, such as pursuing our instincts or our culturally mediated desires. But the wise are aware of these dead-ends and so are stable in meditation and ethics and are unseduced by the myriad possibilities of the world. Free of wavering, they enter nirvana.

52) A Stream Enterer is the first of the four stages of true progress according to Theravadan Buddhism. It is followed by Once Returner, Non Returner and Arahat. A Stream Enterer is freed from belief that appearances have their own fixed identity. They no longer perform rituals and are free of doubts regarding the teaching.

53) The amount of good karma required to gain a human body is vast. For any sentient being it is hard to know that you must die – that the body and habits that you take to be yourself are impermanent and not a true refuge. In the whole of samsara the event of the Dharma being taught is very rare and so to encounter such an event and to be available in oneself to truly listen is hard. Although ignorance and grasping are adventitious and not innate or fundamental they are very familiar in their operation. Letting go of the known, the familiar, the relied on, is hard and for this reason emerging as a Buddha is hard.

54) 'Spiritual asceticism' is the practice to endure whatever arises, whether it provokes desire, aversion, jealousy or other intense responses. Both the stimulating objects and the reactive subjectivity have to be endured without further involvement, neither merging nor rejecting. This is the profound patience which releases us from our attachment to samsara and our helpless participation in it. Hence it is the supreme nirvana. Retaliation, revenge, mindless provocation – there are so many unvirtuous tendencies to be let go of.

55) The Noble Eightfold Path is the fourth of the Four Noble Truths. These truths are:
    1. suffering: pervasive throughout samsara, affecting all sentient beings.

2. the cause of suffering: this is both the ignorance by which we are blind to the truth and our consequent attachment to misleading illusion created by our imagination which obscures awareness.
3. the cessation of suffering: the peace of non-attachment, non-involvement and non-excitation. Suffering ends when the cause of suffering ceases to function.
4. the path: this leads to the cessation of suffering and is called the Eightfold Path.

    This eightfold path is not a set of options – all eight aspects need to be practised. They are:
    i. right knowledge or vision, seeing the fact of impermanence and the absence of inherent existence.
    ii. right intention, deciding to follow the path.
    iii. right speech, clear and undeceiving.
    iv. right action, behaviour guided by the teachings.
    v: right livelihood, supporting yourself with work that is ethical and helpful and not harmful.
    vi: right effort, focusing on developing virtue and diminishing evil and harm.
    vii. right mindfulness, undistracted attention to all details of what is occurring.
    viii. right meditation, concentrating on the practice so that the misleading refuge of thoughts, feelings and sensations can be dispensed with.

56) Beings become sick due to the five poisons. There are also many other more subtle poisons which can make us sick. When we are sick we are incapacitated, full of self-concern and anxiety. To be free of this and to live in health is to be free of ignorance, attachment and craving.

57) Longing is the opposite of contentment. To long for something is to be displaced from where one is and from what is currently available. Longing indicates something is missing: the longing subject hopes for an object that can complete it and bring it happiness. However the happiness referred to in this verse is not dependent on the un-

certainties of finding the 'right' object. It is the happiness which is revealed when the mind relaxes its grasping and finds contentment in mindful presence.

58) The aggregates are the five component factors which constitute sentient beings: form, feeling, perception, propensities or associative constructions, and consciousness.

59) Propensities are the organising attitudes which feed the ripening of full consciousness of an event. Incorporating memories, feelings and thoughts they compound the potential of the event into a sense of something definite.

60) The text uses the term *yoga* to indicate union with something. Linking oneself to activities that do not lead to liberation is a waste of time – and who has time to waste? The mind is fickle and therefore our intention must be strong and clear.

61) The profound happiness of nirvana, a happiness arising from contentment, peace and the absence of longing, is very different from the happiness which arises from momentary contact between a grasping subject and a graspable object. Inner tendencies are unpredictable in their arising and passing and so are outer events. The likelihood that the perfect object can be maintained close to us and kept available is very small. Everything changes and gain and loss fluctuate without ceasing. Therefore seeking happiness in outer objects or in mental objects is not wise.

62) It is not the things or people that we like that are the problem. They are not what has to be discarded. Rather it is our own attachment, investment, and involvement, which binds us to an image of the item or person. Although all phenomena are imperfect and impermanent, with our attachment we create our idea of them, ideas that seems to be outside of time. It is this deluded and seemingly enduring pseudo-object which evokes desire, envy, jealousy, hatred and all the other poisons that are the companions of our chosen sources of happiness.

63) Like a salmon swimming up a rapid river, the one bound upstream goes against the current of samsara and the ignorance and habitual tendencies that maintain it. Their goal lies elsewhere, in the peace of nirvana, and with the stability of their focused intention they will not do anything that would bring about a return to samsara.

64) Identifying forms as things and giving them a name provides the hooks by which you can hold onto them as if they were something real. Name and form keep the drama of samsara running. *See also Note 101, iv.*

65) The changeless state does not react to provocation and so is completely free. Although while on the path to it effort is required to keep one's composure, on arrival all stimuli lose their power and so no more effort is required.

66) Atula was a lay disciple who wished to hear dharma teachings. He visited many of the senior disciples of the Buddha and requested instruction but in each case he was dissatisfied with what he received. He then went to see the Buddha and complained about these teachings of his senior disciples. This verse contains the essence of the Buddha's response.

67) Anger here stands for irritability and agitation. When body and speech and mind are not at peace there is hypersensitivity to the actions of others and a parallel poor level of impulse control.

68) This island rises free of the choppy waters of samsara and so grants some respite from the provocations of daily life. Cutting down worldly involvement to the minimum, one gains time in which to recognise and renounce identification with the taints and faults which have become habitual.

69) 'Ignorance' refers to the ongoing activity of ignoring how things are. It is not an absence of information, but a non-attending to what is occurring in the simplicity of its occurrence. Due to this the actual, although present, is not revealed to us. Instead of attending we

dream of other events, other times, or simply smother what is with our own fantasies of how we think and feel it is. This is the activity of self-blinding which keeps us in the dark forest of samsara.

70) Good qualities are hard won. They do not fall like rain but emerge slowly, aided by the sweat of the brow. Getting lost is easy while staying on track, being reliable and doing what is necessary when it is required, calls for diligence and commitment that often sends the ego into resistance.

71) 'Root' here refers to virtuous roots. When virtuous activity is planted in the soil of clearly seeing phenomena as they actually are, then clarity sprouts and the true path to awakening becomes visible. But if only evil harmful actions are performed by one whose mind is toxic with the five poisons then the sprout shrivels and the root is cut off from its supportive ground.

72) When we have a desire or an agenda and hope it will be fulfilled, we reduce our capacity to open to how life actually is. By comparing what we get with what we would prefer we create agitation and disappointment in ourselves. Cutting off hopes, cutting off mental constructs, letting go of attachment to our sense of how others should behave, brings a sense of freshness to the moment and a mood of humble gratitude for what we are given.

73) Opacity is the hazy, non-transparent density of samsara, the gloom within which everything seems very real. It is the stupidity and mental dullness within which we prefer to imagine rather than to see. In the previous line, the grip is that of the *makara*, a Leviathian-like sea monster with powerful jaws from which no one can escape. Once anger takes hold of us we are not in charge, like a young rider on a wild stallion.

74) Since there is no path in the sky, no matter how long and wide you look you will not find one – it is not there! The world is full of temptations and offers all kinds of excitements and distractions but no matter how long you search there you will not find a basis of spir-

itual practice. Ethics, discipline, concentration and meditation are all to be found only within oneself. The Buddhas are peaceful. They have seen that there is nothing to find and so they have stopped looking and are content.

75) Compounded things do not exist outwith the mind. The mind compounds the traces of events, composing patterns which it holds to be real in themselves, each having their own separate existence. But these composites are mind-made; they are like an illusion, and, arising from causes, they soon vanish. The mind of the Buddha has never been constructed, never alters, and never vanishes.

76) Looking at the Dharma through the body means to not keep it as something abstract or theoretical. It is through looking at one's own embodiment, being mindful of sensation, breath, posture, senses and so on, that impermanence, absence of inherent existence, and suffering are revealed to be the truth of what we take to be our 'existence'. Remembering whatever teachings one has received and applying them moment by moment to illuminate life relieves us of the burden of having to imagine the whole show.

77) Although virtue is better than nonvirtue within the conventional frame of reference, clinging to virtue is also an attachment. It can lead to pride and to further solidification of experience. Therefore both merit and evil are to be discarded as identities and values on which to rest. Although we need self-control and diligence to turn away from evil and towards virtue, we also need to practise meditation in order to relax and release all clinging and craving.

78) The world revealed through good attitudes and actions is not the same as the world encountered by those with evil intentions and actions. The former world is bright and clear even when difficulties occur. The latter is agitated and anxious even when difficulties are absent.

79) *See Note 55*

80) The seer, the one who sees, is the Buddha. With his wisdom eye he sees that everything that occurs, all compounded phenomena, are impermanent and devoid of inherent existence. Seeing this, there is nothing to gain or lose.

81) Seeing clearly or purely is to see the purity of all phenomena. When reification ceases, the fantasy of self-existing objects dissolves and the world is bright and translucent. There is seeing what is without filling it with one's own thickening and dulling interpretations.

82) Mara is the guardian of the ego. As long as the ego is complacent and unquestioning, Mara causes little trouble. But when people make effort to free themselves from dulling habits and start to practice virtue then Mara is actively hostile and tries to catch them and fill them with fear and anxiety. Mara cannot comprehend liberation, awakening, freedom and so when we enter this path he cannot grasp what is going on. The more he tries to understand it the more dazed, bewildered and stupefied he becomes and this makes him more dangerous.

83) Here the Buddha is speaking directly to us. He is teaching from his own experience and knows the validity of what he says. He indicates that he knows well the ground or source out of which all thorns arise: seemingly real objects or entities, in all their myriad forms, have the same ground, ignorance. From ignorance comes deluded imagining followed by grasping at the delusory forms as if they were real and reliable. If ignorance is dissolved in clarity there is no ground to give rise to any thorns, obstacles, poisons, problems and so on.

84) The Tibetan version of this text uses the term *naljor*, (yoga), whereas as the Pali text uses a term for meditation. *Naljor* indicates entering an easy way of being; not struggling, but resting free of attachment and intention. The Tibetan text also says *phuntsok*, flourishing, whereas as the Pali text uses a term for wisdom. When our intention and energy are freed from developing the causes of suffering then our life resources can encourage the flourishing of all that is good.

85) In the dark forest of our imaginings the five poisons flourish. The whole forest must be destroyed along with all the shoots and bushes of habits and tendencies. We cut the forest by cutting off craving through seeing that it operates on false premises. The ego is not real, its desires are like a dream, waking is safer than sleeping.

86) Since death may come at any time we should hold all our plans lightly – they are imaginings, not certainties.

87) 'Small pleasures' refer to those of the senses. They may be intense but they are always fleeting. By not pursuing them the wise man is free to find the unchanging great happiness of liberation from samsara.

88) These enemies are both the people whom you have hurt and who now seek revenge, and the afflictions of your own mind. Your anger and hatred of others gives rise to fear and anxiety in yourself so that you become wary and ill at ease. Now you have enemies outside and inside you, so how will you find peace?

89) This verse is written in code and has to be unpacked. 'Mother' stands for desire, 'father' for ego and anger, 'the two kings' are the extreme views of eternalism and nihilism, 'the country' is all sense objects and sense organs, and 'the inhabitants' are the attachments. 'Killing and destroying' means to make these negative, limiting and deluding factors become inoperable. When they do not operate the Brahman, the meditator, is pure and free of taint.

Such symbolic language uses its disturbing impact to highlight the fact that absolutely all that is perceived to be real and which becomes an object of clinging, whether through desire or anger, has to be killed off. Why? Because it was always only an illusion, like a mirage. A mirage has no real existence and is unborn as a discrete entity. Being unborn, how can it be killed or destroyed? When delusion is destroyed nothing is destroyed except the delusion that there was something which could be destroyed.

In this text the term 'Brahmin' does not refer to the Hindu Brahmin caste but to one who is pure and without any taint or obscuration and is rich in wisdom. *See also note 112.*

90) Again, 'mother' stands for desire, and 'father' for anger, but 'the two holy kings' are ego and jealousy while 'the tiger' is ignorance. Ego and jealousy make us sensitive to our imagined special status as a unique individual and to our consequent fear of losing it. The tiger lives in the jungle and is almost invisible, creeping silently on his prey and devouring it without mercy. This is exactly what ignorance does to us – a hidden force that swallows up our chances of liberation as we wander in confusion in samsara.

91) This verse begins with advice against becoming a sadhu renunciate, a wandering holy person in the Hindu style. Buddhist monks settle in monasteries but freestyle renunciates wander hither and thither and may find nothing but suffering. However to be a married householder is also to be exposed to difficulties and suffering. The Buddhist path is the middle way between these extremes, renouncing attachment to the things and structures of the world while being settled enough to sustain study and meditation.

92) Being self-reliant and self-contained yogis are free of dependence on objects. Passing through the forest of samsara to the very end, their desires, habits and tendencies are gradually extinguished and then they are free wherever they are.

93) The three lower realms of animals, hungry ghosts, and hell realms are not distinguished in this chapter, being referred to simply as 'the states of woe'. It is a great misfortune to be born there. This is not just because of the physical and mental anguish and powerlessness. In these realms there is very little opportunity to gather good karma and merit in order to facilitate rebirth in an upper realm where one might have the leisure and focus to study dharma and apply it in a way that will lead to liberation.

94) Life would be much easier if titles, religious clothing, high status and so on could be relied on to indicate that their possessor was worthy and developed in good qualities. Exploitative bosses wear expensive suits, dictators wear medals of honour, and hypocritical devious people can hide in religious clothing while exploiting oth-

ers. Clearly this is not something new in the world and therefore we have to be heedful and attentive to other people's actual behaviour and not be taken in by mere presentation.

95) Cheating people by pretending to be holy and devoted to the path when you are not, is a grave sin. You deceive them and deepen your own deceitful character – and if they find out it can cause them to doubt all religious people, so that they become wary and anxious and lose their generous open-heartedness.

96) Life in samsara is confusing. Most people have no idea why they were born or what might happen when they die. Such bewilderment is even greater in the non-human realms. The Buddhist teaching offers a map of becoming and shows how to liberate oneself from the endless sequence of life after life. If religious people, who take vows and are supported by alms for the inspiration they represent, act with laziness and deceit, they scatter obscuring dust which hides the true path.

97) The never-reached land is nirvana which one does not arrive at by making a journey from here to there. No matter where you wander in samsara you will not find nirvana. It is not far away yet it is only revealed to those who cut the root of samsara. This root is not cut by pilgrimage. It is cut by sitting on the meditation cushion. We reach the unreachable by not reaching for it.

98) In the time of rutting when its sexual desire is strong the elephant has no self-control. It does not respond to ordinary coercion and has to be tied up. Out of control, yet controlled by impulses it is fused with and seeks to act from, the elephant can be very destructive. This is an image of how we are when we choose to be self-indulgent and avoid self-discipline. At the mercy of our tendencies, we may feel free but are actually prisoners of impulse.

99) The thirty-six currents or streams refers to the forces that can carry us away from steadfast mindful attention to whatever is arising. We are pulled into attachment and involvement in situations and this

creates karma and the thickening of delusion. The thirty-six currents are the six sense organs and their six objects in relation to the three cravings: those for sensual pleasure, for existence, and for nonexistence. The mind or mentation, *manas*, is the sixth of the sense organs.

100) The forest of the afflictions is both terrible and tempting. The excitement of desire, jealousy, anger and so on can be enthralling yet these hot passions end in misery. Human beings have a great capacity for ambivalence. We tend to hedge our bets and so find one-pointed commitment difficult to sustain. We give up smoking then start again; we finally stop an unhealthy relationship but find ourselves phoning them when we are lonely. We will not find the answer in the object because the object is always interpreted by our mental processes. What we take to be an object out there is in fact an aspect of mental experience. We have to awaken to the difference between the clarity of our mind and the stream of mental arisings which flows through it.

101) The famous Wheel of Life, or Wheel of Becoming, illustrates how we move around in the six realms of samsara due to the three root poisons of desire, aversion, and opacity. The momentum of our revolving or ever-changing life is maintained by the unfolding of the Twelve Links or Nidanas. These are:
   i. ignorance of the Four Noble Truths
   ii. constructing arising from subject-object interaction
   iii. consciousness relating to the five senses and to mental functioning
   iv. name and form. Name as the mentality of feeling, perception, intention, contact and attention. Form as the corporality of the four elements: earth, water, fire, air
   v. six-fold sense bases: the five sense organs plus mind/mentation
   vi. contact, the coming together of a sense object, its specific sense organ, and the consciousness belonging to that sense
   vii. feeling/sensation: the pleasant, unpleasant, or neutral sensations that occur when any of the six sense objects meet with their sense organ and its sense consciousness
   viii. craving, longing for more of specific experiences of the objects of the six senses

ix. clinging, holding onto sensual experience, views and beliefs, practices and habits, and the sense of self
x. becoming, karmic force giving rise to rebirth in the lower, upper and highest realms via sensual becoming, form becoming, and formless becoming
xi. birth, emergence in a new form via birth, including birth from an egg. It also refers to the fresh occurrence of any new event.
xii. aging and death, this refers to all the suffering that occurs in a particular life span.

102) Subdue does not indicate crushing the other. Rather it indicates that a person like this does not go under the power of the object. Being bright and radiant and free of need, this wise one offers others no means of gaining control over them. This verse might seem like showing off but it points to the message of the Buddha. He said that he taught us how to identify the root problem and he pointed out the path to freedom but each person has to be a lamp to illuminate their own way on the path. Having received the teaching, the rest is up to us. If we strive we will succeed. The only impediment is ourself. The focus is on looking and learning. The learner, the one who learns about themselves by learning from themselves, can let go of the ego self. No one else can do this for us, so who is the teacher?

103) *See Note 101, item iv.*

104) Associative activity, or compounding, *samskara*, is the unnecessary mental activity of narrative construction. With this, the freshness of the presenting moment is veiled and stalled by the mental activity of trying to make sense of what is going on from the ego's point of view. Due to this, we are conscious of our own creations rather than the simplicity of what is there.

105) The boat stands for all that one clings to as a support for deluded ego identity. Body, family, worldly knowledge, wealth, nationality and all other signifiers of self and place in the world should be released from this perverse usage.

106) The Five to be Cut Off are the lower fetters: belief in inherent existence, doubt in the Buddha, ascetic and ritual practices, sensual desire, and ill will. The Five to be Discarded are the higher fetters of: longing for birth in the form realm, longing for birth in the formless realm, self-conceit, restlessness, and ignorance. The Five Factors to be Cultivated are: faith, vigour, mindfulness, concentration, and wisdom. The Five Impediments are: sensory desire, ill will, sloth and torpor, restlessness and worry, and doubt. They all operate to impede entry into meditative absorption by focusing attention on whatever is arising rather than on calm clarity. Regarding One who has Crossed the Flood, see the *Ogha-tarana Sutta: Crossing over the Flood*.

107) Mental stability is the state where whatever arises is clearly revealed yet without causing disturbance. Clear knowing, or wisdom, is the unchanging experience of the absence of inherent existence in whatever is occurring. Clear knowing is not seduced by how things appear and it does not engage in judging or adopting or rejecting.

108) The empty house has been abandoned. Just as monks in ancient times wore garments of the dead cast off at the burning grounds, so a monk should be able to inhabit a rejected dwelling in an isolated place. To be content with cast-offs is a practice for dissolving pride and the ego-affirmation arising from choice. This parallels the lack of choice in accepting whatever food is put into the monk's begging bowl.

The empty house also stands for non-attachment to the body and its senses since, when those stimuli lose their power to excite, the mind becomes peaceful. The really pure Dharma is the truth of the cause of suffering and the undeniability of the three marks of conditioned existence: suffering, impermanence and absence of inherent existence. The joy that arises from this is not generated by subject/object interaction but is the quality of undisturbed clarity.

109) The aggregates of form, feeling, perception, associations/constructs/compounds, and consciousness are the constituents of sentient beings. They are all impermanent and unreliable. Seeing this,

the meditator is freed from attachment to them and so the truth of how life is is revealed. The ambrosia of the deathless is the liberating elixir that arises from the extinction of the maras, obstacles, karmic traits and so on. They are the maintainers of the cycle of birth and death and when they no longer control us we enter the deathless, nirvana itself.

110) We are the cause of our own misfortune and so it is up to us to stay on the path. The danger does not lie outside ourselves, so when verse says, 'guarding yourself', it indicates guarding, protecting and defending yourself against yourself. That is to say, in samsara we live as divided creatures exhibiting both a lost involvement in the turbulence of stuff and a yearning for clarity. Dharma points out that if we let go of bewilderment and all that arises from it clarity will continue. Thus, we are both death-full and death-less and the choice is ours. If we choose the path of the deathless then we must guard well against our 'own' habitual tendencies to fuse with the deathful.

111) Given that it is customary for Buddhists to begin their practice by reciting three times that they take refuge in the Buddha, the Dharma and the Sangha, this verse may seem strange. Given that I have faults, intense habits, sudden tendencies, and little insight, how can I be my own protector and my own refuge? Well, if we say, "I take refuge in the Buddha", who is doing this? I am. I protect my feet with shoes, my body with clothes, and my mind with Dharma. If I do not put my own shoes on my own feet I will not have protected feet. If I do not do the study, reflection, and meditation my mind will not be protected.

To rely on others is to remain in duality with all the dangers of attachment and aversion. They both stem from the root poison of opacity, the non-translucent quality of duality. Once there is 'this and that', 'me and you', 'me and myself', there is little clarity. I, me, myself operate together as an inner conversation, sometimes encouraging and sometimes criticising. "I don't like myself" means that some activities of body, speech and mind upset the sense of myself that I would like to uphold. This ongoing subject-object dialogue, both inter-personal and intra-psychic, appears to be generating meaning and producing conclusions yet it is impenetrable and opaque. Where do thoughts come from? Where are thoughts when they are 'here'? Where do they vanish to? These are questions the involved ego does not ask and cannot answer. The ego cannot find out who or what it really is, and so invents many identities and stories. Who does this? I do it! But I don't have to. The mind binds us to samsara and the mind frees us in nirvana. This is set out in the first two verses of this text, The Dhammapada. Thus we are our own protector. We are our own refuge.

112) 'Brahmin' in this chapter indicates a pure and holy person. There is an implicit critique of those Hindu priests who are ritual experts. The qualities outlined in this chapter do not refer to them but to one who follows the Buddhadharma in a heartfelt and consistent way. Since most readers are likely to have no cultural association to the term Brahmin, in the remaining verses it is rendered as Holy One. *See also note 89.*

'Awesome presence', *Zilnon* in Tibetan, refers to the capacity to overcome trouble-makers so that they cannot act. Without suggesting threat or attack, the Holy One is so impressive that the minds of others lose their harmful intent. For example, when the serial killer Angulimala met the Buddha on the road he was unable to fulfil his intention of cutting off one of the Buddha's fingers. Just the sight of the Buddha brought about a metanoia, a transformation of the patterns of his mental activity. The finishing of all compounded or conditioned 'things' means that since they are mental phenomena rather than so-called material phenomena, when the mind stops imagining them, they dissolve. Truly, they are mind-forged manacles. They are not intrinsic but adventitious and developed by habit. All sentient beings already have the basis for freedom. The task is to awaken to this.

113) In our familiar dualistic perception, the objects we perceive seem to be out there in the world. This is a delusion. What we experience are the fruits of compounding, of gathering together various aspects of the environment, both outer and inner and patterning them into

the shape of the object, which is then infused with our associations, memories and so on. This arises due to the operation of dependent origination. When this is understood we are in touch with the fact that all appearances are compounded and devoid of inherent existence. All associations, all compoundings, all seemingly fixed and reliable appearances and identities are the work of the mind. That is why they can be fully finished or exhausted (*zadpa* in Tibetan) and this occurs when we cease identifying with the mental activity that generates and maintains them.

114) 'Calm' indicates *shamata*, peaceful abiding, and 'clear' indicates *vipassana*, seeing the actual. With the first, peaceful abiding, we develop stable concentration by focusing on one object e.g. on the sensation of the breath at the nostrils, or on a small rounded pebble. This becomes one's sole focus of attention. With the second, seeing the actual, one brings that focused attention to whatever is arising, usually at first by scanning the body to see what arises there. By simply seeing what is there we awaken to the fact that the actual is impermanent and ungraspable. What appears to be stable and graspable are in fact the concepts we hold about the actual. These two practices take us from the worldly grasping bank of the river of arisings over to the far shore where there is no involvement in the flow. One is then no longer at the mercy of the ever-changing contents of one's mind, for their power has only ever been the power that we invested in them.

115) In this verse in particular, 'this shore' indicates where sentient beings in samsara are trapped in the experience of the six sense organs. The 'far shore' indicates their corresponding six kinds of objects, while 'both' refers to the six sense consciousnesses which bind them together.

116) 'Free of activity' does not mean paralysed. It refers to being free of the unnecessary activity which can arise from the stimulation of the sense organs. When reactivity is pacified, compassionate responsivity is of course still possible as required. Highest value, Tibetan *Don*, is the quality of the unclouded mind. This bright clarity exposes all

the faults of samsara so that without the least regret one can enter nirvana.

117) Washing and ornamenting the body with bones, powdering it with ashes, and presenting an impressive appearance – such an image deludes others and feeds your own egotism: "I am special, look at me!"

118) There are two obscurations. There is the rough obscuration of the five afflictions which in the intensity and persistence of their formulation blinds us to what is beneath our projections and interpretations. Then there is the more subtle obscuration of taking knowledge, information, concepts and so on to be true and reliable so that one cannot penetrate to the non-conceptual, non-conditioned truth of life.

119) The end or cessation of suffering is the heart of the Buddhist teaching. When the truth of the absence of inherent existence is alive in the mind, the burden of the delusion of a grasping subject and a graspable object is laid down forever. Now there is freedom with no need to return as there is no longer 'someone' to be the vehicle for karma accumulated in the past.

120) Consumerist capitalism and consumerist spirituality both offer myriad 'non-paths'. Non-paths seem shiny and useful, even necessary, on first acquaintance. They are often popular and seem validated by the number of followers, yet who amongst the makers and sellers, the teachers and students, is satisfied, deeply contented and at peace? The Buddhadharma has also been marketed as a spiritual add-on to improve one's life. But such cynical corruption of intention will not lead to the enlightenment pointed to by the Buddha.

121) Keeping himself to himself and needing only enough to survive he wanders here and there. He has no plan of where he should go, no preference for here or there. Such aimlessness is hardly imaginable in the modern world where focused intentionality and efficiency drive people from this specific 'here' to that specific 'there'. We trav-

el in order to gain something but the renunciate travels in order to disrupt his patterns of assumption, prediction, and necessity. Wherever he is, he is mindfully present with precise clarity free of all enmeshing involvement.

122) The basis of desire is duality arising from ignorance. Not seeing truthfully but instead imagining entities that seem to have inherent existence, it seems that I am inside me and you are outside me. I am not you, you are not me. You have things, qualities, possessions, functions and so on that I don't have. "Oh, I don't have them but I want them." So now desire is running all over the world, seeking what it likes and ignoring or discarding what it does not like.

123) The foundation on which the world rests is an illusion. Appearances arise in dependent origination. There are no self-existing entities defined by an inner essence or substance which gives them inherent existence. Appearances are empty of self. The foundation of the illusion of self is ignorance, and when that is looked for it cannot be found. When the foundation of all has no foundation, we quickly know all by knowing everything to be an illusion. Looking at the flow of mental activity and seeing its transience, and looking for the mind itself and finding nothing, we gain clarity beyond doubt and this is the deathless, or unchanging clarity, the door to liberation.

124) Although in conventional terms merit and sin are clearly opposites with very different implications, in themselves, in absolute terms they are without any foundation other than their mutual exclusion. By relaxing mental activity the supports of these categories dissolve – they were never more than the play of the mind. Of course until that insight is fully alive and functioning for us all such categories should be attended to carefully since our belief in them drives our actions from which karmic consequences emerge.

125) Wandering in samsara is very hard for all beings but it is even worse without Dharma because then we are lost and don't have a map. The path to liberation is not featured in our cultural conditioning. We follow the tracks that seem meaningful but then they vanish in

the sand: marriages end in divorce, industries become obsolete leaving thousands unemployed, wars evict peaceful people from their homelands and so on endlessly. To get out of samsara, to get free, we need to see what's going on – but we are so full of assumptions that we become bewildered in the face of the truth. The first step to freedom is making contact with the Dharma and developing faith in it.

126) The objects of desire, the things of the world, commodities, material possessions, all the items which stimulate our desires, are not other than illusions generated by mental activity. Surprising and alarming as it may be, they do not exist in themselves. Their 'existence' is dependent on our mind. This is the marvellous basis of liberation since if we cut back on our mental activity, washing off the glue of attachment, we see that when the mind moves the ten thousand things appear. When the mind is at peace there is peace without disturbance. Thus, as is often said, freedom's key is already in the palm of our hand. Calm the subject and the objects go free by themselves.

127) Profound renunciation makes the mind simple and smooth. Free of expectations there is no judgement. Free of hopes there is no disappointment. Wherever we are we are free once the habit of subjective involvement in objects is fully dispensed with.

Section Two

MISTAKEN IDENTITIES

INTRODUCTION TO SHARP WEAPON WHEEL

THIS FAMOUS TEXT BEAUTIFULLY EXPRESSES the inclusive approach of Mahayana Buddhism. Highlighting the inseparability of wisdom and compassion, it shows how seeing things as they truly are and acting for the benefit of all are the two wings of the bird that will fly us to enlightenment.

All sentient beings are precious. All have the same ground or basis which is itself the door to freedom. Yet they wander in samsara activating dualistic intentions under the influence of the five poisons, namely the opacity of mental obscuration, desire, aversion, pride and jealousy. All sentient beings have been our mothers in previous lives and so are equally deserving of our respect and care as we repay our debt of gratitude.

There are no fundamental differences between sentient beings. The diversity of their forms is due to the ripening of their karma. This karma arises from attachment. Attachment arises from ignorance of the ever-open and available ground. This ignorance is adventitious and in no way contaminates the pure ground which is the same for all beings.

True concern for the welfare of beings is necessarily inclusive and not exclusive. To discriminate between beings, doing more for those we like and less for those we do not like, is to act to maintain samsara by privileging the delusion of duality over the actuality of non-duality.

This is very challenging since we have to overcome more than just our everyday biases towards those we care for and those we don't. Ethical concern for others who have been hurt often causes us to have a negative view towards those who torture, rape, exploit and similarly harm others. Especially if we say that torture is done by torturers and that the term 'torturer' really sums up who they are. This way of viewing strengthens our sense of the negativity not only of the action but of the person who acts. They are bad! So, should we act to help 'people like that' gain enlightenment?

Well, 'people like that' have no defining inherent existence. Like everyone else they manifest according to causes and conditions. Their seemingly fixed defining identity as 'torturer', 'rapist', 'terrorist' and so on is an idea arising in our mind. Their own karma will bring them suffering in due course. Our task is not to punish but to see how the potential for enlightenment present in all beings is easily obscured by over-identification with the transient features of each current situation.

All beings are potential buddhas, they are not-yet-buddhas. Buddhahood will manifest following the resolution of their confusion, the dissolving of their karmic tendencies, the ending of their wandering in samsara, and the ripening of their potential for unimpeded clarity and compassion. Moreover, as Shantideva says in ENTERING THE WAY OF THE BODHISATTVA (Ch. 6, v. 113),

> *Thus Buddhahood depends*
> *On beings and buddhas equally.*
> *Which tradition reveres*
> *Buddhas and not beings?*

Without sentient beings there would be no one to become a buddha. Without buddhas who would be able to help sentient beings awaken their own intrinsic buddha-potential and so gain enlightenment? To imagine that buddhas are fundamentally different from the sentient beings who wander in samsara is a great mistake. Beings and buddhas have the same source and all our judgments and discriminations cannot alter this basic fact.

Buddhahood is awakened to by the wisdom conveyed by the teaching of the buddhas and by the compassion evoked by remembrance of both the potential of all sentient beings and the suffering they endure due to ignorance and karmic consequences.

Cherishing all sentient beings, valuing their potential and holding it as more important and definitive of them then their adventitious limitations and tendencies, awakens our own hearts to love and trust. Seeing that they are like us in wishing for happiness and in trying to avoid suffering we can come to see that there is no basis for the judgments we make about them and about ourselves other than our own mental constructs.

Judgment is based on comparing and contrasting, setting this against that. For such an evaluation to occur, 'this' and 'that' need to be different. When we compare and contrast sentient beings we do so not with regard to how they are in themselves but solely with regard to our own interests and concerns. Which person can help me more? Which animal is more delicious for me to eat? This way of examining the qualities of others shows us ourselves, not them. Each and every sentient being is inseparable from emptiness and is therefore incommensurable. All have value yet this is not the value we project into them and then imagine them to inherently possess, but rather it is the intrinsic value of emptiness as set out clearly in the Heart Sutra. Not only are we all empty of inherent existence and so devoid of an enduring defining essence which could be judged to be good or bad but the judging self is also an empty illusion devoid of true authority.

I and all beings wander in samsara due to unawareness of our own mind and the consequent delusion that self and other are really existent. From the single moment of the arising of the idea of an entity existing apart from the ground there is a gradual development of the duality of self and other and the attribution of individual existence and agency to both. The open source, the site of our buddha potential, is never lost; it does not go away from us nor we from it. The ignoring of the ground is the seductive presence of the idea of separateness. There is no actual division yet the idea of self-existing entities develops due to misprisioning the openness. We see right through it without being aware that it is always present.

The focus of our attention and desire is usually on the illusion of substance made ever-more 'real' by our deluded belief in the reality of the separate entities we call 'self' and 'other'. This belief generates us in our 'individuality' at the expense of freedom to relax. We, as pseudo-entities, are now trapped on the treadmill of continuous ego-maintenance, relying on transient phenomena, both the seemingly 'outer' and 'inner', to fill our empty self. Within this delusion we believe in many different objects, animate and inanimate, and experience the apartness of myself, my mind, my body, my world.

Due to this limited understanding we generate some virtue with body, voice and mind and so temporarily inhabit the higher realms of gods, jealous warriors, and humans. We also generate some non-virtue with body, voice and mind and so temporarily inhabit the lower realms of animals, hungry ghosts and hells. None of these realms are final destinations. Each can be experienced by us on the basis of the karmic tendencies which arise for us at the moment we exhaust the cause of inhabiting a form in one particular realm. We then experience a new ripening arising as a consequence of an aspect of our accumulated karma manifesting as identification with a new body and environment.

Seeing that this is the case, if I accept that my experience is generated by my own mind, then there is no one else to blame for my situation. My life is not in the hands of others. Having been born in samsara, all that occurs for me arises from my own past and present actions. If I want freedom from the chain of repeated births I will have to review my life and make the necessary changes. No one can do this for me.

As THE DHAMMAPADA says, verse 165,

> *By oneself alone is evil done.*
> *By oneself is one defiled.*
> *By oneself is evil avoided.*
> *By oneself alone is one purified.*
> *Purity and impurity depend on oneself.*
> *No one can purify another.*

Moreover Nagarjuna says in his LETTER TO A FRIEND,

> *Our liberation depends on us.*
> *No one else can achieve this for us.*
> *Therefore, by study, ethics and non-distraction*
> *Strive to activate The Four Noble Truths.*

Although we vow to cease from causing harm to others and to work for their benefit and welfare, the help we can give is limited. Each sentient being has to awaken by herself or himself. This is because they themselves have to disengage from attachment to thoughts, feelings, memories and all the other constituents of their deluded sense of self. Having done so, they need to awaken their love and compassion by reflecting on the suffering of others, and to dissolve all obscurations in the clarity of unobstructed emptiness.

The mind is primary. When it moves, that is, when thoughts, feelings, sensations, memories, impulses and so on, arise in it, then everything appears and moves. The patterning of my voice and body arise from my mind. Mind is chief. And it is my mind, not as a possession of the ego self, but as the basic field of experience that I, as mental consciousness generating intentions, have access to. The ego is a content of the mind and not the other way round. Mental consciousness can examine the ego, the sense of a continuous permanent self that is cherished above all others. Is it truly what we take it to be? Is it who we truly are? Perhaps it is merely an unexamined assumption. We need to establish this for ourselves. Assumptions or mental obscurations are powerful for they guide our experience and behaviour whether they are actually valid or not.

The absence of inherent self-nature in persons is established through seeing that each of them is a composite of the five components, namely form, feeling tone, identification, augmentation, and conclusive consciousness. These five factors operating together generate the deluded impression of there being people who really exist in and of themselves. However when these five factors and all other phenomena are examined we see that they arise in dependence on other factors. There are no self-existing entities to be found anywhere. All phenomena, including the five components, arise from causes; they have a beginning, a middle and an end. Due to this dependence on factors of creation, maintenance and destruction, phenomena are never independent. To take them as such is the habit of the ego self: I am real, apart, just me and similarly this tree, this apple, this stone, is real, apart and just itself. This misguided and misguiding approach misidentifies appearances and instantiates the fundamental duality of self and other, subject and object, which drives all the confusion and suffering of samsara.

With this unawareness of the functional ground or basis of experience there is no sense of the true status of what is occurring. With this there arises the sense of self and other, both of which are taken to be truly existing. This belief in the inherent existence of phenomena including ourselves is maintained by directing the energy of the mind towards the constructive activity of substantiation. We assume that the objects we encounter, including ourselves, are self-defined in their thingness by an essence and substance which is their personal basis. Thus they appear to be grounded in themselves, of themselves, and so we are blind to the fact that their ground is in fact emptiness.

Emptiness is not a subtle metaphysical essence. The term 'emptiness' does not refer to a 'something', to a refined substance out of which appearances are made. Rather, emptiness is a shorthand term pointing to the absence of inherent existence in everything, including emptiness. In no place and at no time, in either samsara or nirvana, can even one truly autonomous entity be found. Thus, the term 'emptiness' indicates that all that can ever be experienced is devoid of the least independent existence. The whole is undivided; it is not the sum of its parts as there are no parts. The whole is empty and simultaneously full. For this reason, emptiness is beyond concepts and so we require meditation to open us to how it is.

The grasping at existents, at entities, which blocks our awakening to the fact of emptiness, is called *bDag 'Dzin* in Tibetan. *bDag* usually indicates I, the first person singular, but here it indicates the belief in the singularity or unique specificity of just this specific entity. It is this and no other, separate and able to be considered as an independent something. *'Dzin* indicates grasping at and holding onto. Under the deluding power of duality we grasp at entities and come to rely on them as if they truly existed. This becomes the frame of reference within which we pass our lives. Cutting this grasping at entities having inherent existence is the task of dharma practice. When we grasp at entities both the grasper and the grasped at are mere ideas devoid of essence and substance. Since there is no actual duality between self and other all our grasping is just a dog chasing its own tail.

When the open ground, the source, is ignored in favour of what appears, it is as if there is an either/or choice, and on choosing appearance over openness, the non-duality of appearance and the ground is lost touch with. Appearance arises as subject and object, self and other, and neither is independent of the other. The self is always a work in progress, forming and reforming according to the resources available to it.

This ceaseless endeavour of maintenance involves options, selection and our own conscious and not so conscious biases. The subject chooses some items and not others, while each item seems to choose some subjects and not others. Just as we can choose bits of items or objects, so items choose or evoke bits of me. On the sight of a person deemed by me to be beautiful, the erotic aspect of the self is awakened – often to no purpose. Desire and aversion, hopes and fears, are all evoked by the seeming provocation of the other. This is a functional or aesthetic provocation arising from the display of specific aspects of their potential. I take the aspects I encounter to be meaningful and definitive of the 'total' object or person, and then feel provoked by how I have taken them to be.

In truth there is no provoking other and no provoked self, yet within the dream of duality the qualities of the other impact me, often without my wishing it, and perhaps even without my registering the impact.

Believing that I have a body, I am subject to the eight great fears: fire, water, earth, air, elephants, snakes, thieves and kings. I need to breathe, drink, eat and sleep, travel and rest. To gain the resources for this I have to engage with the environment and manage variations in supply of items and in the fads of the culture. I am dependent on so many people and things in so many ways and yet I see myself as apart, separate, autonomous, independent. The dis-owned other, all that is taken to be non-self, cannot be completely rejected as it is needed for survival yet it can be and is ignored, denied and interpreted so that although I functionally rely on it to support my sense of my identity, I can still hold it to be quite apart and other.

To maintain myself I need to control the factors which impinge on me and yet I cannot. I cannot control the appearance and intention of others. I cannot even control my own responses which often arise before I am aware of having a choice. The subject is basically space and so easily fills with transient aspects of wind, fire, water and earth. Space is non-impacted. It is always present within us as the *avadhuti* central channel or middle way. But the other elements are always moving in relationship: they impact and are impacted. We walk in the hills and are refreshed by the views, the colours, the wind and by the movement generated in us by the varied angles, textures and stabilities of the land. Some impacts are sought out and welcomed. Others are enforced, like a series of red traffic lights. While others still are merged with, as if they were our own volition.

To be sensitive is to be touched and moved. This is necessary for compassion but is a tenderness vulnerable to overwhelm and trauma. To defend against it by armour, avoidance, domination and so on, merely sets subject and object in opposition and maintains the delusion of duality. The most useful protection comes not from taking up a position, but from dissolving all positions within the infinity of emptiness. Emptiness is the ground and truth of non-duality, the inclusive whole, free of all splitting and reification. Duality is exclusive, partial, competitive and conflictual, setting this against that. The part cannot encompass the whole, even though it tries to accumulate more and more bits of the world.

Many different descriptions of the patterns of our life energy have evolved over time. For example, the self in its embodiment can be seen to be subject to tendencies of dark and heavy swamp-like sinking, (*tamas*), energetic expansion expressing powerful control (*rajas*), and avoidant purity that remains vulnerable to defilement (*sattva*). This has a parallel description in terms of the tempers, the *doshas*: *vata*, *pitta*, and *kapha*, which can be in balance internally and externally, or not. *Vata* indicates the influence of space and wind, the movement of air; it is enlivening. *Pitta* indicates the influence of fire and water; it is balancing. *Kapha* indicates the influence of water and earth; it is settling. *Dosha* indicates fault or disease since the dynamic nature of these tendencies means that they are rarely balanced either in themselves or as a collective of forces. Our loss of ease or dis-ease arises from their conflicts and contradictions. As long as the individual ignores their actual ground these imbalances in energy will cause problems in body, voice and mind. Energy manifests as the forms of the world of which we are a part. Our individual identity is dependent on both selecting and encountering aspects of the field of manifestation. Since this field is ever-shifting, as are our moods and tendencies, our identity is inherently unstable.

There are so many ways of describing the body yet all seem to point to it as being a dynamic system of communication. It is not a fixed entity. The breath that sustains it manifests as speech, as connectivity, linking words according to grammar and semantics to form patterns that can be comprehended by someone else. The unpredictability of our behaviours lies in the diversity of possibilities inherent in our potential. We are not a singular self but a multiplicity of possibilities each of which is an aspect or mode of what we call 'ourself'. Some aspects are primarily receptive, registering what has happened to 'me'. Others function to interpret and evaluate what has occurred. Further aspects may formulate a response and organise its expression. Hence the aspect of our 'self' which is evoked by the impact of interaction may not be the aspect of self which manifests to generate the response. For example, my vulnerable self-aspect feels hurt when you reject me. Then my defensive aspect concludes that you are horrible which activates my revengeful aspect, allowing 'me' to act in a way that will hurt you.

The integrity of the field is primordial. Only from the confused position of duality does the activity of integrating seem meaningful. The issue is not to try and integrate duality into non-duality – there is no separation. The issue is to desist from the unnecessary and unhelpful arousal which drives the activity of ignoring, forgetting, splitting and reifying. Ending unnecessary effort is the direct path to liberation. When the sole ground is obvious, there is no separate self to provoke or be provoked, to vex or to suffer vexation. All problems are self-liberating in the purity of their own ground. Illusion dissolves like a rainbow in the sky revealing that there are no real obstacles or problems to be worked on. As THE DHAMMAPADA says, verse 170,

> *Look upon the world as a bubble;*
> *Look upon it as a mirage.*
> *One who looks thus upon the world*
> *Cannot be seen by Yama, the King of Death.*

This is largely implicit in this text, SHARP WEAPON WHEEL, where the explicit focus is on grasping at the ego, the specific form of entity that we take to be the self-existing basis of our sense of self. I exist. I am someone. I am me and not anybody else. Cutting this identification frees the mind from the obscuring veil of being taken to be a self. Now the mind, in being awakened to its own intrinsic clarity, can see that all entities are inherently without inherent self-identity.

However, such clarity is unavailable as long as grasping at a self is further intensified by privileging my 'self', seeing 'myself' as the most important self in the world. This self-cherishing, *bDag-gCes*, is our familiar guiding self-preoccupation, the foreclosure that shuts out the vitality of the presence of others. Indeed others are now recruited only for the value they have in maintaining our own sense of specialness and the importance of our desires, projects, status and so on. Love of self has us each living in our own small world, tidying up our ego-garden, planting our favourite pretty flowers and discarding what we take to be weeds.

Life after life can be spent in this way, accumulating the negative karma of not experiencing other beings as an end in themselves, rich in their own value. Rather we see them as a means to fulfilling our own ends and this diminished regard for them allows us to continue in the selfish fantasy of our own supremacy. It is this self-cherishing that is the explicit focus of this text.

Seeing the interconnectedness of all that occurs heals the estrangement experienced by the isolated ego. How sad it is that the very effort to cherish our ego and make it special maintains the pain-inducing delusion of its separate existence and unique value! Not only have all sentient beings been our kind mothers in previous lives but they are inseparably part of the dependent origination that we too are part of. Moreover, we share our inseparability from emptiness and our inalienable buddha potential. With all of this being the case how could any sentient being not be precious to us?

If however I truly want to help all beings I must free my mind from negative tendencies of thought, emotion, speech and activity. I must also develop positive qualities that will enable me to help others and will also inspire confidence in them as to my usefulness and reliability. This is why I will commit myself to mind training, to adopting the good and abandoning the bad. All the buddhas have done this, hence the Tibetan term for buddha, *Sangs-rGyas*. *Sangs* indicates purified and *rGyas*, vast in good qualities. The term for bodhisattva, *Byang-Chub Sems-dPa'*, carries the same connotation, a heroic being committed to purifying limitations, *Byang*, and to becoming complete in all aspects of compassion, *Chub*.

Following in their path I will develop the unflinching honesty of seeing my faults and limitations. Indulging these faults, I deceive myself and others in the process. Therefore I will separate the clarity of my mind from the confusion that arises in it. As my energy is disconnected from identification with the negative it is freed up to be directed towards the positive, towards all that benefits sentient beings.

In the title of the text, SHARP WEAPON WHEEL, 'sharp weapon' refers to ignorance, belief in duality and reification of self and other. This weapon cuts us off from the ground of our presence and traps us in a world of winning and losing permeated by the five poisonous afflictions (mental obscuration, desire, aversion, jealousy and pride) and the ongoing disregarding of cause and effect. 'Wheel' indicates the revolving water-wheel or prayer-wheel where a bucket or an inscription is carried away and then carried back. When cause and effect are ignored there is a sense that one can 'get away with it' if one is not found out in the here and now. But the teachings on karma point out that the consequence of an action often manifests long after the action has been completed. What goes around comes around.

The great beauty of this profound text is the way it shows that we, like the peacock, can learn to thrive on the poison that is toxic for the ego. The ego-self seeks to do as it pleases but has to face the ripening of karmic consequences. However these consequences and their manifestation as life in the six realms of samsara with repeated encounters with Yama, the Lord of Death, also rest on cause and effect. When the absence of inherent existence in beings and phenomena is awakened to, the cause of samsara, ignorance and attachment, is destroyed. Hence, seeing that cause and effect give rise to all conditioned phenomena and that they therefore lack inherent existence, the basis of karmic cause and effect is dissolved. Thus the sharp weapon of karma that torments the ego is itself destroyed by the sharper weapon of wisdom which ends the delusion of the ego and its associated karmic production, thus ending the delusion of samsara.

Only awareness inseparable from emptiness is free of karma and therefore one should take great care until one is fully awakened to ground openness. Our impulses to negative actions are usually infused with the five poisonous afflictions. They are said to be poisonous as they lead us to sin and thereby to suffering.

'Sin' is a term that is hardly used these days but it is useful in highlighting the toxicity of negative action of body, voice and mind. In the Tibetan language the words for scorpion, for poison, and for the toxicity of negative actions are very similar. As verse 1 of THE DHAMMAPADA points out, our mind is our greatest source of benefit but it is also our greatest source of harm:

> *Mind is the forerunner of all things*
> *Mind is the chief and they are mind-made.*
> *If with an impure mind one speaks and acts*
> *Then misery follows, just as the cartwheel follows the ox.*

Karmic consequence is powerful and confusing and difficult to alleviate and so we must take care in everything we do if we are to benefit others and avoid poisoning the world.

Karma means activity which has subsequent consequences as well as immediate outcomes. It is generated when someone is doing something somewhere to someone else with body, speech or mind or with all three. There are four aspects to this. The first is the ground or basis, which is duality. The belief in a separate self as my true identity puts me into a potentially competitive relation with others who are not me. This belief and mode of experience situates me as separate from, yet connected to, others. I wish to gain advantage and to avoid suffering and disadvantage. My focus can be on my benefit alone or on the benefit of others, generating respectively negative or positive consequences. With this as my basis I form an intention: I am going to do something. This could be kind or cruel, selfish or altruistic – the key point is that the intention confirms me as the actor, the one who makes things happen. I am the doer of the deed. The third aspect is the action itself. I am now carrying out my intention. I am conscious of helping or harming. This is what I am doing. The fourth aspect is the conclusion in which I review what I have done and feel satisfied or not with having fulfilled my intention.

When all four aspects or factors are present and in harmony then not only is there the immediate outcome of the action but the basis is laid for consequences to arise at a later stage, usually when I have forgotten about the causal connection.

Therefore as long as we are under the power of duality we have to strive to be mindful of what we do and face up to the deviousness of our own behaviour. We need to recognise that we have a lot to expiate, for as long as we take our self-serving activity to be normal we bind ourselves further into confusion. We need to make use of the potency of the four corrective purifying factors. The first is the potency of the field of activity: visualising Vajrasattva in front of us, connected with us, available to us. He is the presence of the unchanging purity of our own buddha potential and he has the power to remove all adventitious stains. Secondly, we employ the potency of the effective application of the antidotes. We heighten our regret at our confused activity and increase our faith in the cleansing and healing power of the indestructible buddha mind.

Thirdly, we use the potency of complete renunciation. Although selfish behaviour can seem tempting as if it offers true value, with our understanding of karma we need to be clear that the temporary gain arising from putting oneself first will lead to long-term suffering. Self-indulgence is to be renounced in favour of working for the benefit of others. The fourth potency is that of abandoning the return to error. This requires a strong commitment to changing one's tendencies and behaviour and to sustaining the effort that this will require. On a more profound level it requires us to directly awaken to the truth of emptiness so that the illusory quality of all temptations and provocations becomes obvious.

However it is difficult to directly and immediately see the illusory quality of phenomena since the impact of a situation reaches us before we are able to work out what is going on. The impact provokes and evokes responses in us which we and others may well have difficulty in understanding. Even among human beings our responses to what we take to be seemingly the 'same' situation can be very different. Our perceptions, our interpretations and our mobilisations depend on the unique specificity of the factors constituting each of us in each situation. Incidents which provoke me to anger might leave you with indifference. You then think I am making a fuss about nothing while I feel you wilfully misunderstand the situation. Confusion, hurt, and misunderstanding are readily available in human relationships. We need to move beyond the ceaseless pulsation of blaming self/blaming others.

All bad actions and their encouraging five poisons are in fact inseparable from emptiness. To live with the clarity of this insight frees us to be in samsara but not of it. Wisdom is the basis for compassion. As the *Hevajra Tantra* says, *"The one who knows the nature of poison dispels the poison utilising the poison itself."* This view is set out at the beginning of SHARP WEAPON WHEEL in the comparison between the peacock and the crow.

Our afflictions and karmic tendencies make us vulnerable to the four *Maras*, or troublesome forces. They have to be rendered inoperable if we are to awaken. Just as Prince Siddhartha managed under the bodhi tree to avoid the hopes and fears, desires and aversions elicited by the *maras*, so must we. The first set of *maras* manifest as turbulence in the elements, dangerous animals and other threats to life. They also manifest as our friends and enemies evoking emotions of desire and aversion. The second set has no form but arise as our own mental experience of memories, plans and the many kinds of emotional turbulence we are prone to. The third set of *maras* work with the destabilising effects of success, encouraging pride, complacency, disparagement of others and so on. The fourth *mara* is the most dangerous as it feeds the first three. This is the *mara* of belief in the ego. When we are under the power of this delusion we experience all that arises in terms of how it impacts us. This attitude fuels the ceaseless turmoil of hopes and fears and so we are without equanimity.

In this present period of time known as the *kaliyuga*, the period of the demise of the teachings of Shakyamuni Buddha, ethics, analysis of phenomena, and meditation all become corrupted and fade. Behaviours that were formerly carried out in private are enacted in the public sphere so that the shared public space is fragmented into individuals absorbed in their own phone-world and indifferent to their co-presencing with others. The ethical sense of shared obligation and the mood of friendly supportiveness fade as isolation and selfishness creep in under the cover of intimate conversation with those who are not here. Feeling entitled to 'be myself' wherever I am irrespective of the feelings and opinions of those around me, I do not need to reflect on how I might be experienced by others: "That's their business, I'm just being me. If they find me loud, or rude or intimidating or offering too much sexual display, that is nothing to do with me."

The dulling impact of self-preoccupation brings a focus on what I want now so that even if there is any analysis of the factors which generate our world it is unlikely to be informed by any sense of karmic cause and effect. A purely materialistic interpretation of events is put forward by science so that the mind is reduced to electrochemical activity. If my brain made me do it then who is the moral agent? Meditation and calming concentration become rare in this busy world. And if they *are* practised it is only for stress reduction and greater efficiency in worldly pursuits.

When the words 'awakening', 'enlightenment' and 'liberation' are washed free of deep meaning, and the delusion that death is final is held up as the sole truth, then, dear Reader, the sweet balm of dharma is to be applied to the heart daily while we still have the chance.

In order to fulfil this radical reorientation, this transformation of my self-privileging and self-cherishing, I will abandon taking refuge in the objects of this world. No thing can give me the enlightenment I seek, nor the capacity to benefit others. Therefore I will take refuge in the true path to awakening by taking refuge in Buddha, Dharma and Sangha. With the confidence that I am now never alone, that the buddhas and great bodhisattvas are always with me, I can turn towards committing my life to the benefit of others. I will develop this altruistic intention and then activate it by making it inseparable from my meditation practice and every aspect of my life.

With this reorientation our intention shifts from narrow self-focus to infinitely embracing all beings. We can affirm this by ceaselessly bearing in mind The Four Immeasurables:

May all sentient beings have happiness and the cause of happiness.
May all sentient beings be free of suffering and the cause of suffering.
May all sentient beings never be separated from happiness free of suffering.
May all sentient beings abide in the great equanimity free of both attachment to those held close to them and aversion to those kept at a distance.

These four qualities of love, compassion, joy and equanimity are immeasurable because they are offered to all beings and can be enjoyed by all beings. In a deeper sense they are immeasurable when the three wheels of actor, acted upon, and action turn within emptiness. Then we ourselves and our aspirations manifest like a rainbow: a form visible, evident, impactful yet devoid of essence and substance. This applies equally to the objects of our aspiration: all sentient beings, however they appear and live, are like a banana tree, devoid of a centre, core or defining essence. Moreover the activity of making the aspiration is the movement of thoughts, feelings, sensations, breath, sound, none of which can be found as a real existent. The movement of the mind is ever-changing, just as a mirage moves away as we approach it.

We each have had many lifetimes of getting lost and so our tendencies towards self-abandonment within our assumptions and impulses are very powerful. For this reason we need to devote ourselves to dharma study, reflection, and meditation. However we soon encounter the Three Pot Faults. Sometimes we are like an upturned pot and although our body is present it is as if our mind is coated in Teflon and nothing gets in. Sometimes we are like a pot with a hole in it so that all that we train in and commit to leaks away. And sometimes we are like a pot with old food in it – no matter what new delicious dharma we receive we mix it up with our old ideas and so become confused by this toxic meld.

It is time to be less concerned with the never-ending drama of worldly affairs. These issues and problems will never be sorted and so if we attend to them we will be endlessly disturbed. As the Tibetan saying has it, *"It is easier to cover your own feet with leather than to try to cover the whole road."*

To do this we have to be vigilant. As Shantideva says in THE WAY OF THE BODHISATTVA,

> *All you who wish to protect your mind*
> *Must sustain mindfulness and mental vigilance.*
> *Guard both, even at the cost of life and health.*
> *This I request of you with joined hands.*

Generally we need to be mindful of habits, urges, complacency and the many kinds of misleading thoughts and feelings that arise. How many times have we encountered a new situation, a friend, partner, a job and thought that now we were safe, now we were 'sorted'. But all compounded things are impermanent. The outer phenomena of the world and the inner contents of our experience are all impermanent and unreliable. Therefore we have to see, again and again, how we take refuge in the unreliable and forget the true refuge which is reliable.

So when we read or recite this text as a dharma practice we should begin with the refuge and bodhicitta and end with the dedication of merit. Whatever good thoughts and deeds we do, whatever merit and virtue we generate, we offer to others and commit ourselves to their welfare. The deep refuge is to abide in awareness of emptiness. As long as we are struggling to diminish negative thoughts and increase positive thoughts we are like someone trying to destroy a tree by taking off the leaves one at a time. Life is short. We need to cut the root of the tree of duality. We need to constantly attend to the absence of inherent existence in all phenomena: this means our body, voice and mind, all living beings and forms of nature, all rocks, aeroplanes – everything, everything.

This text is easy to understand but difficult to live. It is full of wonderful images through which, without pejorative judgement, all our many faults and foibles are laid bare. In order to let the meaning seep into the marrow of our bones we have to be available and insightful. We promote availability through sitting quietly and focusing on the sensation made by our breath at our nostrils. Whenever our attention wanders we simply bring it back to our intentional focus. The more we do this the more peaceful and less distracted we are and so we become available for dharma and wisdom, and for other beings and compassion. We develop insight or clear seeing by attending to what is actually occurring before we label, interpret and react to what we think is going on. The more we attend to phenomena as they reveal themselves we come to see that our seemingly illuminative commentaries were actually just a veil to the simplicity, beauty and freely given richness of appearance as it is. Now the world can dissolve into the buddha mandala.

Our capacity to comprehend the depth and vastness of this path is supported and nourished when we undertake to practise the six paramitas, the transcendent qualities of generosity, discipline, patience, effort, stability and wise discernment. These are the qualities which free us from the mundane concerns of samsara.

Firstly, we focus on generosity in order to transcend the self-referential desire to hang on to whatever we take to be 'ours'. In samsara our sense of lack has us grasping and clinging to objects which we will lose at the time of death. To share, to give away, to use what we have for the benefit of all others, is not only supportive of others but gives us the blessing of being taken out of ourselves. We move beyond being owners and possessors, to become participants who can experience the sympathetic joy of being pleased at others' good fortune.

Discipline supports us in overcoming impulsivity and self-serving habits. We stay on track and develop the dignity of knowing that we are able to keep our word. Discipline asserts that the rule, the law, the instruction and the method, are all to be privileged above our own ideas, our impulses and our wishes. The path has been set out by the wise and we can only follow it by attending to it and abiding by it. It is difficult to find true freedom if we are unable to align with the teachings. Whimsicality and self-indulgence are obstacles, not freedom.

Patience supports delayed gratification. We learn to wait, to wait until the time is right, until all beings are ripe. To be patient is to align with the speed of the slowest person, to help them as they are and not to subject them to the violence of our wish that they were other than they are. We have to learn to relax frustration and its attendant irritation and anger. We are for the other.

Effort develops as the ability to apply ourselves enthusiastically and energetically to the practice in the face of all the varied conditions we might encounter. Effort requires the harmonisation of the potential of body, voice and mind so that we move beyond reactivity to the fulfilment of our altruistic intention.

Stability arises when our habits of impulse and avoidance are not indulged and we succumb to fewer and fewer incitements to dualistic involvement and thereby experience less and less distraction away from steadily focused attention. A stable mind is like a lamp held in a steady hand; the illumination it gives is regular and focussed and so whatever arises can be seen clearly without inference or speculation.

Wise discernment arises when there is the direct perception of the absence of inherent existence in whatever is occurring. This moves beyond effortful analysis to discernment of emptiness as the ongoing clarity of all one's experience. To see the absence of defining essence and substance in every appearance, whether seemingly outer or inner, is to see the actual truth of oneself and of one's world.

Thus it becomes clear that the deepest, most transformative compassion is that of not doing, not making, not interfering. By not reifying self and other, there is non-confirmation of both the actor and the acted on, the grasper and the object grasped at. The more open we are to the fact that the self is an illusion, the more we see all beings as fundamentally free of self and thus the characteristics we have habitually projected onto self and other, and used as a basis for judging self and other, dissolve like darkness in the dawn light. Our freedom and the freedom of others are inextricable, and so we all awaken together when there is nothing to bind us to false beliefs.

In order to block any backsliding into self-preoccupation we develop the intention and commitment to practise giving others our health and happiness and receiving their pain and difficulties in return. This is the exchange (*gTong-Len*) which cuts the root of self-cherishing and turns ego's values upside down. This practice has been praised and engaged in by the guiding lights of the Mahayana. For example, Nagarjuna in his Precious Garland says: "May their wrongdoing ripen in me and may my virtue ripen in them." Similarly Shantideva in The Way of the Bodhisattva says: "May the pain and suffering of all beings wandering in samsara ripen only in me."

We can decide to make giving happiness and taking on suffering our way of life. Breathing out light from my heart I exhale all my happiness as a gift to all beings. Breathing in the suffering of all beings I take this stream of misery as my own and welcome it into my heart where it melts into the black lump of my selfishness and self-concern which it gradually dissolves. Now my empty open heart is fearless in taking on suffering and offering happiness to all.

Our breath is ceaseless and continuous, so with this visualisation, intention and one-pointed commitment there is not one second of my life in which I am not connected to all beings. Just as breathing is part of life, the very basis of supporting our finite life, so may compassion be part of our life, the very basis of supporting our infinite life.

Whenever I am happy I will give all my happiness to all sentient beings – may they enjoy unlimited happiness. Whenever I have difficulties and feel hurt and sad I will take on all the sorrows and difficulties of all beings – may the ocean of suffering be exhausted.

With these and all other dharma views and methods may I reverse the wish to have the best for myself and less for the rest. May the fixed reference point of 'me first' be dissolved so that my heart is an infinite warmth, a cornucopia of love for all and a great dissolving ocean to cleanse the sufferings and limitations of others.

Renouncing blaming others and seeking for causes outside myself, I accept that I am responsible for the suffering of all beings. I happily accept that this suffering is the consequence of my own previous negative actions. Instead of looking out and judging others I will be mindful of my own tendencies and desist from feeding them further.

Not only will I take on all the sufferings of others but I will take their ignorance, poisons, and karmic accumulations and all the other factors that cause them suffering. I commit myself to awakening to the open emptiness of my mind so that with the vanishing of egoic self-concern the welfare of all can actually be fulfilled. With this I am on the true way and each moment of my life is profoundly meaningful.

The great spiritual friend, the Kadampa Geshe, Langri Thangpa Dorje Senge composed these verses which can express and support our heartfelt intention:

THE EIGHT VERSES OF MIND TRAINING

May I always cherish all sentient beings
With the intention to achieve for them
The highest good which is more precious
Than a wish-fulfilling gem.

Whenever I meet sentient beings,
By seeing myself as inferior to them,
May I always believe all others
To be of the highest value.

In all my activities may I observe my experience and,
Immediately on the arising of the afflictions
Which cause mischief and harm to myself and others,
May I recollect the powerful method and repel them.

When I encounter sentient beings of bad disposition
Who are oppressed by faults and suffering,
May I hold them dear as if
I have met with a precious treasure that is difficult to find.

When, due to jealousy, others revile and
Attack me inappropriately
May I accept their harsh triumph and
Offer the victory to them.

If someone I have helped and
Put my hope and trust in
Acts to harm me in an unfitting way
May I consider them to be my pure spiritual friend.

To be brief, directly and by connection,
May I offer benefit and happiness to all my mothers and
Take all their difficulties and sufferings
Secretly to myself.

With this aspiration never being contaminated
By the defiling attitudes of the eight worldly concerns and
With the clarity of knowing all phenomena to be illusory,
May I be without longing and be freed from all that binds me.

The eight worldly concerns bind us into the polarity of hopes and fears on a daily basis. We have hope of profit and fear of loss; hope of pleasure and fear of pain; hope of fame and fear of defamation; hope of praise and fear of blame. Each time we fall into these potholes of duality we can be grateful for the reminder that all our efforts are vulnerable to distraction and impulse until we are established in the openness of awareness inseparable from emptiness. Emptiness is the one great medicine that cures the sorrows of all beings. The mind inseparable from emptiness is the union of wisdom and compassion. This is the infinite opening in our heart which is the source of all the light and love that we send all beings. It is also the space which can accept and dissolve all the difficulties and sufferings of all beings

At first we are trapped in self-cherishing and so put ourselves first and seek to win. Then we gradually develop the Mahayana attitude of giving victory to the other and taking the last place, the losers place, to ourselves. If someone has to be defeated, unloved, unwanted, let it be me. Dissolving pride, self-esteem and self-referencing we become a vehicle of love and service. The accountant in our head is banished, as we no longer keep score of winning and losing. With this we can move to the third stage of peaceful equanimity free of attraction and aversion. For this to ripen into fruition we must plant the seed of enlightenment in the ever-available, ever-fecund ground of emptiness and water it daily with our loving heart.

With immense gratitude to Dharmarakshita, the author of this text, this translation follows the oral guidance of C R Lama, Chimed Rigdzin Lama Rinpoche. As has been said so often by so many, the kindness of the Guru can never be repaid. Giving everything and asking for nothing except our own efforts on the path, C R Lama opened the dazzling field of dharma to our world-weary eyes.

C R Lama pointed out the tradition of alternative readings that can be made in the earlier verses. He emphasised that the text is one for daily reflection and application, since without love and compassion emptiness can lead us to a desert of the heart.

James Low, 2018

May all merit be shared by all.
May all faults and limitations ripen only in the translator.

FOREWORD BY C R LAMA TO SHARP WEAPON WHEEL

THE TEXT TRANSLATED HERE is a very small book in the original Tibetan yet its meaning is very important. The main teaching it gives is the cutting of the ego, desire, ignorance and so on. This is the principle and most essential point to be understood. Apart from this, the text deals with how to develop a proper, gentle, thoughtful manner and gives important instructions on correct social behaviour.

This book is generally attributed to Jowo Je Paldan Atisha Dipankara Sri Jnana but it originally came from Dharmarakshita who was one of Atisha's twelve principle Gurus. Atisha gave this teaching to 'Brom-sTon-Pa and translated it into Tibetan with him. This text became one of the main teachings of the Khadampa Lamas who often had the custom that one man should get one teaching and do one practice, though some Khadampas also had many different teachings. From the Khadampas, the teaching spread to the Sakyapa, Kargyudpa, Nyingmapa and Gelugpa. Nowadays, some people believe that this is only a Gelugpa text but I do not agree. Though I might also agree, for the Gelugpa mainly do not have any special philosophy or teaching beyond the Tibetan Tripitaka which was largely translated in bSam-Yas Monastery in the presence of Padmasambhava, Santarakshita, Vairocana, Vimalamitra and others. All the religious sects of Tibet, except the Bon, come from these translations and every sect follows the Tibetan Tripitaka. In particular the Tibetan Tripitaka means the scriptures translated from Sanskrit into Tibetan. It includes the work of Lord Buddha and the Indian Pandits but not that of any Tibetan man.

If one does not practise, then one will not get any result. The deep Dharma teaching and the general lay people's advice in this text are not like a strong injection of penicillin. Dharma practice must develop in one's own mind, it is not something that can quickly be pushed in from outside. But, anyway, whatever one's level, if doing Dharma practice then one must have faith in the Buddha, Dharma and Sangha. That is essential.

By the virtues arising from this work may the egoism and ignorance of all sentient beings be finished!

C R Lama, 3rd of April 1979

REFUGE AND BODHICITTA

སངས་རྒྱས་ཆོས་དང་ཚོགས་ཀྱི་མཆོག་རྣམས་ལ།

SANG GYE	CHO	DANG	TSOG	KYI	CHO	NAM	LA
buddha	dharma	and	sangha, assembly	of	supreme, best	(plural)	to

To the Buddha, Dharma and Assembly of the Excellent

བྱང་ཆུབ་བར་དུ་བདག་ནི་སྐྱབས་སུ་མཆི།

JANG CHUB	BAR DU	DAG NI	KYAB	SU	CHI
enlightenment	until	I	refuge	for	go

I go for refuge until enlightenment is gained.

བདག་གིས་སྦྱིན་སོགས་བགྱིས་པའི་བསོད་ནམས་ཀྱིས།

DAG GI	JIN	SOG	GYI PAI	SO NAM	KYI
I by	generosity	other perfections	doing, practising	virtue	through

Through the virtue of practising generosity and the other perfections

འགྲོ་ལ་ཕན་ཕྱིར་སངས་རྒྱས་འགྲུབ་པར་ཤོག།

DRO	LA	PHEN	CHIR	SANG GYE	DRUB PAR	SHO
all beings	to	benefit	in order	buddha	accomplish	may it happen

May I attain buddhahood for the benefit of all beings

I go for refuge to the Buddha, Dharma and Assembly of the Excellent Ones until enlightenment is gained. Through the virtue of practising generosity and the other perfections may I attain buddhahood for the benefit of all beings.

༄༅། །དགྲ་བོ་གནད་ལ་དབབ་པའི་མཚོན་ཆ་འཁོར་ལོ་ཞེས་བྱ་བ།
༄༅། །རྗེ་སྨྲ་བགྱི་ཅས་ཨ་ཏི་ཤ་ལ་གནད་པའི་བློ་སྦྱོང་མཚོན་ཆ་འཁོར་ལོ་བཞུགས་སོ། །

SHARP WEAPON WHEEL

BEING

THE TEACHING ON MENTAL DEVELOPMENT
GIVEN TO ATISHA BY DHARMARAKSHITA

WHICH

ANNIHILATES THE ENEMY

ཁྲོ་བོ་ཆེན་པོ་གཤིན་རྗེ་གཤེད་ལ་ཕྱག་འཚལ་ལོ།

TRO WO	CHEN PO	SHIN JE SHED	LA	CHAG TSHAL LO
wrathful	great (Heruka)	Yamantaka	to	salutation

Salutation to the great Heruka Yamantaka.

བཙན་དུག་ནགས་སུ་རྨ་བྱ་རྒྱུ་བ་ན།

TSAN DUG	NAG	SU	MA JA	GYU WA	NA
aconite (strong poison)	forest	in	peacock	going, moving	if, when

If peacocks who wander in a forest of poisonous aconite

སྨན་གྱི་ལྡུམ་ར་ལེགས་པར་མཛེས་གྱུར་ཀྱང་།

MAN	GYI	DUM RA	LEG PAR	DZAE	GYUR	KYANG
medicine	of	good vegetable garden	useful	beautiful	come	but, yet

Were to come upon beautiful gardens of useful medicines

རྨ་བྱའི་ཚོགས་རྣམས་དགའ་བར་མི་འགྱུར་གྱི།

MA JAI	TSHOG	NAM	GA WAR	MI	GYUR	GYI
peacock	groups	(plural)	happy	not	become	since

They would not be happy there

བཙན་དུག་བཅུད་ཀྱིས་རྨ་བྱ་འཚོ་བ་ལྟར།

TSAN DUG	CHUD	KYI	MA JA	TSO WA	TAR
aconite (strong poison)	juice, essence	by	peacock	thrive, become healthy*	similarly

(* At first when it eats the poisonous plant the peacock becomes sick for a few days but then it starts to shine and will dance and spread its tail. And similarly the pig grows strongly by eating foul things.)

For they thrive on the essence of poisonous aconite.

Salutation to the great Heruka Yamantaka. If peacocks who wander in a forest of poisonous aconite were to come upon a beautiful garden of useful medicines they would not be happy there for they thrive on the essence of poisonous aconite.

Sharp Weapon Wheel

དཔའ་བོ་འཁོར་བའི་ནགས་སུ་འཇུག་པ་ན།

PA WO	KHOR WAI	NAG	SU	JUG PA	NA
hero, bodhisattva	samsara	forest	in	going, enter	if, when

Similarly, when Bodhisattvas enter into the forest of samsara,

བདེ་སྐྱིད་དཔལ་གྱི་ལྡུམ་ར་མཛེས་གྱུར་ཀྱང་།

DE KYI	PAL	GYI	DUM RA	DZAE	GYUR	KYANG
happy (like the joys of samsara)	splendid	of	garden	beautiful	is	yet

Although there are very beautiful and pleasant gardens to be found

དཔའ་བོ་དག་ནི་ཆགས་པར་མི་འགྱུར་གྱི།

PA WO	DAG	NI	CHAG PAR	MI	GYUR	GYI
hero, bodhisattva	(plural)	(emphasis)	involvement, attachment	not	come	thus

Yet they do not become attached to them

སྡུག་བསྔལ་ནགས་སུ་སེམས་དཔའ་འཚོ་བ་ཡིན།

DU NGAL	NAG	SU	SEM PA	TSHO WA	YIN
suffering	forest	in	bodhisattva (awakening being*)	lives	does, is

* Because of being free of desire for his own happiness the Bodhisattva is happy even in hell since his high purpose of helping others keeps his mind free of fear and he knows how to transform all afflictions and difficulties into blessings. They have power and merit enough to remain always in blissful Buddha realms yet they are not attached to this and can cheerfully take on the sufferings of samsara for the sake of others.

For these Bodhisattvas thrive in the forest of suffering.

Similarly, when Bodhisattvas enter into the forest of samsara, although there are very beautiful and pleasant gardens to be found they do not become attached to them for these Bodhisattvas thrive in the forest of suffering.

དེ་ཕྱིར་བདེ་སྐྱིད་ངང་དུ་ལེན་ལེན་པའི།

DE CHIR	DE KYI	NGANG	DU	LEN LEN	PAI
for that reason	happiness	state, nature	in	again and again doing* (* This could also be written bLang-bLang.)	but

Thus, although beings strive constantly to attain a state of happiness

སྔར་མའི་དབང་གིས་སྡུག་ལ་སྐྱེལ་བ་ཡིན།

NGAR MAI	WANG	GYI	DUG	LA	KYEL WA	YIN
former, earlier	power	by	suffering	under	getting	does

They experience suffering due to the power of their former actions,

སྡུག་བསྔལ་ངང་དུ་ལེན་པའི་སེམས་དཔའ་དེ།
DU NGAL   NGANG   DU   LEN PAI   SEM PA   DE
suffering   state   in   practising   bodhisattva   that
                          (i.e. voluntarily enter into)

While the Bodhisattvas who accept the condition of suffering

དཔའ་བོའི་སྟོབས་ཀྱིས་རྟག་ཏུ་བདེ་བ་ཡིན།
PA WOI   TOB   KYI   TAG TU   DE WA   YIN
bodhisattva's   strength   by   always   happy   does

(By searching after ephemeral worldly happiness, sentient beings only become evermore vulnerable to suffering. But the Bodhisattva who willingly accepts suffering for the sake of helping others comes to experience lasting joy in his mind.)

Are always happy due to their strength and courage.

Thus, although beings strive continuously to attain a state of happiness, they experience suffering due to the power of their former actions, while the Bodhisattvas who accept the condition of suffering are always happy due to their strength and courage.

ད་འདིར་འདོད་ཆགས་བཙན་དུག་ནགས་དང་འདྲ།
DAN DIR   DOE CHAG   TSAN DUG   NAG   DANG DRA
now here   desire   aconite   forest   like that

(It is at this time and in this place and in the midst of difficulty and confusion that the Dharma must be practised.)

Here and now desire is like the poisonous forest and

དཔའ་བོ་རྨ་བྱ་ལྟ་བུས་འཇུན་པར་འགྱུར།
PA WO   MA JA   TA BUE   CHUN PAR   GYUR
brave, heroic   peacock   like that,   digested,   becomes
                          equal to/by   disciplined*

(* The Bodhisattva, like the peacock, must be able to use it and not be used by it.)

The Bodhisattva, like the peacock, must be able to make use of it.

སྡར་མ་བྱ་རོག་ལྟ་བུའི་སྲོག་ལ་འཆི།
DAR MA   JA ROK   TA BUI   SOG LA CHI
timid   raven   like that   dies

The timid raven would die if he were to eat such things.

Sharp Weapon Wheel

རང་འདོད་ཅན་གྱིས་དུག་འདི་ག་ལ་འཆུན།

RANG	DOE	CHAN	GYI	DU	DI	GA LA	CHUN
self	desire	one who has	by	poison	this (desire)	now	digest, not be troubled by

(A strong body and a confident healthy attitude are necessary to digest bad food. And a strong clear mind free of doubts and wild tendencies is necessary if one is to use the afflictions creatively. The Bodhisattva understands emptiness and this keeps his compassion free of contamination by desire, anger etc., for these afflictions are then self-liberating.)

Similarly, how could self-focussed people digest the poison of desire?

Here and now desire is like the poisonous forest, and the Bodhisattva, like the peacock, must be able to make use of it. The timid raven would die if he were to eat such things. Similarly, how could self-focussed people digest the poison of desire?

ཉོན་མོངས་གཞན་ལ་འང་དེ་བཞིན་སྦྱར་བ་ན།

NYON MONG	ZHAN LA	ANG	DE ZHIN	JAR WA	NA
afflictions*	other	also	in the same way	use	if

(* anger, ignorance, jealousy and pride)   (i.e. using the same example for the other afflictions)

If the other afflictions are similarly employed in a self-centred way

བྱ་རོག་ལྟ་བུའི་ཐར་བའི་སྲོག་ལ་འབབ།

JA ROG	TA BUI	THAR WAI	SOG LA BAB
raven	like that	freedom	die*

(* Being overwhelmed by the afflictions they will do many sins and gain only bad karma from this life.)

Then those who are like the raven will lose their chance of freedom.

དེ་ཕྱིར་སེམས་དཔའ་རྨ་བྱ་ལྟ་བུ་ཡིས།

DE CHIR	SEM PA	MA JA	TA BU	YI
for that reason	bodhisattva	peacock	similar	by

However the Bodhisattva is like the peacock

དུག་གི་ནགས་དང་འདྲ་བའི་ཉོན་མོངས་རྣམས།

DU	GI	NAG	DANG	DRA WAI	NYON MONG	NAM
poison	of	forest	and	similar	affliction	(plural)

Who consumes the poisons of the forest, for he takes the afflictions and

བཅུད་དུ་སྦྱར་ལ་འཁོར་བའི་ནགས་སུ་འཇུག།

CHUD	DU	JAR LA	KHOR WAI	NAG	SU	JUG
essence*	as	use	samsara	forest	in	enter

(* strong medicine like vitamins)

Using them to nourish his vitality, he enters the forest of samsara.

དང་དུ་བླང་དུག་འདི་གཞོམ་པར་བྱ།

DANG DU LANG	LA	DU	DI	ZHOM PAR	JA
taking, using, adopt enthusiastically	as	poison	this	stop	do

(By not going under the power of the afflictions but making use of their energy, the Bodhisattva is able to increase his power to help others.)

By willingly making use of them the power of the poisons is vanquished.

If the other afflictions are similarly employed in a self-centred way then those who are like the raven will lose their chance of freedom. However the Bodhisattva is like the peacock who consumes the poisons of the forest, for he takes the afflictions and using them to nourish his vitality, he enters the forest of samsara. By willingly making use of them the power of the poisons is vanquished.

དེ་ནི་རང་དབང་མེད་པར་འཁོར་བ་ཡི།

DA NI	RANG	WANG	ME PAR	KHOR WA	YI
now	my	power	not have	samsara, revolving	of

The cause of our revolving powerlessly in samsara

བདག་ཏུ་འཛིན་པ་བདུད་ཀྱི་ཕོ་ཉ་འདི།

DAG	DU	DZIN PA	DUD	KYI	PHO NYA	DI
I, me	to	grasping (belief in a truly existing self)	Mara, demon	of	messenger	this

Is our own adherence to our sense of self, this servant of the demonic Mara.

རང་འདོད་སྐྱིད་འདོད་རོ་དང་ཕར་འབྲལ་ལ།

RANG	DO	KYI	DO	RO	DANG	PHAR TRAL	LA
self, own	benefit	happiness	liking	taste, feeling	and	separate from, stop completely	then

We must completely free ourselves from the attitude of desiring only our own happiness, and then

གཞན་དོན་དགའ་སྐྱིད་དང་དུ་བླང་བར་བྱ།

ZHAN	DON	GA KYI	DANG DU LANG WAR	JA
others	benefit	happily	adopt enthusiastically	do

Happily and enthusiastically strive for the benefit of others.

The cause of our revolving powerlessly in samsara is our own adherence to our sense of self, this servant of the demonic Mara. We must completely free ourselves from the attitude of desiring only our own benefit and happiness and then happily and enthusiastically strive for the benefit of others.

Sharp Weapon Wheel

ལས་ཀྱིས་བདས་ཞིང་ཉོན་མོངས་གོམས་པ་ཡི།
LAE	KYI	DAE SHING	NYON MONG	GOM PA YI
karma	by	driven	afflictions	frequently experiencing

(like a rat chased by a cat)

Being driven on by the force of karma and always experiencing the afflictions,

རིགས་མཐུན་སྐྱེ་དགུ་ཡོངས་ཀྱི་སྡུག་བསྔལ་རྣམས།
RIG	THUN	KYE GU	YONG	KYI	DU NGAL	NAM
family*	in harmony	all beings	all	of	suffering	(plural)

(* who are all in the same situation of desiring happiness yet acting always in ways that bring the opposite)

Is the suffering shared by all beings.

བདེ་འདོད་བདག་གི་སྟེང་དུ་སྤུང་བར་བྱ།
KYI	DOE	DAG GI	TENG DU	PUNG WAR	JA
happiness	desire, liking	me	on top of	heap, accumulate	do

I who like happiness will take all their sorrows upon myself.

གལ་ཏེ་རང་འདོད་འབྲི་བ་བཞུགས་པའི་ཚེ།
GAL TE	RANG DO	TRI WA	ZHUG PAI	TSHE
if	own satisfaction	habit, desire	sit, stay	if, when

If the habit of concern for my own welfare should remain with me,

བཟློག་ལ་རང་གི་བདེ་སྐྱིད་འགྲོ་ལ་སྦྱིན།
DOG LA	RANG GI	DE KYI	DRO LA	JIN
stop, repel	my	happiness	beings to	give

(This verse contains the great mahayana teaching on exchanging one's good position for the bad one of others, also expressed in the following verses.)

Then in order to stop this I will give all my happiness to all beings.

ཇི་ལྟར་བདག་ལ་འཁོར་གྱིས་ལོག་བསྒྲུབས་ཚེ།
JI TAR	DAG LA	KHOR	GYI	LOG	DRUB	TSHE
like that	self to	circle*	by	wrong	practice	if, when

(* one's associates and situation)

In this way, whenever we are troubled by those around us

རང་གིས་(ཉིད་)གཡེང་བས་ལན་ཞེས་(རང་གི་རང་ལ་)སྙིང་ཚིམ་བསྒྲིང་།

RANG   GI   YENG WAE   LAN   ZHE   NYING TSHIM   DRENG
self   by   disturb by   result   call   satisfy, pacify   say strongly to oneself

(If we eat chilli then we should not be surprised if our mouths get hot. So if others trouble us we should recognise this to be the karmic ripening of the harm we have previously wrought. Understanding this we must accept our lot patiently and not seek to harm these others once again. For if we do that the cycle of karma will never end.)

We must encourage ourselves to be patient, recalling that this is the result of our own disturbed actions.

Being driven by the force of karma and always experiencing the afflictions, is the suffering shared by all beings. I, who like happiness, will take all their sorrows upon myself. If the habit of concern for my own welfare should remain with me, then in order to stop this I will give all my happiness to all beings. In this way, whenever we are troubled by those around us we must encourage ourselves to be patient, recalling that this situation is the result of our own disturbed actions.

ལུས་ལ་མི་བཟོད་ན་ཚ་བྱུང་བའི་ཚེ།

LU   LA   MI   ZO   NA TSHA   JUNG WAI   TSHE
body   to   not   endurance   fever, sickness   coming   if, when

When our bodies experience unbearable sickness,

འགྲོ་བའི་ལུས་ལ་གནོད་པ་བསྐྱལ་པ་ཡིས།

DRO WAI   LU   LA   NO PA   KYAL PA   YI
beings who   bodies   to   trouble,   make   by, due to
move in samsara   harm   (i.e. I did this in former times)

This is because we have previously caused harm to the bodies of others.

ལས་ངན་མཚོན་ཆ་རང་ལ་འཁོར་བ་ཡིན།

LAE   NGAN   TSHON CHA   RANG   LA   KHOR WA   YIN
activities,   bad   sharp weapon   self   to   circle, turn   be
deeds   back on

Now the sharp weapon of these bad actions comes turning back upon us.

ད་ནི་ན་ཚ་མ་ལུས་རང་ལ་བླང་།

DA NI   NA TSHA   MA LU   RANG   LA   LANG
from now   sickness*   without   I   to   accept,
            (* of all beings) exception   take

(Previously we harmed others to help ourselves. Now we will give ourselves troubles in order to help others.)

From this time on we will take on ourselves the sicknesses of all beings without exception.

Sharp Weapon Wheel

When our bodies experience unbearable sickness, this is because we have previously caused harm to the bodies of others. Now the sharp weapon of these bad actions comes turning back upon us. From this time on we will take on ourselves the sicknesses of all beings without exception.

(Alternative reading:)

Previously we have caused harm to the bodies of others. Now the sharp weapon of these bad actions comes turning back upon us, so that our bodies experience unbearable sickness. From this time on we will take on ourselves the sicknesses of all beings without exception.

རང་གི་སེམས་ལ་སྡུག་བསྔལ་བྱུང་བའི་ཚེ།

RANG GI	SEM	LA	DU NGAL	JUNG WAI	TSHE
my	mind	to	suffering	arise, come forth	if, when

When suffering arises in our minds,

དེས་པར་གཞན་གྱི་སེམས་རྒྱུད་དཀྲུགས་པ་ཡིས།

NGE PAR	ZHAN	GYI	SEM GYU	TRUG PA	YI
certainly, really	others	of	minds	disturbed, upset	due to

This is because we previously disturbed the minds of others, and

ལས་ངན་མཚོན་ཆ་རང་ལ་འཁོར་བ་ཡིན།

LAE	NGAN	TSHON CHA	RANG	LA	KHOR WA	YIN
deeds	bad	sharp weapons	self	to	turn back on	be

So now the sharp weapon of these bad actions comes turning back upon us.

ད་ནི་སྡུག་མ་ལུས་བདག་ལ་བླང་།

DA NI	DU KHA	MA LU	DAG	LA	LANG
from now	suffering	without exception	I	to	take

From this time on we will take all sufferings on ourselves.

When suffering arises in our minds, this is because we previously disturbed the minds of others and so now the sharp weapon of these bad actions comes turning back upon us. From this time on we will take all sufferings on ourselves.

(Alternative reading:)

Previously we disturbed the minds of others. Now the sharp weapon of these bad actions comes turning back upon us, so that suffering arises in our minds. From this time on we will take all sufferings on ourselves.

རང་ཉིད་བཀྲེས་སྐོམ་དྲག་པོས་གཟིར་བ་ན།

RANG	NYI	TRE	KOM	DRAG POE	ZIR WA	NA
I	self	hunger	thirst	very strong	suffer	when

When we are tortured by intense hunger and thirst,

འཕྲམ་དང་རྐུ་འཕྲོག་སེར་སྣ་བྱས་པ་ཡིས།

TRAM	DANG	KU	TROG	SER NA	JA WA	YI
cheating	and	theft	robbery	avarice	doing	due to

This is because we previously practised cheating, theft, robbery and avarice, and

ལས་ངན་མཚོན་ཆ་རང་ལ་འཁོར་བ་ཡིན།

LAE	NGAN	TSHON CHA	RANG	LA	KHOR WA	YIN
deeds	bad	sharp weapon	self	to	turn back on	be

So now the sharp weapon of these bad actions comes turning back upon us.

ད་ནི་བཀྲེས་སྐོམ་མ་ལུས་དད་དུ་བླང་།

DA NI	TRE	KOM	MA LU	DANG DU LANG
from now	hunger	thirst	without exception	accept, take up willingly

From this time on we will take all hunger and thirst on ourselves.

When we are tortured by intense hunger and thirst, this is because we previously practised cheating, theft, robbery and avarice and so now the sharp weapon of these bad actions comes turning back upon us. From this time on we will take all hunger and thirst on ourselves.

(Alternative reading:)

Previously we practised cheating, theft, robbery and avarice. Now the sharp weapon of these bad actions comes turning back upon us, so that we are tortured by intense hunger and thirst. From this time on we will take all hunger and thirst on ourselves.

དབང་མེད་གཞན་གྱི་བཀོལ་ཞིང་མནར་བའི་ཚེ།

WANG	ME	ZHAN	GYI	KOL ZHING	NAR WAI	TSHE
power	without	others	of	servant	suffer	when

When we suffer powerlessly as the servants of others,

དམན་ལ་སྡང་ཞིང་བྲན་དུ་བཀོལ་བ་ཡིས།

MAN   LA   DANG ZHING   DRAN DUN KOL BA   YI
low*   to   angry   make servants   due to
(* servants, beggars etc.)

This is because we previously acted angrily with the lowly and forced them to work for us, and

ལས་ངན་མཚོན་ཆ་རང་ལ་འཁོར་བ་ཡིན།

LAE NGAN TSHON CHA RANG LA KHOR WA YIN
So now the sharp weapon of these bad actions comes turning back upon us.

དེ་ནི་ལུས་སྲོག་གཞན་དུ་བཀོལ་པར་བྱ།

DA NI   LU   SOG   ZHAN   DU   KOL PAR   JA
from now   body life   others   to   serve   do

From this time on we will use our bodies and lives to serve others.

When we suffer powerlessly as the servants of others, this is because we previously acted angrily with the lowly and forced them to work for us and so now the sharp weapon of these bad actions comes turning back upon us. From this time on we will use our bodies and lives to serve others.

(Alternative reading:)

Previously we acted angrily with the lowly and forced them to work for us. Now the sharp weapon of these bad actions comes turning back upon us, so that we suffer powerlessly as the servants of others. From this time on we will use our bodies and lives to serve others.

མི་སྙན་ཚིག་རྣམས་རྣ་བར་བྱུང་བ་ན།

MI NYAN   TSHIG NAM   NA WA   JUNG WA   NA
not sweet,   words   ear   come, arise   if, when
unpleasant

When we hear sharp, unpleasant words spoken to us,

ཕྲ་མ་ལ་སོགས་ངག་གི་ཉེས་བ་ཡིས།

TRA MA   LA SOG   NGAG   GI   NYE WA   YI
slander   and so on   speech*   of   fault, sin   due to
                           (* lying, rough speech and idle talk)

This is because we previously practised slander and the other sins of speech, and

ལས་ངན་མཚོན་ཆ་རང་ལ་འཁོར་བ་ཡིན།
LAE NGAN TSHON CHA RANG LA KHOR WA YIN
So now the sharp weapon of these bad actions comes turning back upon us.

དེ་བདག་གི་སྐྱོན་ལ་སྨད་པར་བྱ།

DA NI	**DA GI**	**KYON**	**LA**	**MAE PAR**	**JA**
from this time	my	faults	to	make low, humble oneself	do

From this time on we will be humble, knowing our own faults.

When we hear sharp, unpleasant words spoken to us, this is because we previously practised slander and other sins of speech and so now the sharp weapon of these bad actions comes turning back upon us. From this time on we will be humble, knowing our own faults.

(Alternative reading:)

Previously we practised slander and the other sins of speech. Now the sharp weapon of these bad actions comes turning back upon us, so that we hear sharp, unpleasing words spoken to us. From this time on we will be humble, knowing our own faults.

གང་ཡང་མ་དག་ཡུལ་དུ་སྐྱེས་པ་ན།

GANG YANG	**MA**	**DAG**	**YUL**	**DU**	**KYE WA**	**NA**
whenever	not	pure	country	in	born	if, when

When we are born somewhere in a country where everything is impure,

མ་དག་སྣང་བ་རྟག་པར་བསྒོམ་པ་ཡིས།

MA	**DAG**	**NANG WA**	**TAG PAR**	**GOM PA**	**YI**
not	pure	thought, ideas* (* impure relative truth)	continuous, lasting	meditate, imagine	due to

This is because previously we were always cultivating impure ideas, and

ལས་ངན་མཚོན་ཆ་རང་ལ་འཁོར་བ་ཡིན།
LAE NGAN TSHON CHA RANG LA KHOR WA YIN
So now the sharp weapon of these bad actions comes turning back upon us.

དེ་ནི་དག་སྣང་འབའ་ཞིག་བསྒོམས་པར་བྱ།

DA NI	**DAG**	**NANG**	**BA ZHIG**	**GOM PAR**	**JA**
from now	pure	vision* (* vision inseparable from emptiness)	only	meditate	do

From this time on we will cultivate only pure vision.

Sharp Weapon Wheel

When we are born somewhere in a country where everything is impure, this is because previously we were always cultivating impure ideas and so now the sharp weapon of these bad actions comes turning back upon us. From this time on we will cultivate only pure vision.

(Alternative reading:)

Previously we ceaselessly cultivated impure ideas. Now the sharp weapon of these bad actions comes turning back upon us, so that we are born somewhere in a country where everything is impure. From this time on we will cultivate only pure vision.

ཕན་ཞིང་མཛའ་བའི་གྲོགས་དང་བྲལ་བའི་ཚེ།

PHAN ZHING DZE WAI DROG   DANG   DRAL WAI   TSHE
beneficial   good friends, intimates   and   separate from   if, when

When we are separated from dear and beneficial friends,

གཞན་གྱི་འཁོར་རྣམས་གདག་གིས་ཁ་དྲངས་པས།

ZHAN GYI KHOR NAM   DA   GI   KHA DRANG   PAE
others   of   circle,   me   by   persuade   by, this
              associates   (i.e. encouraging them to be my friends instead)

This is because we previously encouraged others to part from their circle of friends and relatives, and

ལས་ངན་མཚོན་ཆ་རང་ལ་འཁོར་བ་ཡིན།

LAE NGAN TSHON CHA RANG LA KHOR WA YIN

So now the sharp weapon of these bad actions comes turning back upon us.

དེ་ནི་གཞན་དག་འཁོར་དང་དབྲལ་མི་བྱ།

DA NI   ZHAN DA   KHOR   DANG DRAL   MI   JA
from now   others   circle   separate   not   do

From this time on we will not separate others from those who care about them.

When we are separated from dear and beneficial friends, this is because we previously encouraged others to part from their circle of friends and relatives and so now the sharp weapon of these bad actions comes turning back upon us. From this time on we will not separate others from those who care about them.

(Alternative reading:)

Previously we encouraged others to part from their circle of friends and relatives. Now the sharp weapon of these bad actions comes turning back upon us, so that we are separated from dear and beneficial friends. From this time on we will not separate others from those who care about them.

དམ་པ་ཐམས་ཅད་བདག་ལ་མི་དགའ་ན།

DAM PA	THAM CHAE	DAG	LA	MI	GA	NA
holy (i.e. gurus)	all	I	to	not	pleased	if, when

When all the holy ones are not happy with us,

དམ་པ་བོར་ནས་གྲོགས་ངན་བསྟེན་པ་ཡིས།

DAM PA	BOR NAE	DROG NGAN	TEN PA	YI
holy people	throw away, abandon	friend bad	having served	due to

This is because previously we have abandoned the holy ones and adopted bad friends and

ལས་ངན་མཚོན་ཆ་རང་ལ་འཁོར་བ་ཡིན།

LAE NGAN TSHON CHA RANG LA KHOR WA YIN

So now the sharp weapon of these bad actions comes turning back upon us.

ད་ནི་ངན་པའི་གྲོགས་རྣམས་སྤང་བར་བྱ།

DA NI	NGAN PAI	DROG NAM	PANG WAR	JA
from now	bad	friends	abandon, discard*	so

(* We do not abandon our vows to help them but we avoid their negative company.)

From this time on we will cease from friendship with those who turn from virtue.

When all the holy ones are not happy with us, this is because previously we abandoned the holy ones and adopted bad friends and so now the sharp weapon of these bad actions comes turning back upon us. From this time on we will cease from friendship with those who turn from virtue.

(Alternative reading:)

Previously we abandoned the holy ones and adopted bad friends. Now the sharp weapon of these bad actions comes turning back upon us, so that all the holy ones are not happy with us. From this time on we will cease from friendship with those who turn from virtue.

Sharp Weapon Wheel

སྐྱོ་བསྐུར་གཞན་གྱིས་སྡིག་གསོག་བྱུང་བའི་ཚེ།

DRO KUR   **ZHAN**   **GYI**   **DIG SOG**   **JUNG WAI**   **TSHE**
incorrect,   others   by   troubled   arise   if, when
false accusation

When we are troubled by the false accusations of others,

གཞན་གྱི་མཁོ་བ་བྱད་དུ་བསད་པ་ཡིས།

ZHAN   **GYI**   **KHO WA**   **KHYE DU SAE PA**   **YI**
others   of   needs,   muddle up and make   due to
                   necessities   unimportant*

(* e.g. if you see a beggar coming and you close your door and pretend you are out)

This is because previously we treated the needs of others as unimportant, and

ལས་ངན་མཚོན་ཆ་རང་ལ་འཁོར་བ་ཡིན།

LAE NGAN TSHON CHA RANG LA KHOR WA YIN

So now the sharp weapon of these bad actions comes turning back upon us.

དེ་ནི་གཞན་གྱི་མཁོ་བ་བསྒྲུབ་པར་བྱ།

DA NI   **ZHAN**   **GYI**   **KHO WA**   **DRU PAR**   **JA**
from now   others   of   needs,   achieve, fulfil   do
                       necessities

From this time on we will satisfy the needs of others.

When we are troubled by the false accusations of others, this is because previously we treated the needs of others as unimportant and so now the sharp weapon of these bad actions comes turning back upon us. From this time on we will satisfy the needs of others.

(Alternative reading:)

Previously we treated the needs of others as unimportant. Now the sharp weapon of these bad actions comes turning back upon us, so that we are troubled by the false accusations of others. From this time on we will satisfy the needs of others.

སེམས་མི་དགའ་ཞིང་སྙིང་མི་གསལ་བའི་ཚེ།

SEM   **MI**   **GA ZHING**   **NYING**   **MI**   **SAL WAI**   **TSHE**
mind   not   pleased, happy   mind, heart   not   clear   if, when

When our minds are not happy and our hearts are troubled

སྐྱེ་བོ་གཞན་ལ་སྡིག་པ་བསགས་པ་ཡིས།

KYE WO	ZHAN	LA	DIG PA	SAG PA	YI
previous lives, (sNgon-Ma)	others	to	sin	collect, gather	due to

This is because previously we accumulated many sins against others, and

ལས་ངན་མཚོན་ཆ་རང་ལ་འཁོར་བ་ཡིན།

LAE NGAN TSHON CHA RANG LA KHOR WA YIN

So now the sharp weapon of these bad actions comes turning back upon us.

དེ་ནི་གཞན་གྱི་སྡིག་རྐྱེན་སྤང་བར་བྱ།

DA NI	ZHAN	GYI	DIG	KYEN	PANG WAR	JA
from now	others	of	trouble	cause, situation	abandon	do

From this time on we will give up all that causes trouble for others.

When our minds are not happy and our hearts are troubled this is because previously we accumulated many sins against others and so now the sharp weapon of these bad actions comes turning back upon us. From this time on we will give up all that causes trouble for others.

(Alternative reading:)

Previously we accumulated many sins against others. Now the sharp weapon of these bad actions comes turning back upon us, so that our minds are not happy and our hearts are troubled. From this time on we will give up all that causes trouble for others.

བྱ་བ་མ་གྲུབ་སེམས་རྩ་དཀྲུགས་པའི་ཚེ།

JA WA	MA	DRUB	SEM	TSA	TRUG PAI	TSHE
deeds	not	accomplish	mind	root	agitated, troubled	if, when

When we cannot perform our tasks and our minds are disturbed,

དམ་པའི་ཆོས་ལ་བར་ཆད་བྱས་པ་ཡིས།

DAM PAI	CHO	LA	BAR CHAE	JAE WA	YI
holy, excellent	Dharma	to	obstructing	do	due to

This is because previously we caused obstacles to the practice of the holy Dharma, and

ལས་ངན་མཚོན་ཆ་རང་ལ་འཁོར་བ་ཡིན།

LAE NGAN TSHON CHA RANG LA KHOR WA YIN

So now the sharp weapon of these bad actions comes turning back upon us.

དེ་ནི་བར་ཆད་ཐམས་ཅད་སྤང་བར་བྱ།

DA NI	BAR CHAD	THAM CHE	PANG WAR	JA
from now	obstructions, interruptions	all	abandon	do

From this time on we will stop creating obstacles.

When we cannot perform our tasks and our minds are disturbed, this is because previously we caused obstacles to the practice of the holy Dharma and so now the sharp weapon of these bad actions comes turning back on upon us. From this time on we will stop creating obstacles.

(Alternative reading:)

Previously we caused obstacles to the practice of the holy Dharma. Now the sharp weapon of these bad actions comes turning back upon us, so that we cannot perform our tasks and our minds are disturbed. From this time on we will stop creating obstacles.

གང་ལྟར་བྱས་ཀྱང་བླ་མ་མ་མཉེས་ཚེ།

GANG TAR	JAE	KYANG	LA MA	MA	NYE	TSHE
whatever	do	although, but	lama, guru	not	happy	if, when

When our Gurus are displeased with us no matter what we do,

དམ་པའི་ཆོས་ལ་དོ་སློག་བྱས་པ་ཡིས།

DAM PAI	CHO	LA	NGO KOG	JAE WA	YI
holy	Dharma	to	open and secret, public and private*	do	due to

(* Deceitful actions, e.g. you say that you do 100,000 prostrations but in fact you are not doing any, or teaching the Dharma only when you get money but not otherwise.)

This is because previously we have acted deceitfully towards the holy Dharma, and

ལས་ངན་མཚོན་ཆ་རང་ལ་འཁོར་བ་ཡིན།

LAE NGAN TSHON CHA RANG LA KHOR WA YIN

So now the sharp weapon of these bad actions comes turning back upon us.

དེ་ནི་ཆོས་ལ་དོ་སློག་ཆུང་བར་(མེད་)བྱ།

DA NI	CHO	LA	NGO KOG	CHUNG WAR	JA
from now	Dharma	to	deceptions	make small	do

From this time on we will remove all deception from our Dharma practice.

When our Gurus are displeased with us no matter what we do, this is because previously we acted deceitfully towards the holy Dharma and so now the sharp weapon of these bad actions comes turning back upon us. From this time on we will remove all deception from our Dharma practice.

(Alternative reading:)

Previously we acted deceitfully towards the holy Dharma. Now the sharp weapon of these bad actions comes turning back upon us, so that our Gurus are displeased with us no matter what we do. From this time on we will remove all deception from our Dharma practice.

སྐྱེ་བོ་ཡོངས་ཀྱིས་ཁ་ཡོག་བྱུང་བའི་ཚེ།

KYE WO	YONG	KYI	KHA YOG	JUNG WAI	TSHE
people	all	by	contradict, oppose	arise	if, when

When everyone acts against us,

ངོ་ཚ་ཁྲེལ་ཡོད་བྱད་དུ་བསད་པ་ཡིས།

NGO TSHA	TREL YOE	KYAE DU SAE PA	YI
feel ashamed (of oneself)	to feel shame at the bad conduct of others	to be indifferent to, not to care about	due to

This is because previously we were not bothered that our actions and those of others were shameful and

ལས་ངན་མཚོན་ཆ་རང་ལ་འཁོར་བ་ཡིན།

LAE NGAN TSHON CHA RANG LA KHOR WA YIN

So now the sharp weapon of these bad actions comes turning back upon us.

ད་ནི་མི་རུང་བ་ལ་འཛེམ་པར་བྱ།

DA NI	MI	RUNG WA	LA	DZEM WAR	JA
from now	not	suitable, right	to	to shun, to be sensitive to	do

From this time on we will shun improper behaviour.

When everyone acts against us, this is because previously we were not bothered that our actions and those of others were shameful and so now the sharp weapon of these bad actions comes turning back upon us. From this time on we will shun improper behaviour.

(Alternative reading:)

Sharp Weapon Wheel

Previously we were not bothered that our actions and those of others were shameful. Now the sharp weapon of these bad actions comes turning back upon us, so that all people act against us. From this time on we will shun improper behaviour.

འཁོར་ཚོགས་འདུས་མ་ཐག་ཏུ་འགྲས་བའི་ཚེ།

KHOR	TSHOG	DU MA THAG TU	DRAE WAI	TSHE
circle	group	just on meeting	feeling uncomfortable, antagonistic, dissatisfied	if, when

When, on first meeting others, there are feelings of discomfort and antagonism

སྔག་གཤིས་ངན་པ་ཕྱོགས་སུ་བཙོངས་བ་ཡིས།

DUG	SHI	NGAN PA	CHOG	SU	TSHONG WA	YI
afflicted	temperament, character	bad	side	to	done (gZham-La Byas-Pa)	due to

This is because previously we have been biased and have acted badly towards certain others, and

ལས་ངན་མཚོན་ཆ་རང་ལ་འཁོར་བ་ཡིན།

LAE NGAN TSHON CHA RANG LA KHOR WA YIN

So now the sharp weapon of these bad actions comes turning back upon us.

དེ་ནི་གང་ལ་འང་མི་གཞི་ལེགས་པར་བྱ།

DA NI	GANG	LA ANG	MI ZHI	LEG PAR	JA
from now	whoever, anyone	also	manner	properly, graceful	do

From this time on we will act with a good attitude towards all.

When, on first meeting others, there are feelings of discomfort and antagonism, this is because previously we have been biased and have acted badly towards certain others and so now the sharp weapon of these bad actions comes turning back on us. From this time on we will act with a good attitude towards all.

(Alternative reading:)

Previously we have been biased and acted badly towards certain others. Now the sharp weapon of these bad actions comes turning back upon us, so that there are feelings of discomfort and antagonism on first meeting others. From this time on we will act with a good attitude towards all.

ཉེ་ཚད་ཐམས་ཅད་དགྲ་བོར་ལངས་པའི་ཚེ།

NYE TSHAD   **THAM CHE**   **DRA WOR**   **LANG WAI**   **TSHE**
all relations   all   enemy, foe   arise, come   if, when

When all our friends and relations become our enemies,

བསམ་པ་ངན་པ་ནང་དུ་བཅུག་པ་ཡིས།

SAM PA   **NGAN PA**   **NANG DU**   **CHUG PA**   **YI**
thoughts, intentions   bad   inside (my mind)   go into, enter   due to

This is because previously bad thoughts and intentions towards others arose in our minds, and

ལས་ངན་མཚོན་ཆ་རང་ལ་འཁོར་བ་ཡིན།

LAE NGAN TSHON CHA RANG LA KHOR WA YIN

So now the sharp weapon of these bad actions comes turning back upon us.

དེ་སྨྲག་སློ་བྱུ་རྣམས་ཆུང་བར་བྱ།

DA NI   **MU KYO GYU NAM**   **CHUNG WAR**   **JA**
from now   deceitful intention   make small   do

From this time on we will cease from deceitful intention.

When all our friends and relations become our enemies, this is because previously bad thoughts and intentions towards others arose in our minds and so now the sharp weapon of these bad actions comes turning back upon us. From this time on we will cease from deceitful intention.

(Alternative reading:)

Previously bad thoughts and intentions towards others arose in our minds. Now the sharp weapon of these bad actions comes turning back upon us, so that all our friends and relations become our enemies. From this time on we will cease from deceitful intention.

བར་གཅོད་ནད་དང་དམུ་ཆུས་ན་བའི་ཚེ།

BAR CHO   **NAE**   **DANG**   **MU CHE**   **NA WAI**   **TSHE**
interrupt   illness   and   water-illness like gout   illness, sickness   if, when

When our lives are disrupted by gout and other illnesses,

ཁྲིམས་མེད་དཀོར་ལ་བག་མེད་འབགས་པ་ཡིས།

TRIM ME	KOR	LA	BAG ME	BAG PA	YI
without vows*	accumulation#	from	careless†	take away, steal	due to

(* and so not being a suitable object for religious offerings)
(# property of the Three Jewels, e.g. money that has been given as an offering to a temple)
(† e.g. we shamelessly accept offerings to which we are not entitled)

This is because previously we were undisciplined and without vows, carelessly misappropriating offerings for the Dharma, and

ལས་ངན་མཚོན་ཆ་རང་ལ་འཁོར་བ་ཡིན།

LAE NGAN TSHON CHA RANG LA KHOR WA YIN

So now the sharp weapon of these bad actions comes turning back upon us.

ད་ནི་དཀོར་འཕྲོགས་ལ་སོགས་སྤང་བར་བྱ།

DA NI	KOR	TROG	LA SOG	PANG WAR	JA
from now	property*	take, deprive	and so on	abandon, stop	do

(* of the Three Jewels)

From this time on we will stop stealing from the Three Jewels and all such behaviour.

When our lives are disrupted by gout and other illnesses, this is because previously we were undisciplined and without vows, carelessly misappropriating offerings for the Dharma and so now the sharp weapon of these bad actions comes turning back upon us. From this time on we will stop stealing from the Three Jewels and all such behaviour.

(Alternative reading:)

Previously we were undisciplined and without vows, carelessly misappropriating offerings for the Dharma. Now the sharp weapon of these bad actions comes turning back upon us, and so our lives are disrupted by gout and other illnesses. From this time on we will stop stealing from the Three Jewels and all such behaviour.

གློ་བུར་འགོ་ནད་ལུས་ལ་ཐེབས་པའི་ཚེ།

LO BUR	GO NAE	LU	LA	THEB PAI	TSHE
suddenly	plague, epidemic*	body	to	reach, touch	if, when

(* like flu or small-pox)

When our bodies are struck by sudden infections,

དམ་ཚིག་ཉམས་པའི་བྱུ་བ་བྱས་པ་ཡིས།

DAM TSHIG	NYAM PAI	JA WA	JAE WA	YI
vows	deteriorate, grows weak	action	done	by, due to

This is because previously we have allowed our tantric vows to decline, and

ལས་ངན་མཚོན་ཆ་རང་ལ་འཁོར་བ་ཡིན།

LAE NGAN TSHON CHA RANG LA KHOR WA YIN

So now the sharp weapon of these bad actions comes turning back upon us.

ད་ནི་མི་དགེ་ལས་རྣམས་སྤང་བར་བྱ།

DA NI	MI GE	LAE	NAM	PANG WAR	JA
from now	unvirtues	deed	all	abandon	do

From this time on we will renounce all unvirtuous activity.

When our bodies are struck by sudden infections, this is because previously we have allowed our tantric vows to decline and so now the sharp weapon of these bad actions comes turning back upon us. From this time on we will renounce all unvirtuous activity.

(Alternative reading:)

Previously we have allowed our tantric vows to decline. Now the sharp weapon of these bad actions comes turning back upon us, so that our bodies are struck by sudden infections. From this time on we will renounce all unvirtuous activity.

ཤེས་བྱ་ཀུན་ལ་བློ་གྲོས་རྨོངས་པའི་ཚེ།

SHE JA	KUN	LA	LO DRO	MONG WAI	TSHE
knowledge, cognisable information	all	to	understanding, intellect	stupid, dull	if, when

When our intelligence dulls as we are trying to learn,

གཞག་ཏུ་འོས་བ་ཆོས་ལ་བྱས་བ་ཡིས།

ZHAG TU OE WA	CHO	LA	JAE WA	YI
be easily satisfied*	Dharma	to	done	due to

(* Although one is not satisfied with eating four times a day, or with having five sets of clothes, one feels one rosary of mantras a day is more than enough.)

This is because previously we were satisfied with the very minimum of Dharma practice, and

ལས་དན་མཚོན་ཆ་རང་ལ་འཁོར་བ་ཡིན།

LAE NGAN TSHON CHA RANG LA KHOR WA YIN

So now the sharp weapon of these bad actions comes turning back upon us.

དེ་ནི་ཐོས་སོགས་ཤེས་རབ་བསྒོམ་པར་བྱ།

DA NI	THOE	SOG	SHE RAB	GOM PAR JA
from now	hearing	and so on	wisdom*	practise meditation

(* *This refers to the wisdom arising from hearing or studying the Dharma, and from reflecting about it, and from meditating on it.*)

From this time on we will focus on developing the wisdom arising from Dharma study, reflection, and meditation.

When our intelligence dulls as we try to learn, this is because previously we were satisfied with the very minimum of Dharma practice and so now the sharp weapon of these bad actions comes turning back upon us. From this time on we will focus on developing the wisdom arising from Dharma study, reflection, and meditation.

(Alternative reading:)

Previously we were satisfied with the very minimum of Dharma practice. Now the sharp weapon of these bad actions comes turning back on us, so that our intelligence dulls as we try to learn. From this time on we will focus on developing the wisdom arising from Dharma study, reflection, and meditation.

ཆོས་ལ་སྒྲུབ་ཚེ་གཉིད་ཀྱིས་ནོན་པའི་ཚེ།

CHO LA	CHOD	TSHE	NYI	KYI	NON PAI	TSHE
Dharma to	practice	when	fall asleep	by	press, force	when

When sleep overwhelms us while practising Dharma,

དམ་པའི་ཆོས་ལ་སྒྲིབ་པ་བསགས་པ་ཡིས།

DAM PAI	CHO	LA	DRIB WA	SAG PA	YI
holy	Dharma	to	obscuration, obstruction	collect, gather	due to

(*We did not have faith and so we built up habits of careless conduct, like not being respectful to Gurus, scriptures, statues, etc, due to our minds feeling little interest or energy towards the Dharma.*)

This is because previously we accumulated obstructions to the holy Dharma, and

ལས་དན་མཚོན་ཆ་རང་ལ་འཁོར་བ་ཡིན།

LAE NGAN TSHON CHA RANG LA KHOR WA YIN

So now the sharp weapon of these bad actions comes turning back upon us.

དེ་ནི་ཆོས་ཕྱིར་དཀའ་བ་སྤྱད་པར་བྱ།

DA NI	CHO	CHIR	KA WA	CHAE PAR	JA
from now on	Dharma	in order to	hard, difficult	practice	do

From this time on we will strive as hard as we can to engage with the Dharma.

When sleep overwhelms us while practising Dharma, this is because previously we accumulated obstructions to the holy Dharma and so now the sharp weapon of these bad actions comes turning back upon us. From this time on we will strive as hard as we can to engage with the Dharma.

(Alternative reading:)

Previously we accumulated obstructions to the holy Dharma. Now the sharp weapon of these bad actions comes turning back upon us, so that sleep overwhelms us while practising Dharma. From this time on we will strive as hard as we can to engage with the Dharma.

ཉོན་མོངས་ལ་དགའ་རྣམ་གཡེང་ཆེས་བའི་ཚེ།

NYON MONG	LA	GA	NAM YENG	CHE WAI	TSHE
afflictions	to	joy, delight	wavering, restless*	great, very strong	if, when

(* as when we meet a person we like and are then happy to have our minds disturbed by all manner of crazy thoughts)

When our minds are very restless and delight in the afflictions,

མི་རྟག་འཁོར་བའི་ཉེས་དམིགས་མ་བསྒོམས་པས།

MI TAG	KHOR WAI	NYE MIG	MA GOM PAE
impermanence	samsara's	retribution	not meditate

(The troubles we experience while revolving in the six realms due to our own bad actions.)

This is because previously we did not meditate upon impermanence and samsara's retribution, and

ལས་ངན་མཚོན་ཆ་རང་ལ་འཁོར་བ་ཡིན།

LAE NGAN TSHON CHA RANG LA KHOR WA YIN

So now the sharp weapon of these bad actions comes turning back upon us.

དེ་ནི་འཁོར་བའི་ཡིད་འབྱུང་ཆེ་བར་བྱ།

DA NI	KHOR WA	YID JUNG	CHE WAR	JA
from now	samsara	renounce, feel repugnance for	great, very strong	do

From this time on we will reject and renounce samsara.

When our minds are very restless and delight in the afflictions, this is because previously we did not meditate upon impermanence and samsara's retribution and so now the sharp weapon of these bad actions comes turning back upon us. From this time on we will reject and renounce samsara.

(Alternative reading:)

Previously we did not meditate upon impermanence and samsara's retribution. Now the sharp weapon of these bad actions comes turning back upon us, so that our minds are very restless and delight in the afflictions. From this time on we will reject and renounce samsara.

ཇི་ལྟར་བྱས་ཀྱང་མར་འགྲོ་ཤོར་བའི་ཚེ།

JI TAR	JAE	KYANG	MAR DRO	SHOR WAI	TSHE
whatever	do	although	go downwards, decline	fall away, be lost*	if, when

(* like a lady who spends a fortune on make-up and beauty treatment but only gets skin diseases as a result)

When all our activities decline and fall away,

ལས་དང་རྒྱུ་འབྲས་ཁྱད་དུ་བསད་པ་ཡིས།

LAE	DANG	GYU	DRAE	KYAE DU	SAE PA	YI
deed	and	cause	result*	distinction	destroy	due to

(* i.e. karma, actions as causes having consequences)

This is because previously we paid little heed to the fact that actions are causes with future consequences, and

ལས་ངན་མཚོན་ཆ་རང་ལ་འཁོར་བ་ཡིན།

LAE NGAN TSHON CHA RANG LA KHOR WA YIN

So now the sharp weapon of these bad actions comes turning back upon us.

དེ་ནི་བཟོད་ལ་(ལས་འབྲས་)སོགས་ལ་འབད་པར་བྱ།

DA NI	ZOE	LA SOG	LA	BAE PAR JA
from now	patience	and so on*	to	exert, strive

(* The six paramitas: generosity, morality, patience, diligence, concentration, supreme knowing. These are the great mahayana method of accumulating merit and wisdom.)

From this time on we will strive in the practice of the six paramitas.

When all our activities decline and fall away, this is because previously we paid little heed to the fact that actions are causes with future consequences and so now the sharp weapon of these bad actions comes turning back upon us. From this time on we will strive in the practice of the six paramitas.

(Alternative reading:)

Previously we paid little heed to the fact that actions are causes with future consequences. Now the sharp weapon of these bad actions comes turning back upon us, so that all our activities decline and fall away. From this time on we will strive in the practice of the six paramitas.

རིམ་གྲོ་བྱས་ཚད་ལོག་པར་སོང་བའི་ཚེ།

RIM DRO	JAE	TSHAE	LOG PAR	SONG WAI	TSHE
religious service, homage etc. to gods and priests	done	whatever quantity	wrong way	gone	when

When all our religious rites and practices turn out badly,

ནག་པོའི་ཕྱོགས་ལ་རེ་ལྟོས་བྱས་བ་ཡིས།

NAG POI	CHOG	LA	RE TOE	JAE WA	YI
black side (i.e. unvirtue)		to	hope, expectation* (* e.g. hoping to become rich by stealing)	do	due to

This is because previously we relied on unvirtuous actions, and

ལས་ངན་མཚོན་ཆ་རང་ལ་འཁོར་བ་ཡིན།

LAE NGAN TSHON CHA RANG LA KHOR WA YIN

So now the sharp weapon of these bad actions comes turning back upon us.

དེ་ནི་ནག་པོའི་ཕྱོགས་ལས་བཟློག་པར་བྱ།

DA NI	NAG POI	CHOG	LAE	DOG PAR	JA
from now	black's	side	deeds	turn, expel	do

From this time on we will turn away from all unvirtuous activity.

When all our religious rites and practices turn out badly, this is because previously we relied on unvirtuous actions and so now the sharp weapon of these bad actions comes turning back upon us. From this time on we will turn away from all unvirtuous activity.

(Alternative reading:)

Previously we relied on unvirtuous actions. Now the sharp weapon of these bad actions comes turning back upon us, so that all our religious rites and practices turn out badly. From this time on we will turn away from all unvirtuous activity.

Sharp Weapon Wheel

དཀོན་མཆོག་གསུམ་ལ་གསོལ་བ་མ་ཐེབས་ཚེ།

KON CHOG   SUM   LA   SOL WA   MA   THEB   TSHE
jewel   three   to   pray   not   appropriate,   if, when
(Buddha, Dharma, Sangha)   suitable
(We do not know their qualities and so do not know why or how to pray. Just as if a beggar does not think that a person is rich or has a good heart then he will have no reason to approach him.)

When we are unable to pray to the Three Jewels,

སངས་རྒྱས་པ་ལ་ཡིད་ཆེས་མ་བྱས་བས།

SANG GYE PA   LA   YI CHE   MA   JAE WAE
Buddhahood*   to   faith, rely on   not   done
(* complete purity with all good qualities)

This is because previously we have not developed deep faith in the Buddha, and

ལས་ངན་མཚོན་ཆ་རང་ལ་འཁོར་བ་ཡིན།

LAE NGAN TSHON CHA RANG LA KHOR WA YIN
So now the sharp weapon of these bad actions comes turning back upon us.

དེ་དཀོན་མཆོག་ཁོ་ན་བསྟེན་པར་བྱ།

DA NI   KON CHOG   KHO NA   TEN PAR   JA
from now   jewel   only, solely   serve   do
From this time on we will rely solely on the Three Jewels.

When we are unable to pray to the Three Jewels, this is because previously we have not developed deep faith in the Buddha and so now the sharp weapon of these bad actions comes turning back upon us. From this time on we will rely solely on the Three Jewels.

(Alternative reading:)

Previously we have not developed deep faith in the Buddha. Now the sharp weapon of these bad actions comes turning back upon us, so that we are unable to pray to the Three Jewels. From this time on we will rely solely on the Three Jewels.

ཉམས་སྒྲིབ་སྒྱིབ་དང་གདོན་དུ་ལངས་པའི་ཚེ།

NYAM   DIG   DRIB   DANG   DON   DU   LANG WAI   TSHE
lapses   sins   obscuration   and   troubles   as   come up   when
in vows

When we lapse in our vows, and our sins, obscurations and disruptions increase,

ཨུ་དང་སྔགས་ལ་སྡིག་པ་བསགས་པ་ཡིས།

LHA	DANG	NGAG	LA	DIG PA	SAG PA	YI
god	and	mantra	to	sin	accumulate	due to

(Khyad-gSad Byed-Pa, not see them as special)

(That is, we had incorrect views and practised wrongly, e.g. destroying thangkas or painting them wrongly or mispronouncing mantras and interspersing them with coughs and talk.)

This is because previously we behaved inappropriately with gods and mantras, and,

ལས་ངན་མཚོན་ཆ་རང་ལ་འཁོར་བ་ཡིན།

LAE NGAN TSHON CHA RANG LA KHOR WA YIN

So now the sharp weapon of these bad actions comes turning back upon us.

ད་ནི་རྣམ་རྟོག་ཐམས་ཅད་གཞོམ་པར་བྱ།

DA NI	NAM TOG	THAM CHE	ZHOM PAR	JA
from now	discursive dualistic thoughts	all	conquer, defeat (not go under the power of)	do

From this time on we will conquer all deluding thoughts.

When we lapse in our vows, and our sins, obscuration and disruptions increase, this is because previously we behaved inappropriately with gods and mantras and so now the sharp weapon of these bad actions comes turning back upon us. From this time on we will conquer all deluding thoughts.

(Alternative reading:)

Previously we behaved inappropriately with gods and mantra. Now the sharp weapon of these bad actions comes turning back upon us, so that we lapse in our vows, and our sins, obscurations and disruptions increase. From this time on we will conquer all deluding thoughts.

དབང་མ་ཐོབ་པར་བྱེས་སུ་འཁྱམས་པའི་ཚེ།

WANG	MA	THO PAR	JAE	SU	KHYAM PAI	TSHE
power	not	get, obtain	abroad, outside	in	wandering*	if, when

(* for example as refugees)

When we are powerless and are forced to wander abroad,

བླ་མ་ལ་སོགས་གནས་ནས་བསྐྲད་པ་ཡིས།

LA MA	LA SOG	NAE	NE	TRAE PA	YI
teacher, guru	and so on	place	from	gone, send away	due to

This is because previously we have expelled gurus and others from their abodes, and

ལས་དན་མཚོན་ཆ་རང་ལ་འཁོར་བ་ཡིན།
LAE NGAN TSHON CHA RANG LA KHOR WA YIN
So now the sharp weapon of these bad actions comes turning back upon us.

དནི་གང་ཡང་ཡུལ་ནས་དབྱུང་མི་བྱ།
DA NI　　GANG YANG　YUL　　　　NAE　　JUNG　　　　　　MI　JA
from now　whoever　　country, place　from　　remove, push out　not　do
From this time on we will never expel anyone from their own place.

When we are powerless and are forced to wander abroad, this is because previously we have expelled gurus and others from their abodes and so now the sharp weapon of these bad actions comes turning back upon us. From this time on we will never expel anyone from their own place.

(Alternative reading:)

Previously we have expelled gurus and others from their abodes. Now the sharp weapon of these bad actions comes turning back upon us, so that we are powerless and are forced to wander abroad. From this time on we will never expel anyone from their own place.

སད་སེར་ལ་སོགས་མི་འདོད་བྱུང་བའི་ཚེ།
SAE　　SER　　SOG　　　　MI　　DOE　　　　　JUNG WAI　　TSHE
frost　　hail　　and so on*　not⁺　liking, desire　comes　　　　when
(* floods, drought, crop-diseases etc.)　(⁺ whatever we dislike)
When we are faced with frost, hail and the many situations we dislike,

དམ་ཚིག་ཚུལ་ཁྲིམས་ཚུལ་བཞིན་མ་བསྲུངས་པས།
DAM TSHI　TSHUL TRIM　TSHUL ZHIN　MA　SUNG PAE
vows　　　　morality　　　properly　　　not　guard, protect
This is because previously we did not guard our vows and morality in the proper way, and

ལས་དན་མཚོན་ཆ་རང་ལ་འཁོར་བ་ཡིན།
LAE NGAN TSHON CHA RANG LA KHOR WA YIN
So now the sharp weapon of these bad actions comes turning back upon us.

དནི་དམ་ཚིག་ལ་སོགས་གཙང་བར་བྱ།
DA NI　　DAM TSHIG　LA SOG　　TSANG WAR　JA
from now　vows　　　　and so on　clean, pure　　do, keep
From this time on we will keep vows and morality pure.

When we are faced with frost, hail and the many situations we dislike, this is because previously we did not guard our vows and morality in the proper way and so now the sharp weapon of these bad actions comes turning back upon us. From this time on we will keep vows and morality pure.

(Alternative reading:)

Previously we did not guard our vows and morality in the proper way. Now the sharp weapon of these bad actions comes turning back upon us, so that we are troubled by frost, hail and the many situations we dislike. From this time on we will keep vows and morality pure.

འདོད་པ་ཆེ་ལ་འབྱོར་བས་ཕོངས་བའི་ཚེ།

DOE PA	CHE	LA	JOR WAE	PHONG WAI	TSHE
desire	great	to	fortune, treasure	poor, needy	if, when

When we indulge our many desires so that our wealth turns to poverty,

སྦྱིན་དང་དཀོན་མཆོག་མཆོད་པ་མ་བྱས་པས།

JIN	DANG	KON CHOG	CHOE PA	MA	JAE PAE
gift (to those in need)	and	excellents* (* the Three Jewels: Buddha, Dharma and Sangha)	offering	not	done

This is because previously we have not been generous and have not made offerings to the Three Jewels, and

ལས་ངན་མཚོན་ཆ་རང་ལ་འཁོར་བ་ཡིན།

LAE NGAN TSHON CHA RANG LA KHOR WA YIN

So now the sharp weapon of these bad actions comes turning back upon us.

དེ་ནི་མཆོད་སྦྱིན་ལས་ལ་བཙོན་པར་བྱ།

DA NI	CHOE	JIN	LAE	LA	TSON PAR	JA
from now	offering	gift	actions	at	strive	do

From this time on we will strive to make offerings and gifts.

When we indulge our many desires so that our wealth turns to poverty, this is because previously we have not been generous and have not made offerings to the Three Jewels and so now the sharp weapon of these bad actions comes turning back upon us. From this time on we will strive to make offerings and gifts.

(Alternative reading:)

Previously we have not been generous and have not made offerings to the Three Jewels. Now the sharp weapon of these bad actions comes turning back upon us, so that we indulge our many desires causing our wealth to turn to poverty. From this time on we will strive to make offerings and gifts.

སྐྱེ་གཟུགས་ངན་ཏེ་འཁོར་གྱིས་བརྙས་པའི་ཚེ།

KYE ZU	NGAN	TE	KHOR	GYI	NYAE WAI	TSHE
body form	bad, ugly	thus, then	circles, associates	by	scorn, despise	if, when

When, having ugly bodies, we are scorned by our associates,

སྐུ་གཟུགས་ངན་ཏེ་ཁོང་ཁྲོས་བསྲེགས་པ་ཡིས།

KU ZU	NGAN	TE	KHONG TRO	SE WA	YI
body* (honorific)	bad	thus	getting angry	destroy with fire⁺	due to

(* Buddha's body, statues, paintings etc.)   (⁺ or any form of destruction)

This is because previously we became angry with badly formed holy images and burned them, and

ལས་ངན་མཚོན་ཆ་རང་ལ་འཁོར་བ་ཡིན།

LAE NGAN TSHON CHA RANG LA KHOR WA YIN

So now the sharp weapon of these bad actions comes turning back upon us.

དེ་ནི་ལྷ་བཞེངས་དང་རྒྱུད་རིང་བར་བྱ།

DA NI	LHA	ZHENG	NGANG GYU	RING WAR	JA
from now	gods	make (statues)	character	long time, patiently	do

From this time on we will make images of the deities and patiently soften our character.

When, having ugly bodies, we are scorned by our associates, this is because previously we became angry with badly formed holy images and destroyed them and so now the sharp weapon of these bad actions comes turning back upon us. From this time on we will make images of the deities and patiently soften our character.

(Alternative reading:)

Previously we became angry with badly formed holy images and destroyed them. Now the sharp weapon of these bad actions comes turning back upon us, so that we have ugly bodies and are scorned by our associates. From this time on we will make images of the deities and patiently soften our character.

གང་ལྟར་བྱས་ཀྱང་ཆགས་སྡང་འཁྲུགས་པའི་ཚེ།

GANG	TAR	JAE	KYANG	CHAG	DANG	TRUG PAI	TSHE
whatever	as	done	still	grasping*	anger, hate	troubles	when

(i.e. however much Dharma we try)

(* No matter how we act towards others we can never gain full satisfaction.)

When, no matter what we do, we are still disturbed by anger and desire,

མ་རུང་རྒྱུད་དན་རིགས་སུ་བཅུག་པ་ཡིས།

MA RUNG	GYU	NGAN	RENG	SU	CHUG PA	YI
atrocious, very wicked	character	bad	rough	to	enter, begin	due to

(e.g. we taunt a wild madman and then laugh at his antics, or we tell untrue stories to stir up the jealousy of a suspicious husband)

This is because previously we have stirred up those who were already rough and vicious, and

ལས་ངན་མཚོན་ཆ་རང་ལ་འཁོར་བ་ཡིན།

LAE NGAN TSHON CHA RANG LA KHOR WA YIN

So now the sharp weapon of these bad actions comes turning back upon us.

ད་ནི་རིངས་ཁྱོད་དྲུངས་ནས་དབྱུང་བར་བྱ།

DA	NI	RENG	KHYOD	DRUNG	NAE	JUNG WAR	JA
from	now	rough, hard	you	exterminate	from	expel	do

From this time on we will completely eliminate all unkindness towards others.

When, no matter what we do, we are still disturbed by anger and desire, this is because previously we have stirred up those who were already rough and vicious and so now the sharp weapon of these bad actions comes turning back upon us. From this time on we will completely eliminate all unkindness towards others.

(Alternative reading:)

Previously we have stirred up those who were already rough and vicious. Now the sharp weapon of these bad actions comes turning back upon us, so that no matter what we do we are still disturbed by anger and desire. From this time on we will completely eliminate all unkindness towards others.

སྒྲུབ་པ་གང་བྱས་དམིགས་སུ་མ་སོང་ཚེ།

DRUB PA	GANG	JAE	MIG	SU	MA	SONG	TSHE
practice	whatever	done	object	to	not	reached, gone to	when, if

When, whatever practice we do, we cannot fulfil our intention,

ལྟ་བ་དམན་པ་ཁོང་དུ་ཞུགས་པ་ཡིས།

TA WA	MAN PA	KHONG DU	ZHU PA	YI
opinion, view*	vulgar, low	inside (mind)	enter	due to

(* of selfishness and sin)

This is because previously we have filled our minds with egotistical attitudes, and

ལས་ངན་མཚོན་ཆ་རང་ལ་འཁོར་བ་ཡིན།

LAE NGAN TSHON CHA RANG LA KHOR WA YIN

So now the sharp weapon of these bad actions comes turning back upon us.

དེ་ནི་ཅི་བྱེད་གཞན་དོན་ཉིད་དུ་བྱ།

DA NI	CHI	JE	ZHAN	DON	NYI DU	JA
from now	whatever	do	others	benefit	truly	do

From this time on, whatever we do will be for the benefit for others.

When whatever practice we do, we cannot fulfil our intention, this is because previously we have filled our minds with egotistical attitudes and so now the sharp weapon of these bad actions comes turning back upon us. From this time on, whatever we do will be for the benefit of others.

(Alternative reading:)

Previously we have filled our minds with egotistical attitudes. Now the sharp weapon of these bad actions comes turning back upon us, so that, whatever practice we do, we cannot fulfil our intention. From this time on whatever we do will be for the benefit of others.

དགེ་སྦྱོར་བྱས་ཀྱང་རང་རྒྱུད་མ་ཐུལ་ཚེ།

GE	JOR	JAE	KYANG	RANG GYU	MA	THUL	TSHE
virtue	practice	done	yet	my mind	not	disciplined*	when

(*e.g. not paying attention to the teaching, or thinking you are the only one who matters)

When, although we have practised virtue, our mind remains undisciplined,

ཚེ་འདི་ཆེ་ཐབས་དང་དུ་བླངས་པ་ཡིས།

TSHE DI CHE THAB DANG DU LANG WA YI
life this proud practise strongly due to

This is because earlier in this life we have striven for worldly success and position, and

ལས་ངན་མཚོན་ཆ་རང་ལ་འཁོར་བ་ཡིན།

LAE NGAN TSHON CHA RANG LA KHOR WA YIN

So now the sharp weapon of these bad actions comes turning back upon us.

ད་ནི་ཐར་པ་འདོད་ལ་བསྒྲིལ་བར་བྱ།

DA NI THAR PA DO LA DRIL WA JA
from now liberate desire to live, behave do

From this time on we will cultivate our longing for liberation.

When, although we have practised virtue, our mind remains undisciplined, this is because earlier in this life we have striven for worldly success and position and so now the sharp weapon of these bad actions comes turning back upon us. From this time on we will cultivate our longing for liberation.

(Alternative reading:)

Earlier in this life we have striven for worldly success and position. Now the sharp weapon of these bad actions comes turning back upon us, so that although we have practised virtues, our mind remains undisciplined. From this time on we will cultivate our longing for liberation.

འདུས་མ་ཐག་ལ་བལྟགས་ཤིང་འགྱོད་པའི་ཚེ།

DU MA THAG LA TA SHING GYO WAI TSHE
assembled immediately to seeing regret* when
(* We feel awkward and guilty with them.)

When we feel awkward as soon as we meet others,

ཁྲེལ་མེད་གསར་འགྲོགས་མཐོ་ཁ་འགྲིམས་པ་ཡིས།

TREL ME SAR DRO THO KHA DRIM PA YI
shameless new friend high, noble diminish* due to
(* i.e. we have acted as if we are much greater than them)

This is because previously we have shamelessly made ourselves out to be great to the new friends we met, and

Sharp Weapon Wheel

ལས་ངན་མཚོན་ཆ་རང་ལ་འཁོར་བ་ཡིན།

LAE NGAN TSHON CHA RANG LA KHOR WA YIN

So now the sharp weapon of these bad actions comes turning back upon us.

དེ་ནི་ཡོངས་ལ་འགྲོགས་ལུགས་གཟབ་པར་བྱ།

DA NI	YONG	LA	DRO	LU	ZAB PAR	JA
from now	all	to	friend	way, manner	careful, well-behaved	do

From this time on we will act mindfully in a friendly way to all.

When we feel awkward as soon as we meet others, this is because previously we have shamelessly made ourselves out to be great to the new friends we met and so now the sharp weapon of these bad actions comes turning back upon us. From this time on we will act mindfully in a friendly way to all.

(Alternative reading:)

Previously we have shamelessly made ourselves out to be great to the new friends we met. Now the sharp weapon of these bad actions comes turning back upon us, so that we feel awkward as soon as we meet others. From this time on we will act mindfully in a friendly way to all.

གཞན་གྱི་སྱུག་སློས་རང་ཉིད་བསླུས་པའི་ཚེ།

ZHAN	GYI	MU KYO	RANG NYI	LU WAI	TSHE
others	of	insult*	self	deceive	when

(* words that trouble and hurt me and my reputation)

When we are cheated by the bad actions of others

རང་ཉིད་ང་རྒྱལ་གཏོགས་འདོད་ཆེ་བས་ལན།

RANG NYI	NGA GYAL	TOG DOE	CHE WAE	LAN
myself	pride	ambition	great	for that reason

This is because previously we were proud and selfishly ambitious, and

ལས་ངན་མཚོན་ཆ་རང་ལ་འཁོར་བ་ཡིན།

LAE NGAN TSHON CHA RANG LA KHOR WA YIN

So now the sharp weapon of these bad actions comes turning back upon us.

དེ་ནི་གང་ལ་འདོད་པ་ཆུང་བར་བྱ།

DA NI	GANG	LA	DOD PA	CHUNG WAR	JA
from now	whatever	to	desire, liking	make small	do

From this time on we will eliminate our desire for whatever appeals to us.

When we are cheated by the bad actions of others, this is because previously we were proud and selfishly ambitious and so now the sharp weapon of these bad actions comes turning back upon us. From this time on we will eliminate our desire for whatever appeals to us.

(Alternative reading:)

Previously we were proud and selfishly ambitious. Now the sharp weapon of these bad actions comes turning back upon us, so that we are cheated by the bad actions of others. From this time on we will eliminate our desire for whatever appeals to us.

ཉན་བཤད་ཆགས་སྡང་གྲོགས་སུ་སོང་བའི་ཚེ།

NYAN	SHA	CHAG	DANG	DROG	SU	SONG WAI	TSHE
hear	tell, discuss	desire, grasping	anger	assistant	as	arise	when

(When I hear things I like or dislike, desire or anger arise, and the things I say cause others to feel desire or anger.)

When desire and anger influence the way we listen and talk,

བདུད་ཀྱི་སྐྱོན་རྣམས་སྙིང་ལ་མ་བསམ་པས།

DU	KYI	KYON NAM	NYING	LA	MA	SAM PAE
mara, demons	of	faults, sins	heart, mind	to	not	think

(i.e. not knowing they were there we made no effort to clear them)

This is because previously we were not aware of the demon-like faults in our minds, and

ལས་ངན་མཚོན་ཆ་རང་ལ་འཁོར་བ་ཡིན།

LAE NGAN TSHON CHA RANG LA KHOR WA YIN

So now the sharp weapon of these bad actions comes turning back upon us.

ད་ནི་འགལ་རྐྱེན་བརྟགས་ནས་སྤང་བར་བྱ།

DA NI	GAL	KYEN	TAG	NAE	PANG WA	JA
from now	wrong, misleading*		situations	recognise	then	abandon	do

(* the wrong views in our minds which lead us to perform all wrong actions)

From this time on we will recognise and abandon all situations that can lead us astray.

When desire and anger influence the way we listen and talk, this is because previously we were not aware of the demon-like faults in our minds and so now the sharp weapon of these bad actions comes turning back upon us. From this time on we will recognise and abandon all situations that can lead us astray.

(Alternative reading:)

Previously we were not aware of the demon-like faults in our minds. Now the sharp weapon of these bad actions comes turning back upon us, so that desire and anger influence the way we listen and talk. From this time on we will recognise and abandon all situations that can lead us astray.

བཟང་བྱས་ཐམས་ཅད་ངན་དུ་ལོག་པའི་ཚེ།

ZANG	JAE	THAM CHE	NGAN	DU	LOG PAI	TSHE
whatever is good	do	all	bad	as	reverse	when

When all the good that we try to do turns out badly,

དྲིན་ལན་ཐམས་ཅད་ལོག་པར་གཞལ་བ་ཡིས།

DRIN	LAN	THAM CHE	LOG PAR	ZHAL WA	YI
kindness	repay	all	reverse*	weighting	due to
			(ungrateful return for a service done)		

(* e.g. someone might lend us money but then we deny this and accuse them of trying to cheat us)

This is because previously we repaid kindness with hurt and harm, and

ལས་ངན་མཚོན་ཆ་རང་ལ་འཁོར་བ་ཡིན།

LAE NGAN TSHON CHA RANG LA KHOR WA YIN

So now the sharp weapon of these bad actions comes turning back upon us.

ད་ནི་དྲིན་ལན་སྤྱི་བོས་བླང་བར་བྱ།

DA NI	DRIN	LAN	CHI WO	LANG WAR	JA
from now	kindness	remember, repay	crown of head (very respectful)	take, accept	do

From this time on we will gratefully and carefully repay all the kindness we receive.

When all the good that we try to do turns out badly, this is because previously we repaid kindness with hurt and harm and so now the sharp weapon of these bad actions comes turning back upon us. From this time on we will gratefully and carefully repay all the kindness we receive.

(Alternative reading:)

Previously we repaid kindness with hurt and harm. Now the sharp weapon of these bad actions comes turning back upon us so that all the good we try to do turns out badly. From this time on we will gratefully and carefully repay all the kindness we receive.

འདོད་དུས་མི་འདོད་ཐོག་ཏུ་བབ་པ་རྣམས།

DOE DU MI DOE THOG TU BAB PA NAM
desire when not like upon descend
(the fruit of our own previous actions)
(I want something but instead I get what I don't like, and the plans I make to get joy merely lead to sorrow.)

When what we desire is smothered by what we find undesirable

མགར་བ་རང་གི་རལ་གྲིས་བསད་པ་ལྟར།

GAR WA RANG GI RAL DRI SAE PA TAR
blacksmith self of sword killed like

We are like a blacksmith who is killed by the sword he himself made, for

ལས་ངན་མཚོན་ཆ་རང་ལ་འཁོར་བ་ཡིན།

LAE NGAN TSHON CHA RANG LA KHOR WA YIN

Now the sharp weapon of our bad actions comes turning back upon us.

ད་ནི་སྡིག་པའི་ལས་ལ་བག་ཡོད་བྱ།

DA NI DIG PAI LAE LA BAG YOE JA
from now sins actions to careful do

From this time on we will take care to avoid unvirtuous activity.

When what we desire is smothered by what we find undesirable, we are like a blacksmith who is killed by the sword he himself has made for now the sharp weapon of our bad actions comes turning back upon us. From this time on we must take care to avoid unvirtuous activity.

ངན་སོང་རྣམས་སུ་སྡུག་བསྔལ་མྱོང་བ་རྣམས།

NGAN SONG NAM SU DU KHA NYONG WA NAM
lower realms* in suffering experience, all
(* hell, hungry ghosts and animal) undergo

When we experience all the sufferings of the three lower realms,

མདའ་མཁན་རང་གི་མདའ་ཡིས་བསད་པ་ལྟར།

DA KHAN RANG GI DA YI SAE PA TAR
arrow-maker self of arrow by killed like

We are like an arrow-maker who is killed by his own arrow, for

ལས་ངན་མཚོན་ཆ་རང་ལ་འཁོར་བ་ཡིན།

LAE NGAN TSHON CHA RANG LA KHOR WA YIN

Now the sharp weapon of our bad actions comes turning back upon us.

དེ་ནི་སྡིག་པའི་ལས་ལ་བག་ཡོད་བྱ།

DA NI	DIG	PAI	LAE	LA	BAG YOE	JA
from now	sin	of	actions	to	careful	do

From this time on we will take care to avoid unvirtuous activity.

When we experience all the sufferings of the three lower realms, we are like an arrow-maker who is killed by his own arrow for now the sharp weapon of our bad actions comes turning back upon us. From this time on we will take care to avoid unvirtuous activity.

ཁྱིམ་གྱི་སྡུག་བསྔལ་ཐོགས་ཏུ་བབ་པ་ཡང་།

KHYIM	KYI	DU NGAL	THOG TU	BAB PA	YANG
house	of	suffering	on top	descend	also

Moreover, when we are oppressed by the troubles and worries of house and family,

བསྐྱངས་བའི་བུ་ཚ་ཕ་མ་གསོད་པ་ལྟར།

KYANG WAI	BU TSA	PHA	MO	SOE PA	TAR
protected	son	father	mother	killed	like

(No matter how much time and money parents spend on their children, there is no certainty that they will be repaid with love, and similarly with our houses and domestic affairs, we can never be sure that they will bring us the happiness that we hope for.)

We are like parents who are killed by the child they have protected and cherished, for

ལས་ངན་མཚོན་ཆ་རང་ལ་འཁོར་བ་ཡིན།

LAE NGAN TSHON CHA RANG LA KHOR WA YIN

The sharp weapon of our bad actions comes turning back upon us.

དེ་ནི་རྟག་པར་རབ་ཏུ་འབྱུང་བར་རིགས།

DA NI	TAG PAR	RAB TU JUNG WAR	RIG
from now	always	become a monk*	family
		(* i.e. renounce samsara)	

From this time on we will always abide in the family of renunciates.

Moreover, when we are oppressed by the troubles and worries of house and family, we are like parents who are killed by the child they have protected and cherished for the sharp weapon of our bad actions comes turning back upon us. From this time on we will always abide in the family of renunciates.

དེ་ལྟར་ལགས་པས་དགྲ་བོ་བདག་གིས་ཟིན།

DE TAR	LAG PAE	DRA WO	DA	GI	ZIN
like that	is and so	enemy, ego-cherishing	me	by	recognise and hold

In this way I come to recognise my enemy.

འཇབ་ནས་བསླུ་བའི་ཆོམ་རྐུན་བདག་གིས་ཟིན།

JAB	NAE	LU WAI	CHOM KUN	DAG	GI	ZIN
disguise, camouflage	from	deceive	robber	me	by	recognise and hold

I recognise this robber in disguise who cheats me.

རང་དུ་བརྫུས་ནས་བསླུ་བ་བདག་གིས་ཟིན།

RANG	DU	DZU	NAE	LU WA	DA	GI	ZIN
self	as	impersonating	from	deceive	me	by	recognise and hold

(The grasping ego pretends it is me; it says, "I am" and, "This is me." But in fact it is my enemy, the source of all my troubles.)

I recognise this deceitful one who impersonates me.

ཨེ་མ་བདག་འཛིན་འདི་ཡིན་ཐེ་ཚོམ་གཅོད།

E MA	DA DZIN	DI	YIN	THE TSOM	CHOE
amazing	self grasping (believing strongly in 'I' and 'mine')	this	is	doubt#	cut

(# All the doubts coming from believing that I am an ego or vulnerable entity requiring protection and special treatment. Now the grasping ego is given no more support by my mind for it is seen clearly to be the source of all my troubles.)

Amazing! I have cut off all doubts regarding the truth about this grasped-at-self!

In this way I come to recognise my enemy. I recognise this robber in disguise who cheats me. I recognise this deceitful one who impersonates me. Amazing! I have cut off all doubts regarding the truth about this grasped-at-self!

དེ་ནི་ལས་ཀྱི་མཚོན་ཆ་ཀླད་ལ་བསྐོར།

DA NI	LAE	KYI	TSHON CHA	LAE	LA	KOR
now*	deeds, karma#	of	sharp weapon	brain, head	around	revolve, swirl

(* Now I cease to rely on the grasping ego and arise in the form of Yamantaka.)

(# All karma, both good and bad, I destroy by removing the concept of a really existing being on whom it could mature. Now I know that this egoism and grasping is not my true identity; I see it clearly for the enemy it is. So keeping my mind free of this grasping, I am not different from Yamantaka who destroys the Lord of Death, the one who terrifies those who believe in the ego.)

Now I swing the sharp weapon of karma around my head,

Sharp Weapon Wheel

ཁྲོས་པའི་ཚུལ་གྱིས་ལན་གསུམ་ཀླད་ལ་བསྐོར།

TRO WAI	TSHUL	GYI	LAN	SUM	LAE LA KOR
khrodha, anger form of Buddha	manner (i.e. with compassion)	by	times	three	swirl around the head

Thrice I swing it around my head in the manner of this fierce Buddha.

བདེན་གཉིས་ཞབས་བགྲད་ཐབས་ཤེས་སྤྱན་མིག་དངད།

DEN	NYI	ZHAB	DRAE	THAB	SHE	CHAN MIG	DENG
truth	two*	feet	wide apart	method	wisdom	eyes	wide open

(* relative and absolute truth)

With my feet of the two truths planted firmly apart, my eyes of method and wisdom are open and glaring.

སྟོབས་བཞིའི་མཆེ་བ་གཙིགས་པ་དགྲ་ལ་བསྔུན།

TOB	ZHI	CHE WA	TSHIG PA	DRA	LA	NUN
power	four*	great	show one's powerful teeth	enemy#	to	pierce

(# grasping at belief in the grasping ego)

(* These are the four essential factors for removing the karmic effects of self-cherishing. Firstly, confess before a pure object, such as Vajrasattva, a statue of Buddha, or the Bodhgaya temple. Secondly, feel intense regret, as if one had eaten poison and might die. Thirdly, confess fully so that all lingering attachment is cut off. Fourthly, promise never to act in this way again.)

My fangs of the four powers pierce the enemy.

Now I swing the sharp weapon of karma around my head; thrice I swing it around my head in the manner of this fierce Buddha. With my feet of the two truths planted firmly apart, my eyes of method and wisdom are open and glaring. My fangs of the four powers pierce the enemy.

དགྲ་བོ་གཟིར་བའི་རིག་སྔགས་རྒྱལ་པོ་ཡང་།

DRA WO	ZIR WAI	RIG	NGAG	GYAL PO	YANG
enemies*	press down, control	awareness	mantra (	king Yamantaka)	also

(* Those who trouble me due to our self-cherishing actions)

I, Yamantaka, king of tantra, crusher of enemies,

འཁོར་བའི་ནགས་སུ་རང་དབང་མ་ཆིས་བར།

KHOR WAI	NAG	SU	RANG	WANG	MA	CHI WAR
samsara's	forest	in	self	power	not	be, have

(Employing the visualisation of ourselves as the powerful terrifying Yamantaka, we arouse the shining power of our intrinsic awareness to destroy the harmful influence of habitual grasping. This section is like Chod cutting practice, in which my awareness is separated from my dualistic consciousness and my ego-cherishing identification with my body.)

Brandish the sharp weapon of karma that keeps beings powerlessly in the forest of samsara.

Yamantaka with buffalo head

ལས་ཀྱི་མཚོན་ཆ་ཐོགས་ནས་རྒྱུག་པ་ཡིས།

LAE	KYI	TSHON CHA	THOG	NAE	GYUG PA	YI
karma	of	sharp weapons	holds up	then	running	by this

Then I come running, trapping

བདག་འཛིན་འགོང་པོ་ཆེས་བའི་གདུག་རྩུབ་ཅན།

DAG DZIN	GONG PO	CHE WAI	DUG TSUB CHAN
grasping at 'I' and 'mine'	demon, trouble maker	called	rough and dangerous

(Self is fabricated with concepts and feelings and then believed in as an unchanging personal essence.)

The very rough and dangerous one called 'the demon of grasping at a self',

རང་གཞན་ཕུང་དུ་འཇུག་པའི་དམ་ཉམས་ཁུག

RANG	ZHAN	PHUNG	DU	JUG PAI	DAM	NYAM	KHUG
self	others	pieces	as	make	vows	lapse, deteriorate	bring

(i.e. losing our vows means losing our chance of enlightenment)

The one who causes deterioration of vows, fragmenting self and others.

I, Yamantaka, king of tantra, crusher of enemies, brandish the sharp weapon of karma that keeps beings powerlessly in the forest of samsara. Then I come running, trapping the very rough and dangerous one called 'the demon of grasping at a self', the one who causes deterioration of vows, fragmenting self and others.

ཁུག་ཅིག་ཁུག་ཅིག་ཁྲོ་བོ་གཤིན་རྗེ་གཤེད།

KHU CHI	KHU CHI	TRO WO	SHIN JE SHE
bring! (ego)	bring!	wrathful, khrodha	Yamantaka

I wrathful Yamantaka, bring the ego! I bring it!

རྒྱོབ་ཅིག་རྒྱོབ་ཅིག་དགྲ་བདག་སྙིང་ལ་བསྣུན།

GYO CHI	GYO CHI	DRA	DA	NYING	LA	NUN
beat!	beat!	enemy	ego	heart	in	pierce, stab

I beat it! I beat it! I stab the enemy, this grasping ego, in the heart!

ཕུང་བྱེད་རྟོག་པའི་མགོ་ལ་ཆེམ་སེ་ཆེམ།

PHUNG	JE	TOG PAI	GO	LA	CHEM SE CHEM
lose, destroy	make	thought	head	on	beat, stomp

(Due to grasping arising from ignorance of emptiness, the true actuality of all phenomena, many thoughts tainted by the five poisons arise. Then, due to acting under their influence, beings build up the karma that brings them to birth in the six realms of samsara.)

I stamp of the head of the thoughts that make me fragment.

Sharp Weapon Wheel

དགྲ་བདག་གཤེད་མའི་སྙིང་ལ་མཱ་ར་ཡ།

DRA DA SHED MAI NYING LA MA RA YA
enemy ego killer# heart in kill†
(grasping at 'I' and 'mine') (i.e. beyond revival)
(# He follows us like an assassin who has stolen our identity and wants to usurp and destroy us.)
(† Ego is killed by the strength of our own wisdom i.e. by ceasing grasping we allow it to dissolve in its own emptiness, vanishing without trace.)

I kill the heart of this murderous enemy, my illusory ego.

I wrathful Yamantaka, bring the ego! I bring it! I beat it! I beat it! I stab the enemy, this grasping ego, in the heart! I stamp on the head of the thoughts that fragment me. I kill the heart of this murderous enemy, my illusory ego!

ཧཱུྃ་ཧཱུྃ་ཡི་དམ་ཆེན་པོ་རྫུ་འཕྲུལ་བསྐྱེད།

HUNG HUNG YI DAM CHEN PO DZU TRUL KYE
* linking deity† great miracle# cause to develop
(* Symbol of the five pristine cognitions; saying this we gain more power to be fully Yamantaka.)
(† A linking deity is one who links us to our buddha potential and helps us to awaken it fully. We are linked to this deity through initiation, vows and practice.)
(# i.e. the power of emptiness)

Hung! Hung! I, the great linking deity, bring forth my miraculous power.

ཛཿཛཿདགྲ་པོ་འདི་ཉིད་དམ་ལ་ཐོགས།

DZA DZA DRA WO DI NYI DAM LA THOG
come! come! enemy this force of with impede
(grasping) your vow
(bind so tightly that he cannot escape)

I am here! I am here! Binding the enemy I render him impotent.

ཕཊ྄་ཕཊ྄་འཆི་བདག་ཆེན་པོས་བསྒྲལ་དུ་གསོལ།

PHAT PHAT CHI DAG CHEN POE DRAL DU SOL
Cut! Cut! death lord great kill please

I cut! I cut! As conqueror of the lord of death, I kill this grasping ego!

ཤིག་ཤིག་འཛིན་པའི་མདུད་པ་བཅད་དུ་གསོལ།

SHIG SHIG DZIN PAI DU PA CHAE DU SOL
release! release! grasping's knot cut please
(By relaxing the fist our hand goes free by itself.)

Freed! Freed! The knot of grasping is cut!

Hung. Hung. I, the great linking deity, bring forth my miraculous power! I am here! I am here! Binding the enemy I render him impotent. I cut! I cut! As conqueror of the lord of death, I kill this grasping ego! Freed! Freed! The knot of grasping is cut!

ཚུར་བྱོན་ཡི་དམ་ཆེན་པོ་གཤིན་རྗེ་གཤེད།

TSHUR	JON	YI DAM	CHEN PO	SHIN JE SHE
to this place	come	linking deity	great	Yamantaka

(The linking deity links or binds our mind back to actuality. The deity cuts through dualistic confusion and deceptive constructed self-identity to reveal the Buddha potential and ripen it in the deity mandala. Now we recite as if we were in our usual body and call on Yamantaka as if he were other than us. In fact we are nondual.)

Great linking deity, Yamantaka, come to this place!

འཁོར་བའི་ལས་ཀྱི་འདམ་རྫབ་སྦྱར་བ་ཡིས།

KHOR WAI LAE	KYI	DAM DZAB	JAR WA	YI
samsara's actions	of	swamp, cesspool	mixture, composed	due to, by

Due to inhabiting this swamp arising from samsaric activity

ལས་དང་ཉོན་མོངས་དུག་ལྔའི་རྐྱལ་བུ་འདི།

LAE	DANG	NYON MONG	DU	NGAI	KYAL BU	DI
deeds	and	afflictions	poison	five*	leather pouch#	this

(* stupidity, anger, desire, pride and jealousy)
(# the skin bag of my body full of impulse and confusion)

I exist as a leather pouch full of the five poisonous afflictions and their activities.

ད་ལྟ་ཉིད་དུ་ཤག་ཤག་དྲལ་དུ་གསོལ།

DAN TAR NYI DU	SHA	SHA	DRAL	DU SOL
now, immediately	quickly	quickly	kill, destroy+	please

(+ Yamantaka, the compassionate manifestation of primordial wisdom uses the bag of our karma (the fruit of the activity of our ego) as a weapon to beat and annihilate our self-cherishing ego, the self-referential offspring of ignorance. Due to his great power and compassion, instead of the returning wheel of the sharp weapon of ignorance, duality and ego-identification causing us ever more suffering, he ensures that this very force of limitation destroys all limitation. In this way poison taken skilfully increases the clarity of the mind in the manner of a peacock.)

Quickly! Quickly! You must immediately destroy all self-cherishing!

Great linking deity, Yamantaka, come to this place! Due to inhabiting this swamp arising from samsaric activity I exist as a leather pouch full of the five poisonous afflictions and their activities. Quickly! Quickly! You must immediately destroy all self-cherishing!

ངན་སོང་གསུམ་དུ་སྡུག་ལ་བསྐྱལ་གྱུར་ཀྱང་།

NGAN SONG	SUM	DU	DUG	LA	KYAL	GYUR	KYANG
lower realms*	three	in	misery	to	put (by grasping)	does	although, but

(* hell, hungry ghost and animal)

Although immersed in the misery of the three lower realms,

Sharp Weapon Wheel

སྲིད་མི་ཤེས་པར་རྒྱུ་ལ་རྒྱུག་པ་ཡིས།

SI	MI	SHE PAR	GYU	LA	GYU PA	YI
possible	not	know	cause (i.e. grasping)	to	return, run to	due to

(excessive desire, like someone eating chilli, burning their mouth and yet still heaping more onto their plate)

I still run after the cause, never feeling I have had enough.

ཕུང་བྱེད་རྟོག་པའི་མགོ་ལ་ཆེམ་སེ་ཆེམ།

PHUNG	JE	TOG PAI	GO	LA	CHEM SE CHEM
lose, destroy	make	thought	head	on	beat, stamp

Stamp on the head of these thoughts that fragment me!

དགྲ་བདག་གཤེད་མའི་སྙིང་ལ་མ་ར་ཡ།

DRA	DA	SHED MAI	NYING	LA	MA RA YA
enemy	ego⁺	trouble-maker	heart	in	kill

(⁺ Although I am making a heartfelt request to Yamantaka to help me find freedom from the limitation of delusion, I make this request with the Mahayana understanding that I am doing so on behalf of all sentient beings and I imagine them all around me making the same request.)

Kill the heart of this killer demon, the ego I believe in!

Although immersed in the misery of the three lower realms, I still run after the cause, never feeling I have had enough. Stamp on the head of these thoughts that fragment me! Kill the heart of this killer enemy, the ego I believe in!

འདོད་ཐག་ཉེ་ལ་སྒྲུབ་པའི་བརྩོན་འགྲུས་ཆུང་།

DOE	THAG	NYE LA	DRUB WAI	TSON	DRUE	CHUNG
desire	quick	close to	practising	effort	diligence	little

(i.e. we want enlightenment in one life-time)

I have great desire for quick results yet I put little effort into my practice, and

བྱ་བྱེད་མང་ལ་གང་ཡང་མཐར་མི་ཕྱིན།

JA	JE	MANG LA	GANG	YANG	THAR	MI	CHIN
deed	do	many to	whatever	yet	in the end	not	reach, come to

Although I engage in many activities, none of them ever comes to completion.

ཕུང་བྱེད་རྟོག་པའི་མགོ་ལ་ཆེམ་སེ་ཆེམ།

PHUNG	JE	TOG PAI	GO	LA	CHEM SE CHEM
destroy		make thoughts	head	on	beat, stamp

Stamp on the head of these thoughts that fragment me!

དགྲ་བདག་གཞེད་མའི་སྙིང་ལ་མ་ར་ཡ།

DRA   DA   SHED MAI   NYING   LA   MA RA YA
enemy ego trouble-maker heart in kill

Kill the heart of this killer demon, the ego I believe in!

I have great desire for quick results yet I put little effort into my practice, and although I engage in many activities, none of them ever comes to completion. Stamp on the head of these thoughts that fragment me! Kill the heart of this killer demon, the ego I believe in!

སྐྱིད་འདོད་ཆེ་ལ་དེ་རྒྱུ་ཚོགས་མི་གསོག

KYI   DOE   CHE LA   DE   GYU   TSHOG   MI   SOG
happiness desire   great to   that   cause   virtues   not   gather,
                                                                accumulate

I have great desire for happiness yet I do not gather the virtues which are its cause, and

སྡུག་བསྔལ་ཆུང་ལ་འདོད་རྣག་དྲགས་སེམས་ཆེ།

DU   SAN   CHUNG LA   DOE   NAG   NGAM   SEM   CHE
misery endure   little to   desire   rough   strong desire   mind   great
(e.g. we want to be yogis but we get tired after a hundred prostrations)

Although I am only able to endure a little suffering, yet my mind is full of great ambitions.

ཕུང་བྱེད་རྟོག་པའི་མགོ་ལ་ཆེམ་སེ་ཆེམ།

PHUNG JE TOG PAI GO LA CHEM SE CHEM

Stamp on the head of these thoughts that fragment me!

དགྲ་བདག་གཞེད་མའི་སྙིང་ལ་མ་ར་ཡ།

DRA DA SHED MAI NYING LA MA RA YA

Kill the heart of this killer demon, the ego I believe in!

I have great desire for happiness yet I do not gather the virtues which are its cause, and although I am only able to endure a little suffering my mind is full of great ambitions. Stamp on the head of these thoughts that fragment me! Kill the heart of this killer demon, the ego I believe in!

གསར་འགྲོགས་ཆེ་ལ་ཁྲེལ་གཞུང་ཕྱི་ཐག་ཐུང་།

SAR   DRO   CHE LA   DREL ZHUNG   CHI   THAG   THUNG
new friends   great to   shameless   later duration   short

I make a great fuss of my new friends but then soon desert them shamelessly.

Sharp Weapon Wheel

བློ་དད་ཆེ་ལ་རྐུ་འཕྲོག་འཚོལ་འགྲོ་རེམ།

TO DAD CHE LA KU TROG TSHOL DRO REM
food desire great to steal rob seeking go always

I have great desire for food and so I go out looking for chances to rob and steal.

ཕུང་བྱེད་རྟོག་པའི་མགོ་ལ་ཆེམ་སེ་ཆེམ།

PHUNG JE TOG PAI GO LA CHEM SE CHEM
Stamp on the head of these thoughts that fragment me!

དགྲ་བདག་གཤེད་མའི་སྙིང་ལ་མ་ར་ཡ།

DRA DA SHED MAI NYING LA MA RA YA
Kill the heart of this killer demon, the ego I believe in!

I make a great fuss of my new friends but then soon desert them shamelessly. I have great desire for food and so I go out looking for chances to rob and steal. Stamp on the head of these thoughts that fragment me! Kill the heart of this killer demon, the ego I believe in!

ཁ་གསགས་གཞོགས་སློང་མཁས་ལ་ཞེ་མུག་ཆེ།

KHA SA	ZHO LONG	KHAE LA	ZHE MU CHE
indirect request*	encouraging charity that will benefit you#	skilful, to expert	attitude anxious very (on tenterhooks, tight with desire)

(* Flattering to get favours. As when you tell someone that the money they gave you last year was very beneficial, and that you used it for the Dharma, so it also generated merit for them. Thus you indirectly encourage them to give it to you again.)

(# For example, you tell someone that Mrs Smith has paid for half the new prayer-wheel but there are no funds left now to complete the work and that this is very sad. Talking thus you encourage the person to be generous to you.)

I am an expert at making indirect requests and encouraging aid and in this way my mind is ever vigilant in seeking my own benefit.

བསྡུ་སོག་རེམ་ལ་ཡོད་ཀྱང་སེར་སྣས་བཅིངས།

DU SO REM LA YONG KYANG SER NAE CHING
collection hoard, gather strong, always to come also avarice* bind
(* i.e. we feel we never get enough)

Although I am always collecting and hoarding, I am still bound by avarice.

ཕུང་བྱེད་རྟོག་པའི་མགོ་ལ་ཆེམ་སེ་ཆེམ།

PHUNG JE TOG PAI GO LA CHEM SE CHEM
Stamp on the head of these thoughts that fragment me!

དགྲ་བདག་གཤེད་མའི་སྙིང་ལ་མ་ར་ཡ།

DRA DA SHED MAI NYING LA MA RA YA

Kill the heart of this killer demon, the ego I believe in!

I am an expert at making indirect requests and encouraging aid and in this way my mind is ever vigilant in seeking my own benefit. Although I am always collecting and hoarding, I am still bound by avarice. Stamp on the head of these thoughts that fragment me! Kill the heart of this killer demon, the ego I believe in!

ཀུན་ལ་བྱས་བ་ཆུང་ཞིང་སྒྲག་ཡུས་ཆེ།

KUN	LA	JE WA	CHUNG	ZHING	DUG	YUE	CHE
all	to	do	little	yet	impressive	claims*	great

(* e.g. A politician actually does nothing for those he represents yet at the time of re-election he says he has done a lot for them and so they must vote for him.)

I do very little for others yet I expect a great deal in return.

རང་ལ་ཁྱེར་ཁ་མེད་ལ་རྔམས་པོ་ཆེ།

RANG	LA	KHYER KHA	ME	LA	NGAM PO	CHE
self	to	empower, mobilise	without	to, with	pride, ambition	great

(We never try properly yet still we wish to be great.)

I never do what I have to, yet I am full of great ambition.

ཕུང་བྱེད་རྟོག་པའི་མགོ་ལ་ཆེམ་སེ་ཆེམ།

PHUNG JE TOG PAI GO LA CHEM SE CHEM

Stamp on the head of these thoughts that fragment me!

དགྲ་བདག་གཤེད་མའི་སྙིང་ལ་མ་ར་ཡ།

DRA DA SHED MAI NYING LA MA RA YA

Kill the heart of this killer demon, the ego I believe in!

I do very little for others yet I expect a great deal in return. I never do what I have to yet I am full of great ambition. Stamp on the head of these thoughts that fragment me! Kill the heart of this killer demon, the ego I believe in!

སློབ་དཔོན་མང་ལ་དམ་ཚིག་ཁུར་ཤེས་ཆུང་།

LOB PON	MANG	LA	DAM TSHIG	KHUR	SHE	CHUNG
teacher	many	to, with	vows	burden	amount	little

I have received tantric vows from many Gurus yet I hardly keep them.

སློབ་མ་མང་ལ་ཕན་ཐོགས་སྐྱོང་རན་དན།

LOB MA	MANG	LA	PHAN THO	KYONG RAN	NGAN
disciple	many	to	benefit	keep	bad

I have many disciples but I do not guard their welfare.

ཕུང་བྱེད་རྟོག་པའི་མགོ་ལ་ཆེམ་སེ་ཆེམ།

PHUNG JE TO PAI GO LA CHEM SE CHEM

Stamp on the head of these thoughts that fragment me!

དགྲ་བདག་གཤེད་མའི་སྙིང་ལ་མུ་ར་ཡ།

DRA DA SHED MAI NYING LA MA RA YA

Kill the heart of this killer demon, the ego I believe in!

I have received tantric vows from many Gurus yet I hardly keep them. I have many disciples but I do not guard their welfare. Stamp on the head of those thoughts that fragment me! Kill the heart of this killer demon, the ego I believe in!

ཁས་བླངས་ཆེ་ལ་ཕན་པའི་ཉམས་ལེན་ཆུང་།

KHAE LANG	CHE	LA	PHAN PAI	NYAM LEN	CHUNG
promise	great	to	beneficial	practice	little

I make big promises but do little beneficial practice.

སྙན་པ་ཆེ་ལ་བརྟགས་ན་ལྷ་འདྲེ་ཁྲེལ།

NYAN PA	CHE	LA	TAG	NA	LHA	DRE	TREL
fame, renown	great	to	think	when	gods (petty, minor gods)	demons	shame

(For example, people may take us to be great meditators and we go along with this encouraging their belief even when we know we have no meditation power at all.)

Although I have great renown if my actual conduct were known it would make even the local gods and demons feel ashamed.

ཕུང་བྱེད་རྟོག་པའི་མགོ་ལ་ཆེམ་སེ་ཆེམ།

PHUNG JE TO PAI GO LA CHEM SE CHEM

Stamp on the head of these thoughts that fragment me!

དགྲ་བདག་གཤེད་མའི་སྙིང་ལ་མུ་ར་ཡ།

DRA DA SHED MAI NYING LA MA RA YA

Kill the heart of this killer demon, the ego I believe in!

I make big promises but do little beneficial practice. Although I have great renown if my actual conduct were known it would make even the local gods and demons feel ashamed. Stamp on the head of these thoughts that fragment me! Kill the heart of this killer demon, the ego I believe in!

ཐོས་རྒྱ་ཆུང་ལ་སྟོང་སྐད་བཏ་ཁམ་ཆེ།

THO	GYA	CHUNG	LA	TONG	KAE	BAE KHAM	CHE
hearing, study		not much	to, with	thousand	sound	shouting, loud	great

I have studied only a little yet I am always talking loudly.

ལུང་རྒྱ་ཆུང་ལ་མི་རྟོག་དགུ་ལ་རྟོག

LUNG	GYA	CHUNG	LA	MI	TOG	GU	LA	TOG
quotations, references		little	with	not	know, think	many	to	think, know

I know only a few quotations yet I give voice to them as if I knew many.

ཕུང་བྱེད་རྟོག་པའི་མགོ་ལ་ཆེམ་སེ་ཆེམ།

PHUNG JE TO PAI GO LA CHEM SE CHEM

Stamp on the head of these thoughts that fragment me!

དགྲ་བདག་གཤེད་མའི་སྙིང་ལ་མུ་ར་ཡ།

DRA DA SHED MAI NYING LA MA RA YA

Kill the heart of this killer demon, the ego I believe in!

I have studied only a little yet I am always talking loudly. I know only a few quotations yet I give voice to them as if I knew many. Stamp on the head of these thoughts that fragment me! Kill the heart of this killer demon, the ego I believe in!

འཁོར་གཡོག་མང་ལ་ཁུར་མཁན་སུ་ཡང་མེད།

KHOR	YOG	MANG	LA	KHUR KHAN	SU	YANG	ME
circle	servant	many	by	respectful	who	even	without

Although I am surrounded by many servants, none of them show me any respect.

དཔོན་པོ་མང་ལ་རྒྱབ་རྟེན་མགོན་དང་བྲལ།

PON PO	MANG	LA	GYAB TEN	GON	DANG DRAL
master, officer	many	with	support	protector	separated from
			(they will not use their power to aid us)		

I have friends in high places yet I have no one to protect me and support my interests.

Sharp Weapon Wheel

ཕུང་བྱེད་རྟོག་པའི་མགོ་ལ་ཆེམ་སེ་ཆེམ།
PHUNG JE TO PAI GO LA CHEM SE CHEM
Stamp on the head of these thoughts that fragment me!

དགྲ་བདག་གཤེད་མའི་སྙིང་ལ་མུ་ར་ཡ།
DRA DA SHED MAI NYING LA MA RA YA
Kill the heart of this killer demon, the ego I believe in

Although I am surrounded by many servants, none of them show me any respect. I have many friends in high places yet I have no-one to protect me and support my interests. Stamp on the head of these thoughts that fragment me! Kill the heart of this killer demon, the ego I believe in.

གོ་ས་ཆེ་ལ་ཡོན་ཏན་འདྲེ་བས་ཆུང་།

GO SA	CHE	LA	YON TAN	DRE	BAE	CHUNG
rank, dignity	great	yet	qualities	mara, demon	(comparative)	little

I hold very high positions yet my qualities are less than those of a demon, and

བླ་མ་ཆེ་ལ་ཆགས་སྡང་བདུད་པས་རྟུབ།

LA MA	CHE	LA	CHAG	DANG	DUE	PAE	TSUB
guru*	great	to	desire	anger	mara, demon	(comparative)	rough

(* or bLa Ming, having the name of being a guru)

Although I appear to be a great guru yet my anger and desire is more intense than that of a disturbing mara demon.

ཕུང་བྱེད་རྟོག་པའི་མགོ་ལ་ཆེམ་སེ་ཆེམ།
PHUNG JE TO PAI GO LA CHEM SE CHEM
Stamp on the head of these thoughts that fragment me!

དགྲ་བདག་གཤེད་མའི་སྙིང་ལ་མུ་ར་ཡ།
DRA DA SHED MAI NYING LA MA RA YA
Kill the heart of this killer demon, the ego I believe in!

I hold very high positions yet my qualities are less than those of a demon, and although I appear to be a great guru yet my anger and desire is more intense than that of a disturbing mara demon. Stamp on the head of these thoughts that fragment me! Kill the heart of this killer demon, the ego I believe in!

ལྟ་བ་མཐོ་ལ་སྤྱོད་པ་ཁྱི་ལས་ངན།

TA WA	THO	LA	CHOE PA	KHYI	LAE	NGAN
view	high	yet	practice	dogs	deeds	worse

I claim to have a very high view yet my deeds are worse than a dog's, and

ཡོན་ཏན་གཞི་མ་ཐམས་ཅད་རླུང་ལ་ཤོར།

YON TAN	ZHI MA	THAM CHAE	LUNG	LA	SHOR
good qualities	ground (i.e. your training)	all	wind (of reckless living)	in	lost

I throw the basis for good qualities into the wind of impulsivity.

ཕུང་བྱེད་རྟོག་པའི་མགོ་ལ་ཆེམ་སེ་ཆེམ།
PHUNG JE TO PAI GO LA CHEM SE CHEM
Stamp on the head of these thoughts that fragment me!

དགྲ་བདག་གཤེད་མའི་སྙིང་ལ་མ་ར་ཡ།
DRA DA SHED MAI NYING LA MA RA YA
Kill the heart of this killer demon, the ego I believe in!!

I claim to have a very high view, yet my deeds are worse than a dog's, and I throw the basis for good qualities into the wind of impulsivity. Stamp of the head of these thoughts that fragment me! Kill the heart of this killer demon, the ego I believe in!

ཞེ་འདོད་ཐམས་ཅད་རང་གི་ཕུགས་སུ་བཅུག

ZHE	DOE	THAM CHAE	RANG GI	PHUG	SU	CHUG
attitude	desireful	all	my	hole	in	put (hide away and keep secret)

(e.g. when a fully ordained monk keeps a secret wife, or when one secretly breaks one's fast with hidden stores of food)

I hide away all my desires and satisfy them in secret.

གྱོང་སྐོར་ཐམས་ཅད་དོན་མེད་གཞན་ལ་བྱེད།

GYONG KOR	THAM CHAE	DON	ME	ZHAN	LA	JED
crooked, confusing, unnecessarily round about	all	meaning	without	others	to	do

(e.g. Two hundred monks each received a very small portion of cloth. Then one of them went to each of the others and said, "Your cloth is so little, please just give it to me!" By collecting all the cloth in this way he acquired a few metres of patches.)

With all my bizarre notions I act meaninglessly towards others.

Sharp Weapon Wheel

ཕུང་བྱེད་རྟོག་པའི་མགོ་ལ་ཆེམ་སེ་ཆེམ།
PHUNG JE TO PAI GO LA CHEM SE CHEM
Stamp on the head of these thoughts that fragment me!

དགྲ་བདག་གཤེད་མའི་སྙིང་ལ་མུ་ར་ཡ།
DRA DA SHED MAI NYING LA MA RA YA
Kill the heart of this killer demon, the ego I believe in!

I hide away all my desires (and satisfy them in secret). With all my bizarre notions I act meaninglessly towards others. Stamp on the head of these thoughts that fragment me! Kill the heart of this killer demon, the ego I believe in!

ངུར་སྨྲིག་གྱོན་ནས་བསྲུང་སྐྱོབ་འདྲེ་ལ་ཞུ།

NGUR MIG	GYON	NAE	SUNG	KYOB	DRE	LA ZHU
monk's robes, dharma robes	wear	then	guard*	protection	demons#	to ask

(* e.g. We do not trust the Buddha to help us when we are sick.)
(# non-buddhist village gods etc.)
I wear Dharma robes yet I look to local gods for protection.

སྡོམ་པ་བླངས་ལ་བསླབ་བྱ་བདུད་དང་བསྟེན།

DOM PA	LANG	LA	LAB JA	DUE	DANG	TEN
ordination vows	take	yet	training	mara, demon	and	compare it to, take it to be

I take ordination yet I feel that my Dharma training is persecuting me like a demon.

ཕུང་བྱེད་རྟོག་པའི་མགོ་ལ་ཆེམ་སེ་ཆེམ།
PHUNG JE TO PAI GO LA CHEM SE CHEM
Stamp on the head of these thoughts that fragment me!

དགྲ་བདག་གཤེད་མའི་སྙིང་ལ་མུ་ར་ཡ།
DRA DA SHED MAI NYING LA MA RA YA
Kill the heart of this killer demon, the ego I believe in!

I wear Dharma robes yet I look to local gods for protection. I take ordination yet I feel that my Dharma training is persecuting me like a demon. Stamp on the head of these thoughts that fragment me! Kill the heart of this killer demon, the ego I believe in!

རྟག་ཏུ་དགོན་པར་བསྡད་ནས་གཡེངས་བས་ཁྱེར།

TAG TU	GON PAR	DAE	NAE	YENG WAE	KHYER
always	quiet place, monastery	stay	then	wavering, laziness, not full application	carried away

I stay in isolated monasteries yet I am easily distracted.

དམ་ཆོས་གཙུག་ལག་ཞུ་ནས་མོ་བོན་སྐྱོང་།

DAM CHO	TSUG LAG	ZHU	NAE	MO	BON	KYONG
holy Dharma	monastery, college	leave (bZhag)	then	prediction with a mala	bonpo*	practice

(* Here Bon does not refer to profound Bonpo practice but to the original cult of local spirits.)

I leave the holy Dharma in the temple and practise prediction and folk religion.

ཕུང་བྱེད་རྟོག་པའི་མགོ་ལ་ཆེམ་སེ་ཆེམ།

PHUNG JE TO PAI GO LA CHEM SE CHEM

Stamp on the head of these thoughts that fragment me!

དགྲ་བདག་གཤེད་མའི་སྙིང་ལ་མ་ར་ཡ།

DRA DA SHED MAI NYING LA MA RA YA

Kill the heart of this killer demon, the ego I believe in!

I stay always in isolated monasteries yet I am easily distracted. I leave the holy Dharma in the temple and practise prediction and folk religion. Stamp on the head of these thoughts that fragment me! Kill the killer demon, the ego I believe in!

ཚུལ་ཁྲིམས་ཐར་བ་བོར་ནས་ཁང་ཁྱིམ་འཛིན།

TSHUL TRIM	THAR WA	BOR	NAE	KHANG KHYIM	DZIN
morality, vows	liberation	throw off	then	household	hold, adopt

(This does not just refer to monks breaking their vows but applies to all kinds of Dharma followers who break their vows and abandon practice and so end up like ordinary people.)

I discard the vows and morality necessary for liberation and follow the lifestyle of worldly people.

བདེ་སྐྱིད་ཆུ་ལ་བོར་ནས་སྡུག་ལ་སྙེག།

DE KYI	CHU	LA	BOR	NAE	DU	LA NYE
happiness	water	in	throw	then	suffering	run after

I throw my happiness in the river and then hasten after sorrow.

Sharp Weapon Wheel

ཕུང་བྱེད་རྟོག་པའི་མགོ་ལ་ཆེམ་སེ་ཆེམ།
PHUNG JE TO PAI GO LA CHEM SE CHEM
Stamp on the head of these thoughts that fragment me!

དགྲ་བདག་གཤེད་མའི་སྙིང་ལ་མུ་ར་ཡ།
DRA DA SHED MAI NYING LA MA RA YA
Kill the heart of this killer demon, the ego I believe in!

I discard the vows and morality necessary for liberation and follow the lifestyle of worldly people. I throw my happiness in the river and then hasten after sorrow. Stamp on the head of these thoughts that fragment me! Kill the heart of this killer demon, the ego I believe in!

ཐར་པའི་འཇུག་རྟོགས་བོར་ནས་ཚོང་ཁེ་བསྒྲུབ།

THAR WAI	JUG NGO	BOR	NAE	TSHONG KHE	DRUB
liberation path	entry point, edge	abandon	then	business	practice

(Not making a firm foundation because of not knowing if one really wants to enter on the path.)

I abandon the path to liberation near the beginning and engage in business instead.

བླ་མའི་ཆོས་ར་བོར་ནས་གྲོང་ཡུལ་འགྲིམ།

LA MAI	CHO RA	BOR	NAE	DRONG	YUL	DRIM
guru's	Dharma site*	abandon	then	village	country	wandering

(* place where there is dharma teaching)

I leave the place where Gurus teach Dharma and then roam the countryside from village to village.

ཕུང་བྱེད་རྟོག་པའི་མགོ་ལ་ཆེམ་སེ་ཆེམ།
PHUNG JE TO PAI GO LA CHEM SE CHEM
Stamp on the head of these thoughts that fragment me!

དགྲ་བདག་གཤེད་མའི་སྙིང་ལ་མུ་ར་ཡ།
DRA DA SHED MAI NYING LA MA RA YA
Kill the heart of this killer demon, the ego I believe in!

I abandon the path to liberation near the beginning and engage in business instead. I leave the place where Gurus teach Dharma and then roam the countryside from village to village. Stamp of the head of these thoughts that fragment me! Kill the heart of this killer demon, the ego I believe in!

རང་གི་འཚོ་བ་བཞག་ནས་འདུ་སྡེ་འཕྲོག

RANG GI	TSHO WA	ZHAG	NAE	DU GO	TRO
my	livelihood, finances	keep	then	sangha	take, pilfer

I have enough to live on but I hoard it and take from the Sangha instead, and

རང་གི་ཁ་ཟས་བཞག་ནས་གཞན་ལ་རྐུ།

RANG GI	KHA ZAE	ZHAG	NAE	SHAN	LA	KU
my	food	keep	then	others	from	steal

I hide my own food and then go stealing from others.

ཕུང་བྱེད་རྟོག་པའི་མགོ་ལ་ཆེམ་སེ་ཆེམ།

PHUNG JE TO PAI GO LA CHEM SE CHEM

Stamp on the head of these thoughts that fragment me!

དགྲ་བདག་གཤེད་མའི་སྙིང་ལ་མུ་ར་ཡ།

DRA DA SHED MAI NYING LA MA RA YA

Kill the heart of this killer demon, the ego I believe in!

I have enough to live on but I hoard it and take from the Sangha instead, and I hide my own food and then go stealing from others. Stamp on the head of these thoughts that fragment me! Kill the heart of this killer demon, the ego I believe in!

ཨེ་མ་སྒོམ་བཟོད་ཆུང་ལ་མངོན་ཤེས་རྗོ།

E MA	GOM	SAN	CHUNG	LA	NGON SHE	NO
difficult, strange	meditation	forbearance	little	yet, with that	intuitive (prediction)	sharp, clever

(We cannot sit for even an hour without becoming restless.)

How strange! I have little patience during meditation yet act as if I am prescient.

ལམ་སྣ་མ་ཟིན་དོན་མེད་ཀང་བ་མགྱོགས།

LAM	NA	MA	ZIN	DON	ME	KANG WA	GYO
paths	ways	not	get and keep	meaning	without	feet	swift, quick

(If you do not know the road then it is best to travel slowly and carefully. Similarly, if you do not understand the basic ideas of the Dharma, like who and what the Buddha is, then there is no point to throw yourself into strong practice for then you may have an accident.)

I do not know the right way yet I rush on meaninglessly.

ཕུང་བྱེད་རྟོག་པའི་མགོ་ལ་ཆེམ་སེ་ཆེམ།

PHUNG JE TO PAI GO LA CHEM SE CHEM

Stamp on the head of these thoughts that fragment me!

དགྲ་བདག་གཤེད་མའི་སྙིང་ལ་མུ་ར་ཡ།

DRA DA SHED MAI NYING LA MA RA YA

Kill the heart of this killer demon, the ego I believe in!

How strange! I have little patience during meditation, yet act as if I am prescient. I do not know the right way yet I rush on meaninglessly. Stamp on the head of these thoughts that fragment me! Kill the heart of this killer demon, the ego I believe in!

ཕན་པར་སྨྲས་ན་སྡང་སེམས་དགྲ་རུ་འཛིན།

PHAN PAR MAE NA DANG SEM DRA RU DZIN
benefit say if angry mind enemy as hold
(like saying you are lazy and should try harder)

If others give me helpful advice I become angry and take them to be my enemy,

མགོ་བསྐོར་བསླུ་ན་སྙིང་མེད་དྲིན་དུ་འཛིན།

GO KOR LU NA NYING ME DRIN DU DZIN
head turning cheat if heart without kind as hold
(confusing talk etc.)
(like someone telling us we are great meditators)

Yet if someone should cheat me with confusing deception, I meekly take this to be a kindness.

ཕུང་བྱེད་རྟོག་པའི་མགོ་ལ་ཆེམ་སེ་ཆེམ།

PHUNG JE TO PAI GO LA CHEM SE CHEM

Stamp on the head of these thoughts that fragment me!

དགྲ་བདག་གཤེག་མའི་སྙིང་ལ་མུ་ར་ཡ།

DRA DA SHED MAI NYING LA MA RA YA

Kill the heart of this killer demon, the ego I believe in!

If others give me helpful advice I become angry and take them to be my enemy, yet if someone should cheat me with confusing deception I meekly take this to be a kindness. Stamp on the head of these thoughts that fragment me! Kill the heart of this killer demon, the ego I believe in!

ནང་མིར་བཏེན་ན་སྙིང་གཏམ་དགྲ་ལ་འཆད།

NANG MIR	TEN	NA	NYING TAM	DRA	LA	CHAE
family man, member of the family group	have	if, yet	confidential, secret	enemy	to	explain, disclose

I am part of a family yet without talking to them, I disclose our private matters to enemies.

ཕེབས་པར་འགྲོགས་ན་ཁྲེལ་མེད་བློ་སྙིང་རྐུ།

PHEB WAR	DROG	NA	TREL ME	LO	NYING	KU
old and true	friend	if, when	shameless	mind	heart	steal
			(acting solely for our own interests)			

I have old and trusted friends yet I shamelessly probe their secrets.

ཕུང་བྱེད་རྟོག་པའི་མགོ་ལ་ཆེམ་སེ་ཆེམ།

PHUNG JE TO PAI GO LA CHEM SE CHEM

Stamp on the head of these thoughts that fragment me!

དགྲ་བདག་གཤེད་མའི་སྙིང་ལ་མུ་ར་ཡ།

DRA DA SHED MAI NYING LA MA RA YA

Kill the heart of this killer demon, the ego I believe in!

I am part of a family yet without talking to them, I disclose our private matters to enemies. I have old and trusted friends yet I shamelessly probe their secrets. Stamp on the head of these thoughts that fragment me! Kill the heart of this killer demon, the ego I believe in!

ཀོ་ལོང་དམ་ལ་རྣམ་རྟོག་སུ་བས་རགས།

KO LONG DAM	LA	NAM TOG	SU	BAE	RAG
orthodox, having many rules of not doing this and that	to	thoughts	who	(comparative)	rough

I am very orthodox in my behaviour, yet my thoughts are worse than those of anyone else.

འགྲོགས་པར་དཀའ་ཞིང་གཤིས་ངན་རྒྱུན་དུ་ལོང་།

DRO PAR	KA ZHING	SHI	NGAN	GYUN DU	LONG
friendly	difficult	temper, character	bad (i.e. angry)	always	develop

I find it difficult to be friendly and allow my bad traits to keep growing.

Sharp Weapon Wheel

ཕུང་བྱེད་རྟོག་པའི་མགོ་ལ་ཆེམ་སེ་ཆེམ།
PHUNG JE TO PAI GO LA CHEM SE CHEM
Stamp on the head of these thoughts that fragment me!

དགྲ་བདག་གཤེད་མའི་སྙིང་ལ་མ་ར་ཡ།
DRA DA SHED MAI NYING LA MA RA YA
Kill the heart of this killer demon, the ego I believe in!

I am very orthodox in my behaviour, yet my thoughts are worse than those of anyone else. I find it difficult to be friendly and allow my bad traits to keep growing. Stamp on the head of these thoughts that fragment me! Kill the heart of this killer demon, the ego I believe in!

བཅོལ་བ་མི་ཉན་བཟློག་ནས་གནོད་པ་སྐྱེལ།

CHOL WA	MI	NYAN	DOG	NAE	NOE PA	KYEL
entrusted matters, instructions (from parents and friends)	not	listen	reverse	then	harm, hurt	bring, employ

Not listening to instructions I do the opposite of what is required and so cause harm.

བཏུད་ན་མི་འདུད་རྒྱངས་ནས་རྩོད་པ་འཚོལ།

TUD	NA	MI	DUE	GYANG NAE	TSOE PA	TSHOL
bow*	if	not	salute	far away	dispute	look for

(* i.e. acting in a friendly way)

When people make friendly gestures I do not respond and, keeping my distance, I pick quarrels.

ཕུང་བྱེད་རྟོག་པའི་མགོ་ལ་ཆེམ་སེ་ཆེམ།
PHUNG JE TO PAI GO LA CHEM SE CHEM
Stamp on the head of these thoughts that fragment me!

དགྲ་བདག་གཤེད་མའི་སྙིང་ལ་མ་ར་ཡ།
DRA DA SHED MAI NYING LA MA RA YA
Kill the heart of this killer demon, the ego I believe in!

Not listening to instructions I do the opposite of what is required and so cause harm. When people make friendly gestures I do not respond and, keeping my distance, I pick quarrels. Stamp on the head of these thoughts that fragment me! Kill the heart of this killer demon, the ego I believe in!

བགའ་བློ་མི་བདེ་འགྲོགས་པར་དཀའ་ཏུ་དཀའ།

KA	LO	MI DE	DROG PAR	TAG TU	KA
difficult	mind*	not happy	friends	always	difficult

(* uncontrolled and not following any fixed systems, e.g. someone who likes to sleep all day and talk all night)

I am unstable and discontented and so am difficult to befriend.

ཕོག་གདུག་མང་ལ་རྟག་ཏུ་འཛིན་པ་དམ།

PHOG	DUG	MANG	LA	TAG TU	DZIN PA	DAM
sensitive	vicious*	much	and, with	always#	holding, grasping	bind, hold

(* easily taking offence and becoming hurt and angry)
(# can never just relax and let the situation go by)

I am oversensitive and retaliatory, always caught up in my own judgments.

ཕུང་བྱེད་རྟོག་པའི་མགོ་ལ་ཆེམ་སེ་ཆེམ།

PHUNG JE TO PAI GO LA CHEM SE CHEM

Stamp on the head of these thoughts that fragment me!

དགྲ་བདག་གཤེད་མའི་སྙིང་ལ་མུ་ར་ཡ།

DRA DA SHED MAI NYING LA MA RA YA

Kill the heart of this killer demon, the ego I believe in!

I am unstable and discontented and so am difficult to befriend. I am oversensitive and retaliatory, always caught up in my own judgments. Stamp on the head of these thoughts that fragment me! Kill the heart of this killer demon, the ego I believe in!

མཐོ་གནོན་ཆེ་ཞིང་དམ་པ་དགྲ་རུ་འཛིན།

THO	NON	CHE SHING	DAM PA	DRA	RU	DZIN
a high position	cling to	greatly	holy gurus (who are great)	enemy, rival	as	hold

Thinking that I am very special I act as if Gurus are my enemies.

འདོད་ཆགས་ཆེ་བས་གཞོན་ནུ་དྲག་ཏུ་ལེན།

DOE CHA	CHE	WAE	ZHON NU	DANG DU LEN
carnal desire, lust	great	by	young people	strongly pursue

Due to my strong carnal desire I chase after young people.

ཕུང་བྱེད་རྟོག་པའི་མགོ་ལ་ཆེམ་སེ་ཆེམ།

PHUNG JE TO PAI GO LA CHEM SE CHEM

Stamp on the head of these thoughts that fragment me!

དགྲ་བདག་གཤེད་མའི་སྙིང་ལ་མ་ར་ཡ།
DRA DA SHED MAI NYING LA MA RA YA

Kill the heart of this killer demon, the ego I believe in!

Thinking that I am very special I act as if Gurus are my enemies. Due to my strong carnal desire I chase after young people. Stamp on the head of these thoughts that fragment me! Kill the heart of this killer demon, the ego I believe in!

ཕྱི་ཐག་ཐུང་བས་སྔར་འདྲིས་རྒྱབ་ཏུ་བསྐྱུར།

CHI	THAG	THUNG	WAE	NGAR	DRI	GYAB DU KYUR
outside	link	short	by	former	friend	cast behind

(quickly encourage friendship)

Quickly starting new friendships, I leave my old friends behind.

གསར་འགྲོགས་ཆེ་བས་ཀུན་ལ་ཁ་བྲོད་འདིངས།

SAR	DRO	CHE	WAE	KUN	LA	KHA DRO	DING
new	friend	great	by	all	to	eagerly	expand

Making fine new friends, I make an impressive show of this to everyone.

ཕུང་བྱེད་རྟོག་པའི་མགོ་ལ་ཆེམ་སེ་ཆེམ།
PHUNG JE TO PAI GO LA CHEM SE CHEM

Stamp on the head of these thoughts that fragment me!

དགྲ་བདག་གཤེད་མའི་སྙིང་ལ་མ་ར་ཡ།
DRA DA SHED MAI NYING LA MA RA YA

Kill the heart of this killer demon, the ego I believe in!

Quickly starting new friendships, I leave my old friends behind. Making fine new friends, I make an impressive show of this to everyone. Stamp on the head of these thoughts that fragment me! Kill the heart of this killer demon, the ego I believe in!

མངོན་ཤེས་མེད་པས་རྫུན་བསྐུར་དང་དུ་ལེན།

NGON SHE	ME PAE	DZUN KUR	DANG DU LEN
prescience	not do	lie, pretence	practise strongly
(supernatural perception like foreknowledge)		(trying to cheat others into believing us)	

I have no powers of prescience yet I pretend that I do.

སྙིང་རྗེ་མེད་པས་བློ་གཏད་སྙིང་ལ་བྲབ།

NYING JE   ME PAE   LO   TAD   NYING   LA   DRAB
compassion not have mind stable heart in thrown

Being without compassion my intellect is clouded by emotional impulses.

ཕུང་བྱེད་རྟོག་པའི་མགོ་ལ་ཆེམ་སེ་ཆེམ།

PHUNG JE TO PAI GO LA CHEM SE CHEM

Stamp on the head of these thoughts that fragment me!

དགྲ་བདག་གཞེད་མའི་སྙིང་ལ་མ་ར་ཡ།

DRA DA SHED MAI NYING LA MA RA YA

Kill the heart of this killer demon, the ego I believe in!

I have no powers of prescience yet I pretend that I do. Being without compassion my intellect is clouded by emotional impulses. Stamp on the head of these thoughts that fragment me! Kill the heart of this killer demon, the ego I believe in!

ཐོས་པ་ཆུང་བས་ཀུན་ལ་སྤུར་ཚོད་བྱེད།

THO WA   CHUNG WAE   KUN   LA   PAR TSHO   JE
study   little   all   to   fighting*   do
                                  (* trying to prove we are the best)

I have studied only a little yet I argue about Dharma with everyone.

ལུང་རྒྱ་ཆུང་བས་ཡོངས་ལ་ལོག་ལྟ་སྐྱེ།

LUNG   GYA   CHUNG WAE   YONG   LA   LOG   TA   KYE
instruction extent little all   to   wrong view raise⁺

(⁺ We mix everything up and so confuse both ourselves and others.)

Having heard only a few teachings I have wrong views about Dharma.

ཕུང་བྱེད་རྟོག་པའི་མགོ་ལ་ཆེམ་སེ་ཆེམ།

PHUNG JE TO PAI GO LA CHEM SE CHEM

Stamp on the head of these thoughts that fragment me!

དགྲ་བདག་གཞེད་མའི་སྙིང་ལ་མ་ར་ཡ།

DRA DA SHED MAI NYING LA MA RA YA

Kill the heart of this killer demon, the ego I believe in!

I have studied only a little yet I argue about Dharma with everyone. Having heard only a few teachings I have wrong views about Dharma. Stamp on the head of these thoughts that fragment me! Kill the heart of this killer demon, the ego I believe in!

ཆགས་སྡང་གོམས་པས་གཞན་ཕྱོགས་ཡོངས་ལ་སྨོད།

CHAG	DANG	GOM PAE	ZHAN	CHO	YONG	LA	MOE
desire	anger	nurture	others	side	all	to	slander, blame

I nurture my desire and anger and disparage all those who differ from me.

ཕྲག་དོག་གོམས་པས་གཞན་ལ་སྐྱོ་སྐུར་འདེབས།

TRAG DO	GOM PAE	ZHAN	LA	DRO KUR	DEB
jealousy	nurture	others	to	insult and deprecate	do

Nurturing my jealousy I insult and demean others.

ཕུང་བྱེད་རྟོག་པའི་མགོ་ལ་ཆེམ་སེ་ཆེམ།

PHUNG JE TO PAI GO LA CHEM SE CHEM

Stamp on the head of these thoughts that fragment me!

དགྲ་བདག་གཤེད་མའི་སྙིང་ལ་མ་ར་ཡ།

DRA DA SHED MAI NYING LA MA RA YA

Kill the heart of this killer demon, the ego I believe in!

I nurture my desire and anger and disparage all those who differ from me. Nurturing my jealousy I insult and demean others. Stamp on the head of these thoughts that fragment me! Kill the heart of this killer demon, the ego I believe in!

སློབ་གཉེར་མ་བྱས་རྒྱ་ཆེན་ཁྱད་དུ་གསོད།

LOB NYER	MA	JAE	GYA CHEN	KHYAE	DU	SOE
student	not	do	very great, deep doctrine	difference	as	destroy (pay no attention to their special qualities)

I have not studied yet I say that the great doctrines have no value.

བླ་མ་མ་བསྟེན་ལུང་ལ་སྨོད་པར་བྱེད།

LA MA	MA	TEN	LUNG	LA	MOE PAR	JE
guru	not	attend to*	instruction, teaching	to	disparage, insult	do

(* serve and receive teachings from)

I do not serve the teacher and I insult her instructions.

ཕུང་བྱེད་རྟོག་པའི་མགོ་ལ་ཆེམ་སེ་ཆེམ།

PHUNG JE TO PAI GO LA CHEM SE CHEM

Stamp on the head of these thoughts that fragment me!

དག་བདག་གཤེད་མའི་སྙིང་ལ་མ་ར་ཡ།

DRA DA SHED MAI NYING LA MA RA YA

Kill the heart of this killer demon, the ego I believe in!

I have not studied yet I say that the great doctrines have no value. I do not serve the teacher and I insult her instructions. Stamp on the head of these thoughts that fragment me. Kill the heart of this killer demon, the ego I believe in!

སྡེ་སྣོད་མི་འཆད་རང་བཟོ་བརྫུན་དུ་སྒྲིག།

DE NOE	MI	CHA	RANG	ZO	DZUN	DU DRIG
tripitaka*	not	explain	self	work	lies	arrange, compile

(* The Buddha's speech, the orthodox Dharma including the Tantras)

I do not teach according to the Buddha's word but instead I present my own creations and lies.

དག་སྣང་མ་འབྱོངས་ལབ་ཚད་འབར་ཤ་མང་།

DAG	NANG	MA	JONG	LAB	TSHAE	BAR SHA	MANG
pure	vision	not	ripen	speech	amount	rough, angry bad things	many

Lacking pure vision, my speech is rough and angry.

ཕུང་བྱེད་རྟོག་པའི་མགོ་ལ་ཆེམ་སེ་ཆེམ།

PHUNG JE TO PAI GO LA CHEM SE CHEM

Stamp on the head of these thoughts that fragment me!

དག་བདག་གཤེད་མའི་སྙིང་ལ་མ་ར་ཡ།

DRA DA SHED MAI NYING LA MA RA YA

Kill the heart of this killer demon, the ego I believe in!

I do not teach according to the Buddha's word but instead I present my own creations and lies. Lacking pure vision, my speech is rough and angry. Stamp on the head of these thoughts that fragment me! Kill the heart of this killer demon, the ego I believe in!

ཆོས་མིན་ལས་ལ་སྨོད་པར་མི་བྱེད་པར།

CHO	MIN	LAE	LA	MOE PAR	MI	JE PAR
Dharma	without	actions	to	slander	not	do

I do not condemn bad worldly actions,

Sharp Weapon Wheel

ལེགས་བཤད་ཡོངས་ལ་སུན་འབྱིན་སྣ་ཚོགས་གཏོང་།

LEG	SHAE	YONG	LA	SUN JIN	NA TSHOG	TONG
good	explain	all	to	insult, dishonour	various, all sorts	give

Yet I insult those who have explained the Dharma well.

ཕུང་བྱེད་རྟོག་པའི་མགོ་ལ་ཆེམ་སེ་ཆེམ།

PHUNG JE TO PAI GO LA CHEM SE CHEM
Stamp on the head of these thoughts that fragment me!

དགྲ་བདག་གཤེད་མའི་སྙིང་ལ་སྨྱུ་ར་ཡ།

DRA DA SHED MAI NYING LA MA RA YA
Kill the heart of this killer demon, the ego I believe in!

I do not condemn bad worldly actions, yet I insult those who have explained the Dharma well. Stamp on the head of these thoughts that fragment me! Kill the heart of this killer demon, the ego I believe in!

ངོ་ཚའི་གནས་ལ་ངོ་ཚར་མི་འཛིན་པར།

NGO TSHAI	NAE	LA	NGO TSHAR	MI	DZIN PAR
shame	places	to	shame	not	hold

(e.g. becoming rich by theft and corruption)
Feeling no shame towards what is shameful, and

ངོ་མི་ཚ་ལ་ངོ་ཚ་ཆོས་ལོག་འཛིན།

NGO MI TSHA	LA	NGO TSHA	CHO	LOG	DZIN
not shameful	to	shame	Dharma	wrong	hold

(e.g. at being poor due to practising the Dharma intensively)   (turn the Dharma upside down)
Feeling ashamed of what is not shameful, I pervert the actual view of Dharma.

ཕུང་བྱེད་རྟོག་པའི་མགོ་ལ་ཆེམ་སེ་ཆེམ།

PHUNG JE TO PAI GO LA CHEM SE CHEM
Stamp on the head of these thoughts that fragment me!

དགྲ་བདག་གཤེད་མའི་སྙིང་ལ་སྨྱུ་ར་ཡ།

DRA DA SHED MAI NYING LA MA RA YA
Kill the heart of this killer demon, the ego I believe in!

Feeling no shame towards what is shameful, and feeling ashamed of what is not shameful, I pervert the actual view of Dharma. Stamp on the head of these thoughts that fragment me! Kill the heart of this killer demon, the ego I believe in!

ཆུས་ན་རུང་བ་གཅིག་ཀྱང་མི་བྱེད་པར།

JAE NA RUNG WA CHI KYANG MI JE PAR
do if proper, one also not do
     suitable (i.e. allowed by the Buddha)

Not doing even one approved activity,

མི་རིགས་བྱ་བ་ཐམས་ཅད་བྱེད་པ་ཡི།

MI RIG JA WA THAM CHAE JE PA YI
not proper deeds all do due to

I do all that is improper.

ཕུང་བྱེད་རྟོག་པའི་མགོ་ལ་ཆེམ་སེ་ཆེམ།

PHUNG JE TO PAI GO LA CHEM SE CHEM

Stamp on the head of these thoughts that fragment me!

དགྲ་བདག་གཤེད་མའི་སྙིང་ལ་སྨྲ་ར་ཡ།

DRA DA SHED MAI NYING LA MA RA YA

Kill the heart of this killer demon, the ego I believe in!

Not doing even one approved activity, I do all that is improper. Stamp on the head of these thoughts that fragment me! Kill the heart of this killer demon, the ego I believe in!

ཨེ་མ་བདག་ལྟའི་འགོང་པོ་འཇོམས་པ་ཡི།

E MA DAG TAI GONG PO JOM PA YI
oh! I, ego view demon, subdue, of
sorrow (grasping) trouble maker destroy

(This is the feeling we have on seeing all the harm that has arisen from self-cherishing.)

Oh, this sorrow! You are the one who subdues the troublesome demon of belief in a real inherent identity.

བདེ་གཤེགས་ཆོས་ཀྱི་སྐུ་མངའ་མཐུ་སྟོབས་ཅན།

DE SHEG CHO KYI KU NGA THU TOB CHAN
Sugata Dharmakaya, energy effective powerful having
Buddha infinite mind   force mind
                         (epithet of Yamantaka)

You are the intrinsic mode of the Buddha's mind, full of strength, force and power!

Sharp Weapon Wheel

བདག་མེད་ཡེ་ཤེས་མཚོན་ཆ་དབྱུག་ཐོ་ཅན།

DAG	ME	YE SHE	TSHON CHA	YUG THO	CHAN
ego, inherent existence	not	original knowing, wisdom	weapon	stick with a skull at the end	having

You wield the skull-headed club, the weapon of original knowing free of belief in autonomous entities!

ཐེ་ཚོམ་མེད་པར་ལན་གསུམ་ཀླད་ལ་བསྐོར།

THE TSHOM	ME PAR	LEN	SUM	LA LA	KOR
doubt, concern	without	times	three	head, around brain	revolve

(Although killing is a sin, killing the ego is not a sin since it has never existed but is merely a reflection of unawareness of the true status of phenomena.)

Swing it thrice around your head without any hesitation!

ངམས་སྟབས་ཆེན་པོས་དགྲ་འདི་བསྒྲལ་དུ་གསོལ།

NGAM	TAB	CHEN PO	DRA	DI	DRAL	DU SOL
impressive, frightening	style	great	enemy	this (illusory ego)	kill	please

(We make this request to inspire and encourage our own wisdom to shine forth.)

With your fearful presence, please kill this enemy!

Oh, this sorrow! You are the one who subdues the troublesome demon of belief in a real inherent identity. You are the intrinsic mode of the Buddha's mind, full of strength, force and power! You wield the skull-headed club, the weapon of original knowing free of belief in autonomous entities! Swing it thrice around your head without any hesitation! With your fearful presence, please kill this enemy!

སྙིང་རྗེ་ཆེན་པོས་ལས་ལ་བསྐྱབ་དུ་གསོལ།

NYING JE	CHEN	POE	LAE	LA	KYAB	DU SOL
compassion	great	by	actions*	to	protect	please

(* i.e. bad karma and its consequential suffering and also our good, yet restrictive, karma)

With your great compassion please protect me from my own karma!

ངེས་པར་བདག་འདི་བརླག་པར་མཛོད་དུ་གསོལ།

NGE PAR	DAG	DI	LAG PAR	DZAE	DU SOL
certainly, surely	ego (grasping)	this	destroy	do	please

You must destroy this ego entity that seems so real!

འཁོར་བའི་ས་ལ་སྡུག་བསྔལ་བ་ཀུན།

KHOR WAI   SA   LA   DU KHA   CHI WA   KUN
samsara   place in   suffering   are   all

Please pile all the sorrows of samsara on top of

བདག་འཛིན་འདི་ལ་ངེས་པར་སྤུང་དུ་གསོལ།

DAG   DZIN   DI   LA   NGE WAR   PUNG   DU SOL
ego   grasping   this   to   really   put on top   please

(Up until now our grasping has brought us endless troubles by leading us into countless lives in samsara. Belief in, and grasping at, self as an autonomous entity automatically gives rise to belief and grasping at other, at all beings and at all phenomena, as autonomous entities. All the troubles of reification arise from belief in oneself as a separate entity. Now that we recognise this belief as our troublesome enemy we must heap all the troubles it has caused right back on its own head.)

My grasping at the idea of being an independent self.

གང་ལ་ཉོན་མོངས་དུག་ལྔ་ཅི་མཆིས་བ།

GANG   LA   NYON MONG DUG   NGA   CHI   CHI WA
whatever,   to   afflictions*   poison   five   whatsoever exist, there is
to whom   (* desire, anger, stupidity, jealousy and pride)

Whatever aspects of the five afflicting poisons are present anywhere,

རིགས་མཐུན་འདི་ལ་ངེས་པར་སྤུང་དུ་གསོལ།

RIG   THUN   DI   LA   NGE WAR   PUNG   DU SOL
group   same   this   to   really   put on,   please
(i.e. they have the same source,   smother
the delusion of reification and duality)

Please pile them on top of this family they are part of.

With your great compassion please protect me from my own karma! You must destroy this ego entity that seems so real! Please pile all the sorrows of samsara on top of my grasping at the idea of being an independent self. Whatever aspects of the five afflicting poisons are present anywhere, please pile them on top of this family they are part of.

འདི་ལྟར་ཉེས་བའི་རྩ་བ་མ་ལུས་པ།

DI TAR   NYE WAI   TSA WA   MA LU PA
like this   trouble, fault   roots   without exception
                (all the causes flow from just this selfish grasping)

In this way the root of all error

ཤེ་ཚོམ་མེད་པར་རིག་པས་ངོས་ཟིན་ཡང་།

THE TSHOM	ME PAR	RIG PAE	NGO ZIN	YANG
doubt	without	vidya, awareness/by	see what it is	yet, but

Is clearly revealed by my unfailing awareness.

ད་དུང་འདི་ཡི་འཇོན་གཤགས་འདེབས་ན།

DA DUNG	DI	YI	KHA DZIN	SHAG DEB	NA
From this time on	this	of	assistant	support	if, when

If however, in future I turn back towards self-cherishing,

འཛིན་མཁན་འདི་ཡང་བརླག་པར་མཛད་དུ་གསོལ།

DZIN	KHAN	DI	YANG	LAG PAR	DZAE	DU SOL
grasper*	agent	this	also	destroy	do	please

(* the one who ties my mind and life in knots)

Please destroy both grasping and grasper.

In this way the root of all error is clearly revealed by my unfailing awareness. If however, in future I turn back towards self-cherishing, please destroy both grasping and grasper.

ད་ནི་ལེ་ལེན་ཐམས་ཅད་གཅིག་ལ་གདའ།

DA NI	LE LEN	THAM CHAE	CHIG	LA	DA
now	causes, reasons	all	one	to	is (selfish grasping)

Now that I see that all troubles arise from the single source of my ego-cherishing,

སྐྱེ་འགྲོ་གཞན་ལ་བཀའ་དྲིན་ཆེ་བར་སྒོམ།

KYE DRO	ZHAN	LA	KA DRIN	CHE WAR	GOM
beings	all	of	kindness	great	meditate, practise

(They have all been our mothers in our past lives and have done many acts of kindness for us.)

I will contemplate the many kindnesses I have received from all sentient beings.

གཞན་གྱི་མི་འདོད་བདག་གི་རྒྱུད་ལ་ལེན།

ZHAN	GYI	MI	DOD	DA	GI	GYUE	LA	LEN
all	of	not	like	I	of	mind	to	take

All that others dislike I will take upon myself.

བདག་གི་དགེ་བ་འགྲོ་བ་ཡོངས་ལ་བསྔོ།

DA GI	GE WA	DRO WA	YONG	LA	NGO
my	virtues	beings	all	to	give, dedicate

All my virtues I dedicate to all beings.

Now that I see that all troubles arise from the single source of my ego-cherishing, I will contemplate the many kindnesses I have received from all sentient beings. All that others dislike I will take upon myself. All my virtues I dedicate to all beings.

DE	TAR	DRO WA	ZHAN	GYI	GO	SUM	GYI
like	that	beings	other	of	doors	three*	by
						(* body, speech and mind)	

All that sentient beings with their body, speech and mind

DU	SUM	GYI WA	DAG GI	LANG WA	YI
three	times	done (sins)	my	receive, take	by
(past, present, future)					

Have done in the three times I take upon myself.

MA JA	DU	GI	DANG	DANG DAN PA	TAR
peacock	poison	by	shining	having	similar

Just as the peacock becomes more radiant from taking poison,

NYON MONG	JANG CHUB	DROG	SU	GYUR WAR	SHO
afflictions	enlightenment	friend, helper	as	become, arise	it must

May I be able to use their afflictions as an aid to enlightenment!

All that sentient beings with their body, speech and mind have done in the three times I take upon myself. Just as the peacock becomes more radiant from taking poison, may I be able to use their afflictions as an aid to enlightenment!

DAG GI	GE	TSA	DRO	LA	JIN PA	YI
my	virtue	root	beings	to	give	by
(Virtues are the root of all happiness.)						

By giving all beings our virtue, the root of happiness,

JA ROG	DU	ZOE	MAN	GYI	SO	TAR	SHO
crow	poison	eat	medicine	by	cured	like	must

May they be cured of their afflictions just as a crow that has eaten poison is cured by medicine.

Sharp Weapon Wheel

སྐྱེ་བོ་ཡོངས་ཀྱི་ཐར་བའི་སྲོག་བཟུང་ནས།

KYE WO	YONG	GYI	THAR WAI	SOG	ZUNG	NAE
beings	all	of	freedom, liberation	life, vital force	hold, take	then

May we support the life-force of liberation of all beings, and thus

བདེ་བར་གཤེགས་པ་སངས་རྒྱས་ཐོབ་པར་ཤོག།

DE WAR SHEG PA	SANG GYE	THOB PAR	SHO
Sugata, Buddha (happily gone from limitation)	Buddhahood	get	must

May they all become Buddhas, the happily gone!

By giving all beings our virtue, the root of happiness, may they be cured of their afflictions just as a crow that has eaten poison is cured by medicine. May we support the life-force of liberation of all beings, and thus may they all become Buddhas, the happily gone!

ནམ་ཞིག་བདག་དང་ཕ་མར་གྱུར་པ་རྣམས།

NAM ZHIG	DAG	DANG	PHA	MAR	GYUR PA	NAM
when	I	and	father	mother	have been (in the three times)	plural

(All sentient beings have each been our own parents during the immeasurable sequence of our sojourn in samsara.)

Until I and all beings, each formerly my parent,

འོག་མིན་གནས་སུ་བྱང་ཆུབ་མ་ཐོབ་པར།

OG MIN	NAE	SU	JANG CHUB	MA	THOB	PAR
Akanishta (the highest buddha realm)	place	in	enlightenment	not	get	until

Have not attained enlightenment in Akanishta, the highest Buddha Realm,

འགྲོ་བ་དྲུག་ཏུ་ལས་ཀྱིས་འཁྱམས་པ་རྣམས།

DRO WA	DRUG	TU	LAE	KYI	KHYAM PA	NAM
beings, those in samsara	six	in	deeds, karma	by	wander	(plural)

As we wander through the six realms of samsara due to our karma,

ཕན་ཚུན་གཅིག་སེམས་གཅིག་གིས་འཛིན་པར་ཤོག།

PHAN TSHUN	CHIG	SEM	CHIG	GI	DZIN PAR	SHO
each other	one	mind	wholly (full attention)	by	hold, keep on the good way	must

May we be of one mind in helping and encouraging each other!

Until I and all beings, each formerly my parent, have not attained enlightenment in Akanishta, the highest Buddha Realm, as we wander through the six realms of samsara due to our karma, may we be of one mind in helping and encouraging each other!

དེ་ཚེ་འགྲོ་བ་གཅིག་གི་དོན་དུ་ཡང་།

DE TSHE   DRO WA   CHIG   GI   DON DU   YANG
that time   being   one   of   benefit   also

(From this point on the text is written with the view of one who has already gained understanding of emptiness.)

During this time, for the benefit of even one being,

ངན་སོང་གསུམ་དུ་བདག་གིས་ཡོངས་ཞུགས་ནས།

NGAN SONG SUM   DU   DAG GI   YONG   ZHUG   NAE
three lower realms*   in   I by   fully, really   enter   then
(* animal, hungry ghost, hells)

May I willingly enter the three lower realms, and then,

སེམས་དཔའ་ཆེན་པོའི་སྤྱོད་པ་མ་ཉམས་པར།

SEM PA   CHEN POI   CHOE PA   MA   NYAM PAR
mind   great   practice,   not   defiled, deteriorated
(bodhisattva's)   conduct

(Only by the power of understanding emptiness can we be certain to always maintain bodhicitta. As long as situations are perceived as being real and substantial we will be trapped in subject/object conceptualisation and so start protecting ourselves at the expense of others.)

Maintaining my faultless bodhisattva practice,

ངན་སོང་སྡུག་བསྔལ་བདག་གིས་འདྲོངས་བར་ཤོག

NGAN SONG   DU NGAL   DAG GI   DRONG WAR   SHO
lower realms   suffering   I by   pull, guide   must!

May I be a guide to all who suffer there.

During this time, for the benefit of even one being, may I willingly enter the three lower realms, and then, maintaining my faultless bodhisattva practice, may I be a guide to all who suffer there.

དེ་མ་ཐག་ཏུ་དམྱལ་བའི་སྲུང་མ་རྣམས།

DE MA THAG TU   NYAL WAI   SUNG MA   NAM
immediately   hell's   guards   (plural)

Immediately on arriving in the hells may the guards

Sharp Weapon Wheel

བདག་ལ་བླ་མའི་འདུ་ཤེས་སྐྱེས་གྱུར་ཏེ།

DAG	LA	LA MAI	DU SHE	KYE	GYUR	TE
I	as	guru's	association	born, arise	become	thus

(i.e. we will have enough spiritual power to turn their minds from the wrong way)
Come to regard me as their guru, so that

མཚོན་ཆ་རྣམས་ཀྱང་མེ་ཏོག་ཆར་དུ་གྱུར།

TSHON CHA NAM	KYANG	ME TOG	CHAR	DU	GYUR
sharp weapons	also, even	flower	rain	as	become

Even their sharp weapons will turn into a rainfall of flowers.

གནོད་པ་མེད་པར་ཞི་བདེས་བསིལ་བར་ཤོག།

NO PA	ME PAR	ZHI	DE	SIL WAR	SHO
evil, harm	without	peaceful, calm	happy	cool, refreshing	must be!

Freed of harmful intent, may they be cooled, peaceful and happy.

Immediately on arriving in the hells may the guards come to regard me as their guru, so that even their sharp weapons will turn into a rainfall of flowers. Freed of harmful intent, may they be cooled, peaceful and happy.

ངན་སོང་བ་ཡང་མངོན་ཤེས་གཟུངས་ཐོབ་ནས།

NGAN SONG WA	YANG	NGON SHE	ZUNG	THOB	NAE
lower realms	also	prescience	memory	get	then

May the beings in the lower realms gain clairvoyance and good memories, and then,

ལྷ་མིའི་ལུས་བླངས་བྱང་ཆུབ་སེམས་བསྐྱེད་དེ།

LHA	MI	LU	LANG	JANG CHUB SEM	KYE	DE
gods	human	body	get, take	enlightened attitude in mind, bodhicitta	develop	this

Taking birth as gods or humans, may they develop the spirit of enlightenment.

བདག་གིས་དྲིན་ལན་ཆོས་ཀྱིས་གསོར་གྱུར་ཅིག།

DAG GI	DRIN	LAN	CHO	KYI	SO	GYUR CHI
my	kindness* (* when they were my parents)	repay	Dharma	by	foster	must be!

May I repay their kindness by nourishing them with the Dharma.

བདག་ལ་བླ་མར་གཟུང་ནས་བསྟེན་པར་ཤོག

DAG LA   LA MAR   ZUNG   NAE TEN PAR   SHO
I   as   guru   hold   then serve, respect must!
(The service that a disciple does for their Guru is actually for the benefit of the disciple, since the disciple needs blessing and teaching, while the Guru, being free of worldly desire, is pleased by the faith and aspiration of the disciple rather than by any material gifts.)

Taking me as their Guru, may they serve me with respect.

Then may the beings in the lower realms gain clairvoyance and good memories, and then, taking birth as gods or humans, may they develop the spirit of enlightenment. May I repay their kindness by nourishing them with the Dharma. Taking me as their Guru, may they serve me with respect.

དེ་ཚེ་མཐོ་རིས་འགྲོ་བ་ཐམས་ཅད་ཀྱང་།

DE TSHE   THO RI   DRO WA   THAM CHAE   KYANG
that time heaven beings   all   also*
(* the upper realms of humans, jealous gods and gods)

At that time all beings in the upper realms

བདག་དང་མཚུངས་པར་བདག་མེད་རབ་བསྒོམ་ནས།

DAG DANG   TSHUNG WAR   DAG   ME   RAB   GOM   NAE
I and   equal   ego   not fully meditate then*
(* do the same deep practice as me)

Will be like me in meditating deeply on the absence of inherent existence.

སྲིད་དང་ཞི་བདེ་རྣམ་པར་མི་རྟོག་པར།

SI   DANG   ZHI   DE   NAM PAR   MI   TOG PAR
samsara   and   peace happy   fully   not   thinking
              (nirvana of the arhats) (not making these their object)

Then, without thinking of either samsara or nirvana,

མཉམ་པ་ཉིད་དུ་ཏིང་འཛིན་སྒོམ་པར་ཤོག

NYAM PA NYI   DU   TING DZIN   GOM PAR   SHO
equalness, evenness in samadhi, absorbed meditate   must!
(emptiness)   contemplation

May they meditate in the absorbed contemplation of perfect equality!

Sharp Weapon Wheel

མཉམ་པ་ཉིད་དུ་རང་ངོ་འཕྲོད་པར་ཤོག།

NYAM PA NYI   DU   RANG   NGO   TROD PAR SHO
equalness   in   self   own   face, truth   recognise   must
(In the non-arousal of evenness there is the clarity that our mind itself is inseparable from emptiness. This is our original face.)

Within this perfect equality may they see their original face!

At that time all beings in the upper realms will be like me in deeply meditating on the absence of inherent existence. Then without thinking of either samsara or nirvana, may they meditate in the absorbed contemplation of perfect equality! Within this perfect equality may they see their original face!

དེ་ལྟར་བྱས་ན་དགྲ་འདི་ཆོམས་པར་འགྱུར།

DE TAR   JAE   NA   DRA   DI   CHOM PAR   GYUR
like that   do   if   enemy   this   finished,   become
                    (i.e. grasping)   defeated

If we act in this way the enemy, our grasping, will be rendered powerless.

དེ་ལྟར་བྱས་ན་རྣམ་རྟོག་ཆོམས་པར་འགྱུར།

DE TAR   JAE   NA   NAM TOG   CHOM PAR   GYUR
like that   do   if   errant, discursive   finished,   become
                    thoughts*   defeated
(* the thoughts that chase each other creating endless self-deception)

If we act in this way all discursive thoughts will be rendered powerless.

མི་རྟོག་ཡེ་ཤེས་བདག་མེད་བསྒོམས་གྱུར་ནས།

MI TOG   YE SHE   DAG ME   GOM   GYUR   NAE
not think*   original   self without   contemplate   become   then
             knowing   (egolessness)   (rest in dharmakaya)
(* no disturbance from creating misleading ideas)

Resting in the contemplation of the absence of inherent existence there is the original knowing free of discursive thought, and with this

གཟུགས་སྐུའི་རྒྱུ་འབྲས་ཅི་སྟེ་ཐོབ་མི་འགྱུར།

ZUG KUI   GYU   DRAE   CHI TE   THOB   MI   GYUR
form body   cause   effect   if, but   get   not   become
(rupakaya, i.e. both sambhogakaya and nirmanakaya)
(By maintaining non-grasping and penetrating to the empty ground of all, the dharmakaya mind of the buddha is revealed. From this the rupakaya flows out naturally as the sambhogakaya speech of the buddha and the nirmanakaya body of the buddha.)

The cause of the manifest bodies of the Buddha will surely ripen.

If we act in this way the enemy, our grasping, will be defeated. If we act in this way all discursive thoughts will be defeated. Resting in the contemplation of the absence of inherent existence there is the original knowing free of discursive thought, and with this the cause of the manifest bodies of the Buddha will surely ripen.

ཀ་ཡེ་དེ་དག་ཐམས་ཅད་རྟེན་འབྲེལ་ཡིན།

KA YE	DE DA	THAM CHAE	TEN DREL	YIN
(vocative)	these	all	connected,	are
		(everything mentioned above)	interrelated	
			(interdependent, not self-existing)	

Well now! All that has been described is interrelated.

རྟེན་འབྲེལ་སྟོབས་པ་རང་ཆགས་མེད་པ་ཡིན།

TEN DREL	TOE PA	RANG	TSHUG	ME PA	YIN
connection,	going	self	shaping,	without	is
interrelated	together		defining		
(	like pillar and beam	)			

(In all this flow of interconnected events, ego and its objects cannot be found to be existing anywhere in truth. They cannot function by themselves)

In the connectivity of interdependence no appearance has its own inherent shape, identity or essence.

ཕར་བསྒྱུར་ཚུར་བསྒྱུར་རྫུན་སྣང་སྒྱུ་མ་ཡིན།

PHAR	GYUR	TSHUR	GYUR	DZUN	NANG	GYU MA	YIN
there	change	here	change	lie	appearance*	illusion	is

(* not of something but of emptiness)
(All the appearances of samsara and nirvana are endlessly changing and can never actually be found to be existing as substantial entities. Actually it is the content of our mind that is changing, saying, "It is good", "It is bad", "It is mine", "It is yours" – and thus we deceive ourselves endlessly with this unceasing flow of deceptive notions.)

Changing here, changing there, all appearances are deceptive, being mere illusions.

མགལ་མེ་བཞིན་དུ་སྣང་བའི་གཟུགས་བརྙན་ཡིན།

GAL ME	ZHIN DU	NANG WAI	ZUG NYAN	YIN
fire-trail*	as, like	appearances	reflected image,	is
(* seeming circle made by swirling a burning stick)			without substance or essence	

Just as a swirling firebrand creates the semblance of a circle of fire, so all appearances are mere reflections.

Well now! All that has been described is interrelated. In the connectivity of interdependence no appearance has its own inherent shape, identity or essence. Changing here, changing there, all appearances are deceptive, being mere illusions. Just as a swirling firebrand creates the semblance of a circle of fire, so all appearances are mere reflections.

Sharp Weapon Wheel

ཆུ་ཤིང་བཞིན་དུ་སྲོག་ལ་སྙིང་པོ་མེད།

CHU SHING	ZHIN DU	SOG	LA	NYING PO	ME
banana tree	as, like	life-force*	to	essence#	not

(* the force that keeps our life together) (# i.e. not permanent, easily destroyed)

Like the banana tree our life force has no sustaining essence.

ལྦུ་བ་བཞིན་དུ་ཚེ་ལ་སྙིང་པོ་མེད།

BU WA	ZHIN DU	TSHE	LA	NYING PO	ME
bubble	as, like	lifespan	to	essence	not

Like bubbles our lifespan has no sustaining essence.

ཁུག་སྣ་བཞིན་དུ་བཏུད་ན་འཇིག་པ་ཡིན།

KHUG NA	ZHIN DU	TUE	NA	JIG PA	YIN
flower	as, like	subdued, crushed	if	destroyed	be

Like flowers, if crushed we are destroyed.

སྨིག་རྒྱུ་བཞིན་དུ་བརྒྱུད་ནས་མཛེས་པ་ཡིན།

MI GYU	ZHIN DU	GYU NAE	DZE PA	YIN
mirage	as, like	lives as	beauty	is

(Our lives are endlessly fascinating yet their beauty is essentially empty and unsatisfying like that of a mirage.)

Our lives have the beauty of a mirage.

Like the banana tree our life force has no sustaining essence. Like bubbles our lifespan has no sustaining essence. Like flowers, if crushed we are destroyed. Our lives have the beauty of a mirage.

མེ་ལོང་གཟུགས་བརྙན་བཀྲ་ལྟ་བུར་བདེན་བདེན་འདྲ།

ME LONG	ZUG NYAN	TA BUR	DEN DEN	DRA
mirror	reflection	like	true true	as, like

All appearances have as much truth to them as reflections in a mirror.

སྤྲིན་དང་ན་བུན་བཞིན་དུ་སྡོད་སྡོད་འདྲ།

TRIN	DANG	NA BUN	ZHIN DU	DOD DOD	DRA
cloud	and	fog, mist	as, like	stay stay	similar

They abide only in the manner of clouds and mist.

དགྲ་བདག་གཤེན་མ་འདི་ཡང་དེ་བཞིན་དུ།

DRA	DAG	SHE MA	DI	YANG	DE ZHIN DU
enemy	ego grasping	butcher, dangerous form	this	also	like this

Our enemy, the murderous belief in inherent existence, is also not other than this.

ཡོད་ཡོད་འདྲ་སྟེ་ནམ་ཡང་ཡོད་མ་མྱོང་།

YOE YOE DRA TE NAM YANG YOE MA NYONG
have, have, like this never exist not had, experience
exist exist

Although it seems to really exist, in fact it has never been experienced as really existing.

All appearances have as much truth to them as reflections in a mirror. They abide only in the manner of clouds and mist. Our enemy, the murderous belief in inherent existence, is also not other than this. Although it seems to really exist, in fact it has never been experienced as really existing.

བདེན་བདེན་འདྲ་སྟེ་གང་དུ་འང་བདེན་མ་མྱོང་།

DEN DEN DRA TE GANG DU ANG DEN MA NYONG
real real like this wherever, whatever real not experience

(Appearances, emotions, etc. all seem to us to really exist, yet if we examine them dispassionately, free of the grasping notion that we need and rely on them, they will be found to be quite empty, insubstantial and powerless.)

All that seems to be really existing and reliable has never had the least reality that could be experienced.

སྣང་སྣང་འདྲ་སྟེ་བློ་སྐུར་ཡུལ་ལས་འདས།

NANG NANG DRA TE DRO KUR YUL LAE DAE
appearance* appearance like this mere opinion# object from gone

(* They appear: relative truth. They are not real: absolute truth.)
(# Saying it is this or that but not knowing exactly, or not knowing at all yet giving some strong opinion.)

Although appearances seem to be the appearance of something, in fact they are intrinsically free of being substantial objects supporting definite knowledge.

དེ་ལས་ལས་ཀྱི་འཁོར་ལོ་གང་ཞིག་ཡོད།

DE LA LAE KYI KHOR LO GANG ZHIG YOE
this* to deeds, of wheel, cycle# which, whatever have
 karma

(* the deceptive appearances of samsara)
(# i.e. The flow of karmic events is ever-changing and empty like a reflection in a mirror. But the ego believes in the reality of these appearances.)

Since this is the case, whatever manifests from the wheel of karma

འདི་ན་དེ་ལྟར་རང་བཞིན་མེད་ན་ཡང་།

DI NA DE TAR RANG ZHIN ME NA YANG
still like that quality without anyway

Is similarly without any inherent self-definition.

Sharp Weapon Wheel

ཆུར་ན་ཟླ་བའི་དཀྱིལ་འཁོར་ཤར་བ་ལྟར།

CHU	NANG	DA WAI	KYIL KHOR	SHAR WA	TAR
water	in	moon's	circle	rise	like

Although appearances do manifest they do so in the manner of the reflection of the full moon in water.

ལས་འབྲས་འདི་ནི་རྫུན་པ་སྣ་ཚོགས་བཀྲ།

LAE	DRAE	DI NI	DZUN PA	NA TSHOG	TRA
deeds (karma)	result	this	lies, false (devoid of true validity)	all, variety	variegated

The results of karmic actions manifest as infinitely varied deceptions.

སྣང་བ་ཙམ་དུ་བླང་དོར་བྱ་བོ་ཨང་།

NANG WA	TSAM DU	LANG	DOR	JA	O ANG
appearance	only	take,* accept	throw out, cast out	do	(imperative)

(* This is necessary until enlightenment is reached in order to keep us strongly on the quick path. Even after the illusoriness of all appearances is awakened to, one must still act outwardly in a virtuous way so as to inspire others and lead them into the Dharma.)

Although these are mere appearances it is vital to adopt virtue and abandon nonvirtue.

All that seems to be really existing and reliable has never had the least reality that could be experienced. Although appearances seem to be the appearance of something, in fact they are intrinsically free of being substantial objects supporting definite knowledge. Since this is the case, whatever manifests from the wheel of karma is similarly without any inherent self-definition. Although appearances do manifest they do so in the manner of the reflection of the full moon in water. The results of karmic actions manifest as infinitely varied deceptions. Although these are mere appearances it is vital to adopt virtue and abandon nonvirtue.

རྨི་ལམ་ཡུལ་དུ་ལ་མའི་མི་འབར་ཚེ།

MI LAM	YUL	DU	LA MAI	ME	BAR	TSHE
dream	object	in	beautiful woman's hair	fire burn	blaze	if, when

When a woman dreams that her beautiful hair is burning

རང་བཞིན་མེད་ཀྱང་ཚ་བས་འཇིགས་པ་ལྟར།

RANG ZHIN	ME	KYANG	TSHA WAE	JIG PA	TAR
actual existence	not	yet, also	heat	fear, terrified	similar

She is terrified by the heat, although the fire does not really exist.

དམྱལ་ཁམས་ལ་སོགས་རང་བཞིན་མེད་ན་ཡང་།

NYAL KHAM LA SOG RANG ZHIN ME NA YANG
hell　realm　and so on　existence　not　yet, but

The hells and other realms are similarly without inherent existence, yet

བཙོ་བསྲེག་ཚོགས་ལ་འཇིགས་པས་སྤང་བར་བྱ།

TSO SE TSHOG LA JIG PAE PANG WAR JA
boil, cook　roast burn,　all this　to　fear　abandon　do
(of bodies)　　　　　　　　　　　　　(sins and their root of grasping)

(It is our belief in the reality of these horrors which is the cause of our terror. When we see that they are an illusion we start to relax. The same applies if watching a horror film.)

We are frightened by the roasting and burning. Therefore we must abandon the beliefs and actions which lead us there.

When a woman dreams that her beautiful hair is burning she is terrified by the heat, although the fire does not really exist. The hells and other realms are similarly without inherent existence, yet we are frightened by the roasting and burning. Therefore we must abandon the beliefs and actions which lead us there.

ཚད་པས་འཁྲུལ་ཚེ་མུན་ནག་ཡོངས་མེད་ཀྱང་།

TSAD WAE TRUL TSHE MUN NAG YONG ME KYANG
heat　mistaken,　then　dark,　black　all　not　also
　　　deluded　　　obscured

When we are delirious with fever, although we have not blacked out,

གཏིང་རིང་ཡུགས་སུ་རྒྱུ་ཞིང་འཚུབ་པ་ལྟར།

TING RING YUG SU GYU ZHING TSHUB WA TAR
deep　long　unconsciousness　　　　suffocated,　like, as
(and so we require help and medicine)　choked

Yet we feel dizzy and about to pass out and require help.

མ་རིག་ཚོགས་ལ་རང་བཞིན་མེད་ན་ཡང་།

MA RIG TSHOG LA RANG ZHIN ME NA YANG
ignorance　and so on　to　self-existence　not　yet

Similarly, although ignorance and its associated factors are without inherent existence,

ཤེས་རབ་གསུམ་གྱིས་འཁྲུལ་བ་བསལ་བར་བྱ།

SHE RAB SUM GI TRUL WA SAL WAR JA
wisdom*　three　by　delusion　clear away　do

(* arising from study, reflection and meditation. It is through hearing the teaching that this wisdom is developed.)

Our consequent delusion must be cleared away with the true knowing arising from study, reflection and meditation.

Sharp Weapon Wheel

When we are delirious with fever, although we have not blacked out, yet we feel dizzy and about to pass out and require help. Similarly, although ignorance and its associated factors are without inherent existence, our consequent delusion must be cleared away with the true knowing arising from study, reflection and meditation.

རོལ་མོ་མཁན་གྱིས་པི་ཝང་གླུ་བླངས་ཚེ།

ROL MO KHAN	GYI	PI WANG	LU LANG	TSHE
musician	by	16 stringed lute	singing	is, when

When a musician is playing the lute and singing,

དཔྱད་ན་སྒྲ་དེ་རང་བཞིན་མ་མཆིས་མོད།

CHAE	NA	DRA	DE	RANG ZHIN	MA	CHI	MOE
examine[+] if		sound	this	self-existence	not	exist	is

([+] Examine the sound to see if it is a mere temporary and empty effect of various causes operating together, like the strings of the lute, the musician's hand, his knowledge and so on. These causes also are not ultimate existents but are themselves also the result of other situations – and so on, in the great web of interrelation.)

If we examine the sound it will be seen to be without inherent self-existence.

མ་དཔྱད་ཚོགས་པས་སྙན་པའི་སྒྲ་འབྱུང་བས།

MA	CHAE	TSHOG PAE	NYAN PAI	DRA	JUNG	WAE
not	examine	all	pleasing, sweet sound		arise	by

(That is, it appears to us to be something, 'a pleasant sound', and so we feel desire to hear more of it.)

Those who do not examine what is occurring hear the sweet sounds

སྐྱེ་པོའི་སེམས་ཀྱི་གདུང་བ་སེལ་བ་ལྟར།

KYE POI	SEM	KYI	DUNG WA	SEL WA	TAR
peoples'	mind	of	sorrow	remove	like

Which dispel sorrow in peoples' minds.

ལས་དང་རྒྱུ་འབྲས་ཡོངས་ལ་དཔྱད་པ་ན།

LAE	DANG	GYU	DRAE	YONG	LA	CHAE PA	NA
actions	and	cause (karma)	effect	all	to	examine	if

(For an act to be fully karmic the following four factors must be present: 1) an object, e.g. an enemy; 2) an intention, e.g. the desire to kill him; 3) the instrument and the act, e.g. taking the knife and stabbing him; 4) the completion of the act, e.g. seeing that he is dead and being happy at this. The strength of karma depends on the intensity of each of these factors.)

Similarly, if we examine all our actions and see that they are the consequences of causes and that they in turn act as causes generating further consequences,

གཅིག་དང་ཐ་དད་རང་བཞིན་མེད་ན་ཡང་།

CHIG DANG THA DAD RANG ZHIN ME NA YANG
one and various self-existing not if also
(e.g. The body is not a thing in itself for it is composed of parts, and these parts are not things in themselves for they are all functioning together and are also composed of still further parts.)

We will see they lack inherent self-existence either as a singularity or in their diverse aspects.

སྣང་སྣང་ལྟ་བུར་ཆོས་རྣམས་སྐྱེ་འཇིག་བྱེད།

NANG NANG TA BUR CHO NAM KYE JIG JE
appearance* appearance like phenomena, all born# destroy do
dharmas⁺

(* all that can be seen and known) (⁺ all that can be conceptualized)
(# Our own ignorant grasping makes appearances seem real. They actually offer no true basis for our attachment.)

When we take appearances to be separate and substantial entities they become phenomena which are created and destroyed.

ཡོད་ཡོད་ལྟ་བུར་བདེ་སྡུག་སྣ་ཚོགས་མྱོང་།

YOE YOE TA BUR DE DUG NA TSHOG NYONG
really like happiness suffering many, experience
existing various
(i.e. we wander in samsara)

When we take these seeming entities to be really existing, we experience many different forms of joy and sorrow.

When a musician is playing the lute and singing, if we examine the sound it will be seen to be without inherent self-existence. Those who do not examine what is occurring hear the sweet sounds which dispel sorrow in peoples' minds. Similarly, if we examine all our actions and see that they are the consequences of causes and that they in turn act as causes generating further consequences, we will see they lack inherent self-existence either as a singularity or in their diverse aspects. When we take appearances to be separate and substantial entities they become phenomena which are created and destroyed. When we take these seeming entities to be really existing, we experience many different forms of joy and sorrow.

ཆུ་ཡི་ཐིག་པས་བུམ་པ་འགངས་བ་ན།

CHU YI THIG PAE BUM PA GANG WA NA
water of drop pot full if

When a pot is filled by drops of water,

Sharp Weapon Wheel 227

ཆུ་ཐིག་དང་པོས་བུམ་པ་མི་ཁེངས་ཤིང་།

CHU	THIG	DANG POE	BUM PA	MI	KHENG	SHING
water	drop	first	pot	not	fill	...ing

It is not the first drop of water which fills the pot,

ཐ་མ་ལ་སོགས་རེ་རེས་མ་ཡིན་མོད།

THA MA	LA SOG	RE RE	MA YIN MOE
last	and so on	one by one	not done

Nor is it the last, nor any one of the separate drops that enter it.

རྟེན་འབྲེལ་ཚོགས་པས་བུམ་པ་གང་བ་ལྟར།

TEN DREL	TSHOG PAE	BUM PA	GANG WA	TAR
interdependence, interrelation	connectivity, accumulation	pot	full	like

(In fact the fullness of the pot is just a temporary condition dependent on the conjunction of various incidental factors such as there being a pot, and drops of water entering it in sufficient quantity that they gradually cause it to fill up before they evaporate or leak away.)

It is the accumulation of drops arising in dependent origination that bring about the filling of the pot.

བདེ་སྡུག་འབྲས་བུ་གང་གིས་མྱོང་བ་ན།

DE	DU	DRAE BU	GANG	GI	NYONG WA	NA
happiness	sorrow	result*	whatever	by	experience	then

(* of our past virtuous and sinful actions)

Similarly, whatever we experience of consequent happiness and sorrow

རྒྱུ་ཡི་སྐད་ཅིག་དང་པོས་མ་ཡིན་ཞིང་།

GYU	YI	KAE	CHIG	DANG POE	MA YIN ZHING
cause	of	moment	one	first	is not

Did not come from just the first moment of the cause,

ཐ་མའི་སྐད་ཅིག་སོགས་ཀྱིས་མ་ཡིན་ཀྱང་།

THA MAI	KAE CHIG	SOG	KYI	MA YIN	KYANG
last	moment	and so on	by	not do	but

(i.e. all the moments between first and last)

Nor from just its last moment, nor from any of the others,

རྟེན་འབྲེལ་ཚོགས་པས་བདེ་སྡུག་མྱོང་བར་འགྱུར།

TEN DREL	TSHOG PAE	DE	DU	NYONG WAR	GYUR
interdependence	connected	happiness	suffering	experience*	arise

(* The happiness and sorrow are themselves not substantial entities with a self-existence of their own. They are mere temporary occurrences that exist briefly with the conjunction of certain factors. They are thus always open to change, since both they and the contributory factors, having had a beginning, must also have an end. Both cause and result being dynamic, it is like the insubstantial flow of a dream or a cinema picture. The vastness of complexity of the web of interdependence means that it is as if samsara has no beginning or end.)

For it is the connectivity of all the various moments and factors that gives rise to experiences of happiness and sorrow.

When a pot is filled by drops of water, it is not the first drop of water which fills the pot, nor is it the last, nor any one of the separate drops that enter it. It is the accumulation of drops arising in dependent origination that bring about the filling of the pot. Similarly, whatever we experience of consequent happiness and sorrow did not come from just the first moment of the cause, nor from just its last moment, nor from any of the others, for it is the connectivity of all the various moments and factors that gives rise to experiences of happiness and sorrow.

ཨེ་མ་མ་བརྟགས་གཅིག་བོར་ཉམས་དགའ་བའི།

E MA	MA TAG	CHIG BOR	NYAM GA WAI
wonderful	not mental activity	alone, uninvolved	pleasant, delightful

How amazing! When we are alone and free of mental activity,

སྣང་བ་འདི་ལ་སྙིང་པོ་མ་མཆིས་མོད།

NANG WA	DI	LA	NYING PO	MA	CHI MOE
appearance	this	to	essence	not	have
			(i.e. without real existence)		

This pleasant experience has no identity or existence of its own.

འོན་ཀྱང་ཡོད་པ་ལྟ་བུར་སྣང་བ་ཡི།

ON KYANG	YOE PA	TA BUR	NANG WA	YI
however	exist	like	appearance	of

However we seem to experience something that exists.

ཆོས་འདི་ཟབ་སྟེ་དམན་པས་མཐོང་བར་དཀའ།

CHO	DI	ZAB	TE	MAN PAE	THONG WAR	KA
Dharma	this	deep	thus	low, stupid	understand, see	difficult

This deep Dharma is hidden by our obscurations.

Sharp Weapon Wheel

How amazing! When we are alone and free of mental activity, this pleasant experience has no identity or existence of its own. However we seem to experience something that exists. This deep Dharma is hidden by our obscurations.

དེ་ནི་ཏིང་འཛིན་མཉམ་པར་འཇོག་པ་ན།

DA NI	TING DZIN	NYAM PAR JOG PA	NA
now	samadhi, absorbed contemplation	entering the state of equality	if, when

Now when we abide evenly in profound non-disturbance

དེས་པར་སྣང་བ་ཚམ་ཡང་ཅི་ཞིག་ཡོད།

NGE WAR	NANG WA	TSAM	YANG	CHI ZHIG	YOE
true, certain	appearance, experience	whatever	also	what	have (i.e. none)

Do we find any real existence in anything that occurs?

ཡོད་པ་ཅི་ཡོད་མེད་པ་འང་ཅི་ཞིག་ཡོད།

YOE PA	CHI	YOE ME PA	ANG	CHI ZHIG	YOE
exist	what	non-exist	also	what	have

Is there anything that could be said to exist or not exist?

ཡིན་མིན་དམ་བཅའ་གང་དུ་སུ་ཞིག་ཡོད།

YIN	MIN	DAM CHA	GANG DU	SU ZHIG	YOE
is	isn't*	conviction, strong belief	whatever	whoever	have

(* good, bad, mine, yours etc.)

Who could propose definitive assertion or negation?

ཡུལ་དང་ཡུལ་གྱི་ཆོས་ཉིད་མ་མཆིས་ཤིང་།

YUL	DANG	YUL	GYI	CHO NYI	MA	CHI SHING
object	and	object	of	dharmaness⁺	not	exist

(⁺ Dharmaness, dharmata, is the root of phenomena (dharma) and it seems to validate or support their existence. However the emptiness of dharmaness reveals the emptiness of all phenomena.)

There are no real objects nor is there a common substantial basis for objects.

བླང་དོར་ཀུན་བྲལ་སྤྲོས་དང་བྲལ་བ་ཡི།

LANG	DOR	KUN DRAL	TROE	DANG	DRAL WA	YI
take	reject	all free of (judgment and selectivity)	conceptual elaboration, deluding imagination	and	free of	of

Being free of accepting and rejecting, and free of conceptual elaboration,

གཉུག་མའི་ངང་དུ་བློ་གྲོས་མ་བཅོས་པར།

NYUG MAI   NGANG   DU   LO DRO   MA   CHO WAR
unchanging   abiding   in   intellect not   artificial

We abide in the intrinsic, free of the artifice of the intellect.

ལྷན་ནེ་གནས་ན་སྐྱེས་བུ་ཆེན་པོར་གྱུར།

LHA NE   NAE NA   KYE BU   CHEN POR   GYUR
peaceful,   stay if   person   great   become
relaxed   (i.e. great beings able to help others)

Remaining relaxed, we become great beings.

Now when we abide evenly in profound non-disturbance do we find any real existence in anything that occurs? Is there anything that could be said to exist or not exist? Who could propose definitive assertion or negation? There are no real objects nor is there a common substantial basis for objects. Being free of accepting and rejecting, and free of conceptual elaboration, we abide in the intrinsic, free of the artifice of the intellect. Remaining relaxed, we become great beings.

དེ་ལྟར་ཀུན་རྫོབ་བྱང་ཆུབ་སེམས་དང་ནི།

DE TAR   KUN DZOB JANG CHUB SEM   DANG NI
like that   relative   bodhicitta   and

In this way the relative truth spirit of enlightenment

དོན་དམ་བྱང་ཆུབ་སེམས་ལ་སྦྱངས་པ་ཡིས།

DON DAM   JANG CHUB SEM   LA   CHAE PA   YI
absolute   bodhicitta   to   practice   by

And the absolute truth spirit of enlightenment,

ཚོགས་གཉིས་བར་ཆད་མེད་པར་མཐར་ཕྱིན་ནས།

TSHOG   NYI   BAR CHAE   ME PAR   THAR CHIN   NAE
accumulation   two   obstruction   without   fulfilment   then
(i.e. merit and wisdom)

The two accumulations will be completed without difficulty, and

རང་གཞན་དོན་གཉིས་ཕུན་སུམ་ཚོགས་པར་ཤོག།

RANG   ZHAN   DON   NYI   PHUN SUM TSHOG PAR   SHO
self   others   benefit   both   all good things   must
(i.e. complete enlightenment for all beings)   intend to

There will be the wonderful richness of benefit for others and ourselves.

In this way with the relative truth spirit of enlightenment and the absolute truth spirit of enlightenment, the two accumulations will be completed without difficulty, and there will be the wonderful richness of benefit for others and ourselves.

དགྲ་པོ་གནད་ལ་དབབ་པའི་མཚོན་ཆའི་འཁོར་ལོ་ཞེས་བྱ་བ། འཇིགས་པའི་གཅན་ཟན་སྣ་ཚོགས་རྒྱུ་བའི་ནགས་ཁྲོད་དུ། ཡང་དག་རྟོགས་པའི་རྣལ་འབྱོར་བ་སྔ་མ་རྣམ་དཔྱོད་ཅན་པོ་དེས་བླ་མ་དམ་པའི་གསུང་ལྟར་བསླབས་ནས། དུས་ཀྱི་སྙིགས་མ་ལ་འཇིགས་པ་དང་བཅས་པའི་ནགས་ཁྲོད་དུ་ཉམས་སུ་བླངས་པའོ།། དེས་ཇོ་བོ་ཨ་ལ་གནང་ནས། ཨ་ཏི་ཤས་ཀྱང་གདུལ་དཀའ་བའི་སེམས་ཅན་མང་པོ་འདུལ་བའི་ཕྱིར། ཕྱོགས་མཚམས་མེད་པར་ཉམས་སུ་བླངས་བས་རྟོགས་པ་འབྱུངས་པའོ། ཚིགས་ས་བཅད་པ་འདི་གསུངས་སོ།།

Regarding this text, THE SHARP WEAPON WHEEL STRIKING THE HEART OF THE FOE, in the forest retreat where fearful beasts prowl, the yogi Dharmarakshita, who was both a scholar and a sage, composed it on the basis of his own guru's teaching. In this present dark age he put it into practice in his fearsome forest retreat. He gave this teaching to Atisha, and Atisha also gained clarity by practising it wherever he went in order to discipline those beings who were difficult to educate. He said as follows:

ཁོ་བོས་རྒྱལ་སྲིད་སྤངས་ནས་དཀའ་བ་སྤྱད་པའི་ཚེ།

KHO WOE	GYAL SI	PANG	NAE	KA WA	CHAE WAI	TSHE
by me	kingdom	abandon	then	difficult	practice	when

When I abandoned my kingdom and practised intensely

བསོད་ནམས་བསགས་པས་བླ་མ་མཆོག་དང་འཇལ།

SO NAM	SAG PAE	LA MA	CHOG	DANG	JAL
merit	collect	guru	excellently	and	meet

I collected merit enough to meet my most excellent guru

དམ་ཆོས་བདུད་རྩི་འདི་བསྟན་ཆོས་དབང་བསྐུར།

DAM CHO	DU TSI	DI	TAN	CHO	WANG KUR
holy Dharma	liberating elixir	this	doctrine	Dharma	initiation, empowerment

Who taught me the liberating elixir of this holy Dharma and gave me empowerment.

དེང་སང་གཉེན་པོ་ཐོབ་ནས་ཚིག་ཀྱང་བཟུང་།

DENG SANG	NYEN PO	THOB	NAE	TSHIG	KYANG	ZUNG
nowadays	antidote* (* remedy for the kleshas)	got	then	words	also	hold

Now I have truly gained this antidote and teach it to others.

གྲུབ་པའི་མཐའ་ལ་ཕྱོགས་རིས་མ་མཆིས་པས།

DRUB PAI THA	LA	CHOG RE	MA	CHI	PAE
philosophy, view	to	bias, narrow, selection and exclusion	not	do	by

By not being biased in my philosophical view,

བློ་གྲོས་བཀྲམ་ནས་ཀུན་ལ་བསླབ་པའི་ཚེ།

LO DRO	TRAM NE	KUN	LA	LAB WAI	TSE
intelligence	spread	all	to	teach	when

With matured intelligence I have given this teaching to all, and

ཡ་མཚན་དཔག་མེད་བདག་གིས་མཐོང་མོད་ཀྱིས།

YA TSHAN	PAG ME	DAG GI	THONG MO	KYI
wonderful	measureless	me by	saw	therefore

Have seen the immeasurable wonderful results.

སྙིགས་མའི་དུས་འདིར་ཆོས་འདི་ཕན་པར་འབྱུང་།།

NYIG MAI DU	DIR	CHO	DI	PHAN PAR	JUNG
degenerate time	here	Dharma	this	benefit	arise

In these degenerate times this Dharma teaching brings benefit!

When I abandoned my kingdom and practised intensely I collected merit enough to meet my most excellent guru who taught me the liberating elixir of this Holy Dharma and gave me empowerment. Now I have truly gained this antidote and teach it to others. By not being biased in my philosophical view and with matured intelligence, I have given this teaching to all, and have seen the immeasurable wonderful results. In these degenerate times this Dharma teaching brings benefit!

ཞེས་གསུངས་ནས། རྒྱ་བོད་ན་སློབ་མ་བསམ་གྱིས་མི་ཁྱབ་པའི་ནང་ནས། བཅོམ་ལྡན་འདས་རྗེ་བཙུན་སྒྲོལ་མ་ལ་སོགས་པ་ཡི་དམ་གྱི་ལྷ་དཔག་ཏུ་མ་མཆིས་པས་ལུང་བསྟན་པའི་སློབ་མ་སྨྱོ(སྟོན)དང་ལྡན་པ་ཨུ་བ་སི་ཀ་ལ། དེས་མཐར་བོད་ཀྱི་གདུལ་བྱ་མ་རུངས་བ་འདུལ་བའི་ཆེས་སུ་གནད་བསྟེ། ལོ་པ་ཉ་ཅུང་རྒྱལ་བ་ཡབ་སྲས་ཉིད་ཀྱིས་མཛད་དོ།།

Thus he said. "The enlightened one, noble Tara, and innumerable linking deities had all predicted that amongst all the countless disciples of Atisha in India and Tibet Upasaka 'Brom-sTon-Pa would be the most suitable disciple. Atisha gave this teaching to 'Brom-sTon-Pa in order to pacify the rough disciples in Tibet. This book was translated from Sanskrit into Tibetan by Atisha and 'Brom-sTon-Pa.

Translated into English by C R Lama and James Low in 1979 in Santiniketan, India.
Revised by James Low in June 2018.

DEDICATION OF MERIT

GE WA   DI   YI   NYUR DU   DAG
virtue   this   by   quickly   I
By this virtue may I quickly

PAD MA JUNG NE   DRUB   GYUR   NAE
Padmasambhava,   established   become,   and then
Guru Rinpoche   attain
Become inseparable from the Lotus Born and then,

DRO WA   CHIG   KYANG   MA   LU PA
beings   one   even   without   exception
All beings without exception,

DE   YI   SA   LA   GOE PAR   SHO
that   of   state, level   into   place, lead   may it happen
May I establish them in that situation.

By this virtue may I quickly become inseparable from the Lotus Born. Then may I establish all beings without exception in that same situation.

ཕན་པར་བསམས་པ་ཙམ་གྱིས་ཀྱང་།

PHEN PAR　SAM PA　TSAM GYI　KYANG
benefit　think　only　also

When merely the thought of helping others

སངས་རྒྱས་མཆོད་ལས་ཁྱད་འཕགས་ན།

SANG GYE　CHO　LAE　KYA PHAG　NA
buddhas　offering　than　excellent　thus

Is more excellent than the worship of the Buddhas,

སེམས་ཅན་མ་ལུས་ཐམས་ཅད་ཀྱི།

SEM CHEN　MA LUE　THAM CHE　KYI
sentient beings　without　all　genitive

It is unnecessary even to mention the greatness of striving

བདེ་དོན་བརྩོན་པ་སྨོས་ཅི་དགོས།།

DE DON　TSON PA　MOE CHI GOE
benefit　do　not necessary to mention

For the happiness and welfare of all beings without exception.

When merely the thought of helping others is more excellent than the worship of the Buddhas, it is unnecessary even to mention the greatness of striving for the happiness and welfare of all beings without exception.

སྤྱོད་འཇུག་ལས། *(Verse from Entering the Way of the Bodhisattva by Shantideva)*

Section Three

SWEET SIMPLICITY

INTRODUCTION TO SWEET SIMPLICITY

DAWN LIGHT, THE FIRST SHADING IN THE BLACK of the receding night, is soft and understated. There is illumination but not the intensity of the noonday sun. A gentle lightening touches the latency of appearances and seems to bring them to life. Samantabhadra, the original and unchanging Buddha, the source of the Dzogchen teachings, is dark blue in colour, just a few shades away from black, the colour of the early dawn. He is present, always, but non-insistent, non-demanding, available for those who wish to find dawn light in their own hearts and eyes.

All the polarities, including light and dark, good and bad, are pacified in the presence of Samantabhadra, the indivisible integrating of all. He is the unchanging ground and source and space of all that seems to come and go. Unarisen yet present he is forever apart from the delusion of splitting that manifests with ignoring of the ground. His name means always good, a good beyond the relativity of polarities. All is present within his unfragmented wholeness. Nothing enters it, nothing leaves it. Everything that is possible is nothing other than the radiance of his unchanging awareness. Beyond all extremes and beyond the conflicts of duality, untouched and undefined by all he effortlessly displays, Samantabhadra is the heart and source of all sentient beings.

The Dzogchen teaching set out in these texts all point to the fact that that which is unbroken needs no repair. The effort of trying to fix the world and fix oneself is misguided and can bring only transient relative benefits. The original, the unchanging, the ever pure, the ever open, is our own source and origin moment by moment. Disregarding it, we are in a world of things, and the multiplicity of items is paralleled by the multiplicity of our own moods, thoughts, emotions and so on.

However if we attend to the unchanging we slip free of immersion in the flow of becoming and find ourselves open and relaxed, present and available, without having the least fixed essence or inherent existence. Freedom is the ground on which we build our prison – so don't try to get through the walls to somewhere else. Simply open to the groundless ground that has supported you forever.

The first text in this section, *The Lamp Clarifying the Essentials of the of Meditation*, is very condensed and to the point. It was written by Tulku Tsulo, the root guru of my own guru, C R Lama.

The focus of this text is on the status of experience. Whatever we experience through the senses, and however we interpret and respond to it, is a movement of the mind. We seem to experience 'things'; something is happening. There is a knower and a known. The source of all knowables (*dharmas*, *Chos* in Tibetan, phenomena) is called *dharmata* in Sanskrit and *Chos Nyid* in Tibetan. This term indicates *dharma*-ness, thing-ness appearance-ness, experienced-ness i.e. the essence of all that is encountered. This source or ground or basis of things is not a thing; it is an aspect of emptiness and is therefore without inherent existence or real identity. It is inseparable from the ground (*gZhi*).

Similarly all that seems to be part of the knower, the transient thoughts, feelings, memories and so on have their source in what is known as *chittata* in Sanskrit, *Sems Nyid* in Tibetan, i.e. mind-ness which is the essence of all we take to be the encounterer. This source or ground or basis of knowing and experiencing is not an entity or a thing apart; it is an aspect of emptiness and therefore without inherent existence or real identity.

Clear understanding of this based on and mediated by concepts is the orientation by which we can enter direct revelation through opening in non-dual meditation. Emptiness is beyond thought yet is the ground of everything, whether it seems to be 'object' or 'subject'. There are no essences, islands of real stuff, self-existing substances or entities. In every situation whether sitting on a meditation cushion or arguing with a partner there is only the non-dual, non-separated display of the energy of the ground. The light or illumination of the ground is called *vidya* in Sanskrit, *Rigpa* in Tibetan, awareness, the lucidity of space.

Emptiness is fullness. Nothing is everything and everything is nothing. This fact shows us how the infinite potential of emptiness/openness/infinity gives rise to incomprehensible riches of appearance filling space and time. This is clear within the mirror-like clarity of empty awareness which never seeks to appropriate, identify with, or rely on any mode of arising. This is freedom itself. Conceptual interpretation, on the other hand, building up images of what is going on, is a thankless task since all such constructs are inherently impermanent. If the difference between intrinsic non-dual clarity and the effortful 'making sense of what is going on' becomes obvious for you and you can maintain that in all situations, then dzogchen practice is truly accessible.

When we seem to be apart from and different from all we encounter, we are a thing in a world of things. We then encounter things changing into other things. Hence if A becomes B and B has a real existence different from that of A, then the change would be irreversible, for example, an essential oil of jasmine cannot be turned back into jasmine flowers. In this way every development and gain also involves a loss. To get what you did not have you have to give up what you did have. This is the feeling tone of the material world, a domain in which change is primarily from one fixity to another.

However if A only appears to be different from B, if A only appears to be A and B only appears to be B then the transformation of A to B is not of one thing becoming another. Water, ice, mist, steam, cloud – all can be said to be 'water' taking on different appearances due to causes and conditions. However, if we say they are forms of water that is to privilege water over the other forms as if it was somehow valid as the one true or definitive mode rather than just being one of a range of possible manifestations. Recognising this, we can see that various forms manifest without having an inherent existence. They are form and emptiness, known as *sNang-sTong* in Tibetan. All appearances are the appearance of the open empty ground and the myriad forms they show establish no entities or separate real things.

The world is seamless, the mind is seamless, moreover world and mind have no seam or border between them. This is the intrinsic integrity of non-duality, the one truth that dispels all darkness.

The second text in this section is *The Evocation of Samantabhadra*, spoken by the primordial Buddha Samantabhadra himself, transmitted by Padmasambhava and revealed as the treasure text by Rigdzin Godem. This wonderful short text gives a precise account of the open ground, the ground of everything we know, everything we can imagine, and all that we are. This ground is the same for all, whether what appears seems to be the radiance of the ground or a dull denial of its presence.

The ground is the key to practice. For as long as we take the myriad forms of display offered by the ground to be real independent entities, its emergence which never emerges as something separate, will be misunderstood. The misunderstander, the seemingly autonomous, self-directing ego self, is ceaselessly imagining 'things' which are actually illusions. The non-duality of appearance and emptiness, if appreciated as it is, is the liberating clarity of emptiness. However if it is grasped at there is an experiential though not actual loss of integrity in the whole. We are then mere fragments in a fragmented world buffeted hither and thither by events.

To open to and abide with the ground, in the ground, as the ground, is liberation itself. To continue to ignore this ever-open, ever-available freedom is to find oneself wandering in the six realms of samsara. Liberation is then so near and yet so far. To have this text is to be able to consult an accurate map that will always show you exactly where you truly are no matter what appearances arise.

The third text is by Gonpo Wangyal, son of Tulku Tsulo. It is a section from his beautiful Cutting or *gCod* text, *Opening the Door to Liberation*. In this short text we find a more practice-oriented account of the view presented in the two previous texts. The starting point is an active critique of our usual sense of materiality as something irreducible. Active investigation cuts through the jungle of delusion, opening a clearing in which the actual ground is visible. Clearing habit formations, cutting them down by leaf, stem, branch, trunk and root uncovers the unchanging presence of the ground.

With direct seeing of the naked fresh ground, liberating clarity arises like the dawn. All obscurations and confusions have the same ground as luminous awareness! The concepts we became familiar with in *The Evocation of Samantabhadra* and which we have used to support our investigation dissolve into the open lucidity of the unchanging sphere, the inseparability of the infinite hospitality of the *dharmadhatu* and the ungraspable presence of awareness.

Relaxing in non-dual spaciousness there is no need to get involved with anything that occurs. All arisings, whether seemingly on the object 'side' or the subject 'side' are self-liberating. Arising without effort and vanishing without effort, this is the effortless pulse of the energy of the Buddha's heart. Free of dualistic intention and all concern with gain and loss, karmic accumulation has nowhere to ripen and dissolves like morning dew. Thus we come to live the three statements of Garab Dorje: opening to how it is; not harbouring doubts about how it is; and continuing in the effortless presence of how it is. No ignorance, no leaking, and no faults since there is no ego actor to make self-referential choices obscuring the sky-like mind which welcomes all without holding on to anything. Within this limitless field of clarity, movement arises as compassionate or liberating connectivity in the manner of a dream.

The fourth and final text in this section is the only one in the whole book written by a woman: having it come last is not an oversight but rather an honouring of the fact that it is a synopsis of all that has come before. This amazing yogini lived a life of profound practice without drawing attention to herself. She gave this short teaching to Namkhai Norbu Rinpoche and he has transmitted it in the West many times. Every word she offers is precise and to the point. If we follow her instructions she will lead us to the open infinite that cannot be closed. Everything that occurs is always already within it. Neither one nor many, the non-dual ground displays the unborn variety of vibrant empty light.

She highlights the importance of not doubting the non-conceptual. We are so used to having concepts as the validators of experience. We have learned to use them to reach conclusions, to establish facts and build up pictures. But she shows the delusional quality of this unnecessary activity. Concepts do not come from on high, from some superior place outside wholeness. Although they present themselves as true, powerful and honest judges they are actually the activity which maintains our alienated suffering. Everything is within the single *thigle*, the one sphere free of corners and fissures. Seeing that our mind is without limit it is clear that we cannot be caught by a thought unless through misguided identification we have become merely the thought forms 'I, me myself'. Thoughts catch thoughts but awareness is open, empty and other than all we can think or imagine.

To meet the *Dharma* is to have a chance, one that is rare and precious in this world of deceit. Knowing the *Dharma* is knowing that the knowable ego-self is not who we are. True knowledge leads to not knowing and in this strange darkness, if we trust, the dawn light reveals the sweet simplicity of Samantabhadra.

THE LAMP CLARIFYING THE ESSENTIALS OF THE WAY OF MEDITATION

BY TSULTRIM ZANGPO

༄༅། །སྒོམ་གྱི་ལམ་གནད་གསལ་བའི་སྒྲོན་མེ་བཞུགས།

༄༅། །དངོས་གྲུབ་སྐྱེད་སྟོབས་བུལ་ཆོས་ཀྱི་སྐུ། །མདངས་མ་འགགས་གསལ་བ་ལོངས་སྤྱོད་རྫོགས། །རྩལ་རིས་མེད་འཆར་བ་སྤྲུལ་པའི་སྐུ། །སྐུ་གསུམ་གྱི་བདག་ཉིད་བླ་མར་འདུད། །དབྱིངས་སྟོང་པའི་ཡེ་ཤེས་བླ་མར་མཆོད། །ལྷུན་གྲུབ་ཀྱི་རང་བཞིན་ཡི་དམ་ལྷ། །ཕྱགས་རྗེ་ཡི་རྩལ་མདངས་མཁའ་འགྲོ་སྟེ། །རྩ་གསུམ་གྱི་བདག་ཉིད་རང་རིག་རྒྱལ། །འདིར་ཆོས་ཀྱི་གནས་ལུགས་མཐར་ཐུག་ནི་སེམས་ཉིད་རང་བྱུང་གི་ཡེ་ཤེས་ཤུག་གཅིག་ཡིན་ལ། དེ་མཛོད་དུ་བྱས་ན་འཁོར་འདས་ཀྱི་གནས་ལུགས་མཛོད་དུ་གྱུར་བར་འཛིན་ནུས་ཏེ། ཆོས་ཉིད་ཀྱི་རང་བཞིན་ལས་མ་འདས་པའི་ཕྱིར་རོ། །དེའི་ཚུལ་ཡང་ཀུན་བྱེད་ཀྱི་ཆོས་ཀྱི་རང་བཞིན་མཐའི་སྟོབས་པ་ལས་གྲོལ་བའི་སྟོང་པ་ཉིད་ལོ་ན་སྟེ། སྟོང་པ་དེར་མཐར་གཏུགས་ན་སེམས་ཀྱི་རང་བཞིན་དུ་བཞུགས་པའི་སྟོང་པ་རིག་པའི་སྙིང་པོ་ཅན་ལས་རྒྱུང་ཆད་

245

དུ་རྟོགས་པ་མེད་དེ། རྣལ་འབྱོར་པས་སེམས་ཉིད་ལ་མཉམ་པར་བཞག་པ་ན་འགྱུར་འདས་ཀྱི་ཆོས་རྣམས་སྟོང་པའི་ཡེ་ཤེས་དེའི་རྣམ་རོལ་དུ་འཆར་བ་ཡིན་པས་སོ། །སེམས་ཉིད་ལ་མ་ལྟོས་པའི་ཆོས་ཉིད་བྱུང་བ་ཞིག་ཡོད་ན། ཆོས་ཉིད་དེའི་ཆོས་ཅན་ཡང་སེམས་ཉིད་ལས་ཐ་དད་པར་རང་དབང་བའི་ཆོས་སུ་འགྱུར་བ་ཞིག་ན། དེ་བཞིན་གྲུབ་ཏུ་འཇོག་པ་ལས་འོས་མེད། དེ་ལྟར་ན་ཆོས་ཉིད་ཡང་བདེན་སྟོང་དུ་མི་འཐད་པས། བདེན་གྲུབ་ཉིད་ཆོས་ཉིད་དུ་ཐལ་བའོ། །དེས་ན་རྒྱལ་སྲས་ཐམས་ཅད་རིགས་པའི་རྣ་འཕུལ་ལས་གཞན་དུ་མ་གྲུབ་པས་ཡུལ་ཅན་སྣང་ཡང་རིག་པ་མི་ལྡན་ལྟ་བུ་ལས་ཕར་ཕྱིན་མ་གཏོགས་འཆར་གཞི་ཚོགས་ཐྲུབས་ཀྱིས་གྲུབ་པའི་ཆོས་ཞིག་ཡོད་ནས་ཚོར་ཕྱིན་མ་ཡིན་ནོ། །དེ་ལྟ་ན་དགག་མ་དགག་པའི་ཆོས་རྣམས་རིག་པའི་སྟོབས་ཤུགས་ལས་ཕྱིན་ཅིད་དོ། །དེའི་ཕྱིར་ན་སེམས་སྟོང་པའི་ཡེ་ཤེས་སུ་མཉམ་པར་བཞག་ཅིང་དེ་རྟོགས་ནས་ཆོས་ཐམས་ཅད་མེད་སྣང་སྟོང་པའི་གཟུགས་སུ་འཆར་འོང་བ་ཡིན། འོན་སེམས་ཉིད་ལ་མཉམ་པར་འཇོག་ཚུལ་ནི། དཔེར་སེམས་འདི་ཉིད་ཞིན་འཛིན་དམིགས་གཏད་ཅན་དུ་མ་ཆེད་བཞིན་པའི་རང་དུས་ནས་ཀྱང་ཤེས་པའི་རང་རོ་ཞིན་འཛིན་གྱི་རྟོགས་དང་བྲལ་བའི་ཟེར་ཐལ་བའི་དང་ནས་གཡོ་མ་སྐྱོང་བར་ཡོད་པས། དེ་མ་ཟིན་དུ་བྱུས་ཏེ་འཇོག་དགོས་ལ་དེའང་རང་གི་རོ་བོ་དེ་རྟོག་བྲལ་སྟོང་པའི་ཆ་དང་། གཡོ་མེད་གནས་པའི་ཆ་དང་། གསལ་བ་བདེ་བའི་ཆ། གསལ་བ་ཤེས་རབ་ཀྱི་ཚོགས་ཡོན་ཏན་དུ་མའི་བདག་ཉིད་དུ་ཡེ་རྟོགས་ལྷུན་གྲུབ་ཏུ་ཡོད་པས་རིག་པ་མངོན་དུ་གྱུར་འོང་ཚོར་གྱི་ཡོན་ཏན་དེ་རྣམས་རང་ཤུགས་ཀྱིས་མངོན་དུ་མི་འགྱུར་མི་སྲིད་པས། དེའི་སྐབས་སུ་བདེ་གསལ་སོགས་ཡོན་ཏན་དེ་དག་གང་དུ་ཤར་ཀྱང་། དེར་དམིགས་གཏད་ཀྱིས་མི་བཀླག་ཞིང་དེའི་དང་ལ་མི་གནས་པར་རྟོག་བྲལ་ཤེས་ཙམ་པའི་ཤེས་རབ་ཀྱི་ཚད་རིག་ཚཟེར་བས་དེ་ཀ་རང་གི་ཐོག་ཏུ་མ་བརྗེད་མ་བོར་ཙམ་བྱས་ཏེ་བཅོས་མེད་རང་བབས་སུ་འཇོག་དགོས་པ་ཡིན། དེ་ལྟར་རང་དོ་ཤེས་ཙམ་མ་བརྗེད་ཙམ་གྱི་རྒྱུན་སྐྱོང་བ་ནི། རང་བབས་ཀྱི་ཡེ་བསྐོམ་ལ་ཡང་བསྐོམ་གྱིས་བཅོས་བསྐྲུན་མེད་པའི

དང་ལ་རྒྱན་མར་གནས་ནུས་ན་ཡེངས་སུ་མེད་ཅིང་དམིགས་གཏད་ཀྱི་སྒོམ་དུ་མེད་པ་ལ་ཚོས་ཆིད་གཞུག་མའི་དུས་ཞེས་བྱ་ལ། མ་ཡེངས་པའི་དུས་ན་མ་བརྗེད་ཙམ་དང་ཞེས་ཅམ་མ་བོར་བར་ཡོད་པ་དེ་དང་། གཡེང་བའི་དུས་ན་རང་དོ་ཞེས་ཙམ་ནས་གཡེང་མཁན་བོར་ཏེ་ཞེས་ཅམ་པ་དང་དབྱེར་མེད་ཐ་མི་དད་དུ་འགྲོ་བ་ནི་དུན་སྣང་ཡེ་ཤེས་སུ་འཆར་བའི་མགོ་བཙུགས་པ་ཡིན་པར་གསུངས་པས་ལྟ་བྱ་ལྟ་བྱེད་གནས་བྱ་གནས་བྱེད་སྒོམ་བྱ་སྒོམ་བྱེད་ཐ་དད་དུ་མ་སོང་བར། རང་ངོ་མཐོང་ཙམ་པ་དེའི་དང་ལ་རྩོལ་མེད་རང་བཞག་གི་རྒྱུན་བསྐྱངས་ན། ཡེངས་ཡུལ་ཚོས་ཅིད་དུ་ཟད་དེ་དབྱིངས་གཅིག་གི་རང་བཞིན་ལས་མི་འདའ་བས། མཉམ་རྗེས་གང་གི་དུས་སུའང་རྟོག་དཔྱོད་ཕྱེ་ཚོམ་ཡིན་མིན་གྱི་འཆིང་ཞེན་ཐམས་ཅད་རང་གྲོལ་ལ་སོང་ནས། ནམ་མཁའི་ནལ་འབྱོར་ཞེས་གྲགས་པ་ཡིན། རིག་ཆ་དེས་ཅི་ཞེས་ན་ཞེས་རབ་ལྷག་མཐོང་དུ་འགྱུར་རམ་སྙམ་ན། དེའི་ཞེས་བྱ་རིག་བྱེ་རིག་པ་རང་གི་དབྱིངས་སྟོང་པ་དེ་ཉིད་ཡེ་ནས་མངོན་དུ་བྱས་དེ་ནམ་ཡང་དབྱིངས་དེ་ལས་གཡོ་འཕོ་སྐྱེད་ཅིག་ཙམ་ཡང་བྱེད་མི་ནུས་བ་ཡིན་པས། ད་ལྟ་མཉམ་པར་བཞག་སྐབས་སུ་ཡང་རིག་པ་ལ་སྟོང་པའི་ལྷན་པ་གསར་དུ་འདེབས་མི་དགོས་པར་རིག་པ་ཁོའི་སྟེང་ལ་རང་བབས་སུ་ཅིག་བཞག་བྱས་པ་གཅིག་པུའི་མཐུ་ལས་སྟོང་པ་རྒྱུ་དུ་རྟོགས་འགྲོ་བ་ཡིན་ནོ། །སྟོས་བྲལ་གྱི་རིག་པ་ཅུ་རེ་བ་རང་བབས་སུ་འཇོག་པའི་སྒོམ་པ་དེ། ཐ་མལ་བའི་ཞེས་པ་སྐྱོང་བ་ཡིན། ཡུལ་རྗེས་སུ་པར་ལ་མ་འབྲམས་ཤིང་། རིག་ཅམ་པའི་དང་དུ་ཆུར་གནས་ཏེ་སྟོང་ཆགས་པའི་དུན་པ་བསྟེན་པ་གཅེས། མཉམ་བཞག་དང་རྗེས་ཐོབ་གང་གི་དུས། དུན་ཅམ་གྱི་དང་ལས་མ་གཡོས་ན། །མི་བསྒོམ་པའི་བསྒོམ་པ་ཆེ་ཞེས་གྲགས། །དུས་ཀུན་ཏུ་མ་བརྗེད་བཙོན་པར་རིས། །དགེ་འདིའི་མཐུས་མ་རྒྱུན་སེམས་ཅན་ཀུན། །བྱང་ཆུབ་ཀྱི་གོ་འཕང་མྱུར་ཐོབ་ཤོན། །ཞེས་པ་འདིའང་གདོང་སྨྲ་རྒྱན་ལོ་དང་བཙུན་པ་ཡི་ལོའི་དོར་ཆུལ་མིད་པས་སྐུལ་པ་དགེ་ལེགས་འཕེལ། །རྟོགས་ཆེན་གྱི་བསྟན་པ་ཕྱོགས་མེད་དུ་འཕེལ་བར་ཤོག །

Intrinsic mode, unborn space free of conceptual elaboration,
Enjoyment mode, radiance of unceasing clarity,
Emanation mode, impartially available contact –
Presence of these three modes, my guru, I bow to you.

The guru is seen in the original knowing of empty space.
The meditation deity is its quality of instant presence.
The dakinis are the bright energy of its connectivity.
These three roots are our own regal awareness.

THE ULTIMATE WAY OF ABIDING of all phenomena is simply the self-arising original knowing of the mind itself (*sems nyid*). When this becomes clear, you will have the ability to settle in the clarity of how samsara and nirvana abide since this does not stray from the quality of the actuality or truth of phenomena (*chos nyid*).

Further to this, emptiness free of limiting concepts is the truth (*rang bzhin*) of all the phenomena manifesting from the maker of all (*kun byed*). Conclusively this emptiness abides as the truth of the mind, the heart of the inseparability of awareness and emptiness. If one is cut off from this there is no awakening. However if a yogi rests without disturbance in the mind as it is (*sems nyid*) all the phenomena of samsara and nirvana appear as the play of the intrinsic knowing of emptiness.

If there was separate phenomenaness (*chos nyid*) independent of mind as it is (*sems nyid*) then any phenomena within that phenomenaness would be separate from mind as it is, and such phenomena would have their own agency. Due to this one would have to consider them to be really existent. If it were like that, then phenomenaness also would not be empty of real existence. Real existence would then be the condition of that phenomenaness.

However all the appearances of energy are not other than the magical display of awareness and so the appearances which arise as objects do not manifest outside of mirror-like awareness. The existence of a basis for arisings other than that (empty awareness), one which would give rise to real entities, does not occur.

Hence all phenomena, whether (deemed) pure or impure, manifest solely through the power and force of awareness. Due to this, if you avail yourself of resting evenly in the original knowing of the empty mind then you will find that all phenomena do not really exist and that all that appears is merely empty form.

Well, what is the way to settle evenly in the mind itself? Your mind as it presents itself right now, with its longing and attachment, its reliance on concepts and all that occurs for it at this moment, (is an experience of knowing) and the truth (*rang ngo*) of this knowing is free of the disturbance of longing and attachment as it never wavers from unobstructedness (*zang thal*).

You need to experience this directly. Moreover the simplicity (*ngo bo*) of your mind has an empty aspect free of thought, a still aspect free of movement, a bliss aspect which is experienced, and an aspect of precise knowing (*shes rab*) which is clarity. These many qualities have been complete and effortlessly present from the very beginning. Therefore when awareness becomes fully present for you it is not possible that these qualities would not automatically manifest for you. At that time, whichever of these qualities, bliss, clarity and so on, arise for you, do not make them something that you focus on and do not merge into these experiences. Without forgetting or discarding the aspect of precise knowing, simple knowing free of thoughts which is also referred to as the aspect of awareness, settle in relaxed free-flowing non-contrivance.

In this way, free of forgetfulness, by ceaselessly sustaining awareness of the truth of one's being (*rang ngo shes*), you abide in free-flowing original meditation free of the contrivance and corruption of added-on meditation.

If you have the capacity to abide ceaselessly in the state then, without wavering, you will have recollection of the unchanging emptiness of phenomena (*chos nyid*) free of the meditation which relies on fixed objects. Then, without distraction, without abandoning simple awareness, when wavering occurs simply be aware of the truth of your own being (*rang ngo shes*) and discard (identification with) the one who wavers. Continuous inseparability from simple awareness free of division is said to be the beginning of the arising of recollection and appearance as original knowing. So do not make any distinction between the looker and the object of looking, between the one who abides and the site of abiding, between the one who protects and sustains and what is sustained.

If you continuously maintain effortless self-settling in the state of simply seeing one's own true being, any objects of distraction will vanish in the truth of phenomena (*chos nyid*) *and* you and they will not pass beyond the expanse of the sole openness (*dharmadhatu*). Whether evenly abiding or in post-meditation allow all conceptual distinctions, doubts and attachments binding one to ideas of existing and non-existing to self-liberate. This is known as the yoga of the sky (or the relaxed non-duality of space). One might enquire whether with this aspect of awareness whatever is known (experienced) will be the clear vision of true knowing (*shes rab lhag mthong*)? All that it encounters, or is aware of, is primordially manifesting within the givenness (*de nyid*) of the inherent empty spaciousness of awareness. For not even an instant have these objects/experiences moved out of this space.

Therefore, at the present moment as we settle in evenness there is no need to freshly apply emptiness to awareness. Settling into awareness itself, simply open to the non-arousal of free-flow and this itself will quickly bring you to the revelation of emptiness. Entering the meditation (or rest) which is the vivid (*hu re*, alert) uninterruptedness of awareness free of conceptual elaboration, allows one to sustain ordinary knowing (*tha mal bai shes pa*) (without getting lost). Then you will not go wandering outside following after objects. You will remain right here in the state of simple awareness, diligent in being supported by relaxed stable recollection (of empty awareness).

> *Whether in meditation or post-meditation,*
> *If you do not waver from the state of simple recollection,*
> *This is the great meditation of non-meditation.*
> *Never be distracted from this and attend to it always.*

By the power of this virtue may all sentient beings, my previous mothers, quickly gain the level of awakening!

I, known as Tsul, said this in response to requests from Dongna Gyenlo and Tsunpa Yilo.

May virtue and goodness spread!
May the teachings of dzogchen spread everywhere!

Written by Tsultrim Zangpo, also known as Tulku Tsulo
Translated by James Low, May 2018

༄༅། །ཀུན་ཏུ་བཟང་པོའི་སྨོན་ལམ།

THE EVOCATION OF SAMANTABHADRA

THE POTENTIAL OF THE GROUND

ཧོཿ་སྣང་སྲིད་འཁོར་འདས་ཐམས་ཅད་ཀུན༔

HO	NANG	SRI	KHOR	DAE	THAM CHE	KUN
expressive	appearance	becoming, existing	samsara, revolving	nirvana, beyond	all	all

Ho! All the possible appearances and existences of samsara and nirvana

གཞི་གཅིག་ལམ་གཉིས་འབྲས་བུ་གཉིས༔

ZHI	CHIG	LAM	NYI	DRAE BU	NYI
ground, basis, source	one	path	two	result	two

Have the same source, yet two paths and two results arise

རིག་དང་མ་རིག་ཆོ་འཕྲུལ་ཏེ༔

RIG	DANG	MA	RIG	CHOM THRUL	TE
awareness	and	not	aware	miraculous magical display	regarding
		ignoring			

As the magical display of awareness and unawareness.

1

2

3

གུན་ཏུ་བཟང་པོའི་སྨོན་ལམ་གྱིས༔

KUN TU ZANG POI	MON LAM	GYI
always good in every way, Samantabhadra	wish, path evocation	by

4

By this evocation of Samantabhadra

ཐམས་ཅད་ཆོས་དབྱིངས་ཕོ་བྲང་དུ༔

THAM CHE	CHOE YING	PHO DRANG	DU
all	dharmadhatu, all-encompassing space, infinite hospitality	palace	in

5

In the palace of infinite hospitality

མངོན་པར་རྫོགས་ཏེ་འཚང་རྒྱ་ཤོག༔

NGON PAR	DZOG	TE	TSANG GYA	SHO
fully	complete, perfect	then, hence	enlightened, awakened, buddhahood	may!

6

May all beings awaken to full enlightenment.

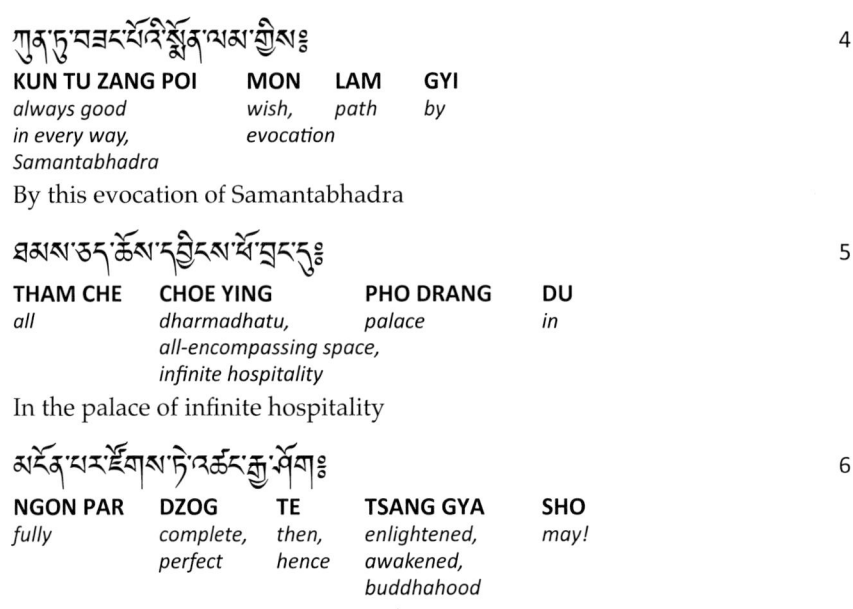

Ho! All the possible appearances and existences of samsara and nirvana have the same source, yet two paths and two results arise as the magical display of awareness and unawareness. By this evocation of Samantabhadra may all beings awaken to full enlightenment in the security of infinite hospitality.

HOW THE GROUND IS

ཀུན་གྱི་གཞི་ནི་འདུས་མ་བྱས༔

KUN	GYI	ZHI	NI	DUE	MA	JAE
all	of	basis, ground	regarding	gathered together, uncomposed, uncreated	not	done

7

The source of all is uncompounded,

རང་བྱུང་ཀློང་ཡངས་བརྗོད་དུ་མེད༔

RANG	JUNG	LONG YANG	JO DU	ME
self	arising, arisen	vast expanse, infinity	express ineffable	beyond

8

Self-arisen, infinite, inexpressible and

འཁོར་འདས་གཉིས་ཀའི་མིང་མེད་དོ༔ 9

KHOR	DAE	NYI KAI	MING	ME DO
samsara	nirvana	both	name,	without
			designate or label	

Impossible to label as 'samsara' or 'nirvana'.

དེ་ཉིད་རིག་ན་སངས་རྒྱས་ཏེ༔ 10

DE NYI	RIG	NA	SANG GYE	TE
that itself,	aware	if	buddhahood,	yet
suchness			awakening	

Awareness as this suchness is buddhahood.

མ་རིག་སེམས་ཅན་འཁོར་བར་འཁྱམས༔ 11

MA RIG	SEM CHEN	KHOR WAR	CHAM
not aware,	sentient beings	in samsara,	wander
ignoring		round and round	

Unaware of this, sentient beings wander in samsara.

ཁམས་གསུམ་སེམས་ཅན་ཐམས་ཅད་ཀྱིས༔ 12

KHAM	SUM	SEM CHEN	THAM CHE KYI
realms	three*	sentient beings	all by
(* desire, form and formless)			

May all beings in the three realms

བརྗོད་མེད་གཞི་དོན་རིག་པར་ཤོག༔ 13

JO	ME	ZHI	DON	RIG PAR	SHO
express,	without	basis,	truth,	be aware	may!
describe		source	meaning		

Be aware in the truth of the ineffable base!

The source of all is uncompounded, self-arisen, infinite, inexpressible and impossible to label as 'samsara' or 'nirvana'. With awareness of this there is buddhahood. Unaware of this, sentient beings wander in samsara. May all beings in the three realms be aware in the truth of the ineffable base!

THE QUALITIES OF AWARENESS OF THE GROUND

ཀུན་ཏུ་བཟང་པོ་ང་ཡིས་ཀྱང་༔ 14

KUN TU ZANG PO	NGA YI	KYANG
Samantabhadra	I, me by	also

I, Samantabhadra, affirm

The Evocation of Samantabhadra

རྒྱུ་རྐྱེན་མེད་པ་གཞི་ཡི་དོན༔ 15

GYU **KYEN** **ME PA** **ZHI** **YI** **DON**
causal *conditions* *without* *ground,* *of* *truth, presence,*
source *actuality, quality*

The truth of the source free of causes and conditions.

དེ་ཉིད་གཞི་ལས་རང་བྱུང་རིག༔ 16

DE NYI **ZHI** **LAE** **RANG** **JUNG** **RIG**
thatness, *ground,* *from,* *self* *arising* *awareness*
thusness *source* *in, as*

Awareness is intrinsically present with the source itself,

ཕྱི་ནང་སྒྲོ་སྐུར་སྐྱོན་མ་བཏགས༔ 17

CHI **NANG** **DRO KUR** **KYON** **MA** **TAG**
outer *inner* *exaggerate,* *faults* *not* *named,*
fabrication of *defined*
affirmation and denial

Untouched by the faults of separating outer and inner, and employing biased judgements, and

དྲན་མེད་མུན་པའི་དྲི་མ་བྲལ༔ 18

DREN **ME** **MUN PAI** **DRI MA** **DRAL**
recollection, *without* *darkness* *stain,* *free of*
unconsciousness *taint*

Untainted by the darkness of the loss of recollection.

དེ་ཕྱིར་རང་སྣང་སྐྱོན་མ་གོས༔ 19

DE CHIR **RANG** **NANG** **KYON** **MA** **GOE**
therefore *self* *appearance* *faults* *not* *touched,*
obscured

And so spontaneous appearance is free of faults.

རང་རིག་སོ་མ་གནས་པ་ལ༔ 20

RANG **RIG** **SO MA** **NAE PA** **LA**
self, *aware* *fresh* *abide* *then*
intrinsic

Intrinsic awareness is fresh and unchanging.

སྲིད་གསུམ་འཇིག་ཀྱང་དངངས་སྐྲག་མེད༔ 21

SI **SUM** **JIG** **KYANG** **NGANG TRAG** **ME**
worlds *three** *destroyed,* *yet* *panic, fear* *without*
(* gods, humans, nagas) *collapsed*

It is free of fear and panic even if the three worlds are destroyed.

སྣང་སེམས་གཉིས་སུ་མེད་པ་ལ༔ 22A

NANG SEM NYI SU MED PA LA
appearance mind two as not then, with

With the non-duality of appearance and mind, there is

འདོད་ཡོན་ལྔ་ལ་ཆགས་པ་མེད༔ 22B

DO YON NGA LA CHAG PA ME
sensory objects five to attached without

No attachment to the pleasures of the five senses,

རྟོག་མེད་ཤེས་པ་རང་བྱུང་ལ༔ 23

TOG ME SHE PA RANG JUNG LA
thought without awareness self arising to, with
non-conceptual spontaneously arisen

Self-arising awareness is free of concepts, and so

གདོས་པའི་གཟུགས་དང་དུག་ལྔ་མེད༔ 24

DOE PAI ZUG DANG DUG NGA ME
material, forms and poisons* five without
solid (* assumption, desire, aversion, pride, jealousy)

Is free of material form and the five poisons.

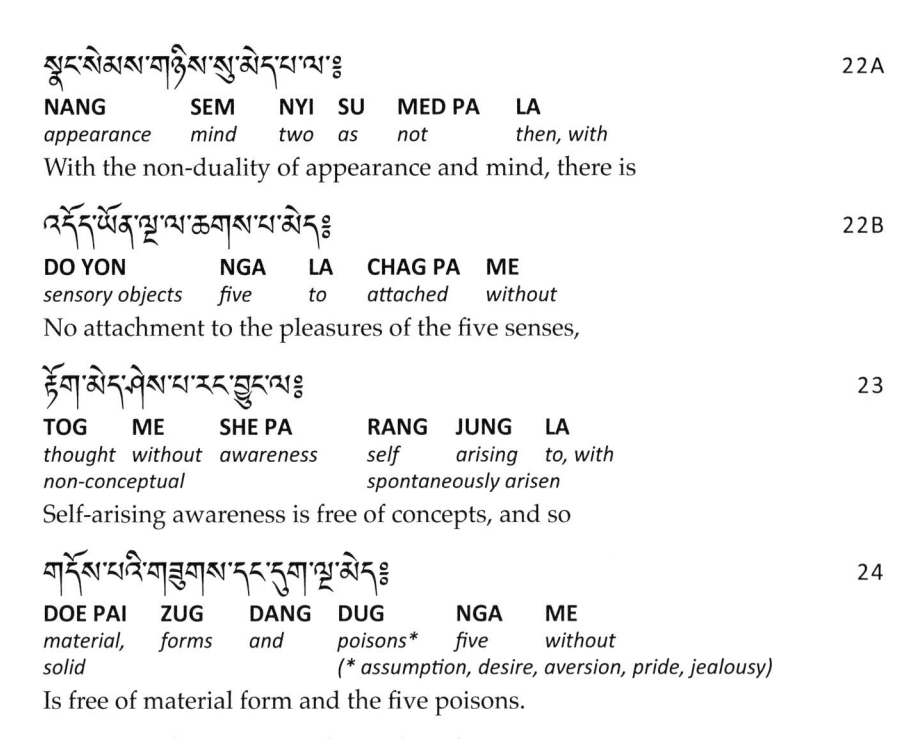

I, Samantabhadra, affirm the truth of the source free of causes and conditions. Awareness is intrinsically present with the source itself, untouched by the faults of separating outer and inner, and employing biased judgements, and untainted by the darkness of the loss of recollection and so spontaneous appearance is free of faults. Intrinsic awareness is fresh and unchanging. It is free of fear and panic even if the three worlds are destroyed. With the non-duality of appearance and mind, there is no attachment to the pleasures of the five senses. Self-arising awareness is free of concepts and so is free of material form and the five poisons.

THE RADIANCE OF AWARENESS

རིག་པའི་གསལ་ཆ་མ་འགགས་པ༔ 25

RIG PAI SAL CHA MA GAG PA
awareness clarity, aspect without interruption, ceasing
lucidity

The clarity aspect of awareness is uninterrupted,

The Evocation of Samantabhadra

དོ་བོ་གཅིག་ལ་ཡེ་ཤེས་ལྔ༔ 26

NGO WO   **CHIG**   **LA**   **YE SHE**   **NGA**
original face,   *single,*   *as*   *pristine knowing,*   *five*
essence   *one*   *illumination from awareness*

A single essence with five illuminations.

ཡེ་ཤེས་ལྔ་པོ་སྨིན་པ་ལས༔ 27

YE SHE   **NGA PO**   **MIN PA**   **LAE**
pristine knowing   *five*   *ripening,*   *with*
illumination   *blossom*

The five illuminations ripen as

ཐོག་མའི་སངས་རྒྱས་རིགས་ལྔ་བྱུང༔ 28

THOG MAI   **SANG GYAE**   **RIG**   **NGA**   **JUNG**
primordial   *buddha*   *families*   *five*   *arise*

The emanation of the five primordial buddha families.

དེ་ལས་ཡེ་ཤེས་མཐའ་རྒྱས་པས༔ 29

DE   **LAE**   **YE SHE**   **THA GYAE**   **PAE**
that   *from*   *pristine knowing,*   *expands,*   *by*
         illumination   *develops fully*

From this, illumination spreads out as

སངས་རྒྱས་བཞི་བཅུ་རྩ་གཉིས་བྱུང༔ 30

SANG GYE   **ZHIB CHU TSA NYI**   **JUNG**
buddhas   *forty-two*   *arise*
(peaceful)

The arising of the forty-two buddhas.

ཡེ་ཤེས་ལྔ་ཡི་རྩལ་ཤར་བས༔ 31

YE SHE   **NGA**   **YI**   **TSAL**   **SHAR**   **WAE**
pristine knowing,   *five*   *of*   *energy,*   *arising*   *by*
illumination   *expression*

Due to the rising energy of the five illuminations

ཁྲག་འཐུང་དྲུག་ཅུ་ཐམས་པ་བྱུང༔ 32

THRAG THUNG   **DRUG CHU**   **THAM PA**   **JUNG**
blood-drinking   *sixty*   *all*   *arise*
herukas

The sixty herukas manifest.

དེ་ཕྱིར་གཞི་རིག་འཁྲུལ་མ་མྱོང་༔ 33

DE CHIR	ZHI	RIG	THRUL	MA	NYONG
due to this	ground, source	awareness	deluded	not	influenced, taken over by, experienced

Due to this, awareness inseparable from the source never experiences delusion.

The clarity aspect of awareness is uninterrupted, a single essence with five illuminations. The five illuminations ripen as the emanation of the five primordial buddha families. From this, illumination spreads out as the arising of the forty-two buddhas. Due to the rising energy of the five illuminations the sixty herukas manifest. Due to this, awareness inseparable from the source never experiences delusion.

EVOCATION OF SAMANTABHADRA

ཐོག་མའི་སངས་རྒྱས་ང་ཡིན་པས༔ 34

THOG MAI	SANG GYAE	NGA	YIN	PAE
primordial, first, original	buddha	I	am	by

I am the primordial buddha, and so,

ང་ཡི་སྨོན་ལམ་བཏབ་པ་ཡིས༔ 35

NGA YI	MON LAM	TAB PA	YI
my	evocation	express	by

By expressing my evocation

ཁམས་གསུམ་འཁོར་བའི་སེམས་ཅན་གྱིས༔ 36

KHAM	SUM	KHOR WAI	SEM CHEN	GYI
realms	three	samsara, revolving	sentient beings	by

May all sentient beings in the three realms of samsara

རང་བྱུང་རིག་པ་ངོ་ཤེས་ནས༔ 37

RANG	JUNG	RIG PA	NGO	SHE	NE
self	arisen	awareness	face	see, awaken to	then

Awaken to their intrinsic self-arisen awareness and

ཡེ་ཤེས་ཆེན་པོ་མཐའ་རྒྱས་ཤོག༔

YE SHE — pristine knowing, illumination **CHEN PO** — great **THA GYE** — expand, vast, infinite **SHO** — may!

Find themselves in the infinity of great illumination!

ང་ཡི་སྤྲུལ་པ་རྒྱུན་མི་ཆད༔

NGA YI — my **TRUL PA** — emanations **GYUN** — stream **MI CHED** — not cut, unceasing

My emanations are unceasing:

བྱེ་བ་ཕྲག་བརྒྱ་བསམ་ཡས་འགྱེད༔

JE WA THRAG — trillions **GYA** — hundreds **SAM YAE** — inconceivable **GYE** — send out

Inconceivable trillions of diverse forms radiate,

གང་ལ་གང་འདུལ་སྣ་ཚོགས་སྟོན༔

GANG LA GANG — according to individual need **DUL** — help, train **NA TSOG** — various, diverse **TON** — show

Appearing according to the requirements of beings.

ང་ཡི་ཐུགས་རྗེའི་སྨོན་ལམ་གྱིས༔

NGA YI — my **THUG JE** — compassionate **MON LAM** — evocation **GYI** — by

Through my compassionate evocation

ཁམས་གསུམ་འཁོར་བའི་སེམས་ཅན་ཀུན༔

KHAM — realm **SUM** — three **KHOR WAI** — samsara, revolving **SEM CHEN** — sentient beings **KUN** — all

May all sentient beings revolving in the three realms

རིགས་དྲུག་གནས་ནས་འཐོན་པར་ཤོག༔

RIG — domain **DRUG** — six* **NAE** — places **NAE** — from **THON PAR** — escape **SHO** — may!
(* gods, jealous gods, humans, animals, hungry ghosts, hells)

Escape from the six domains of samsara!

I am the primordial Buddha, and so, by expressing my evocation may all sentient beings in the three realms of samsara awaken to their intrinsic self-arisen awareness and find themselves in the infinity of great illumination! My emanations are unceasing: inconceivable trillions of diverse forms radiate, appearing according to the requirements of beings. Through my compassionate evocation may all sentient beings revolving in the three realms escape from the six domains of samsara!

THE ARISING OF SENTIENT BEINGS

དང་པོ་སེམས་ཅན་འཁྲུལ་པ་རྣམས༔ 45

DANG PO   **SEM CHEN**   **THRUL PA**   **NAM**
beginning,   sentient beings   delusion,   all
at first   confusion

Deluded beings begin

གཞི་ལ་རིག་པ་མ་ཤར་བས༔ 46

ZHI   **LA**   **RIG PA**   **MA**   **SHAR**   **WAE**
ground, source   to   awareness   not   arise   by this

When awareness of the source does not arise.

ཅི་ཡང་དྲན་མེད་ཐོམ་མེ་བ༔ 47

CHI YANG   **DREN ME**   **THOM ME WA**
completely,   unconsciousness,   blankness
anything at all   no recollection

With no recollection at all there is blankness and

དེ་ཀ་མ་རིག་འཁྲུལ་པའི་རྒྱུ༔ 48

DE KA   **MA RIG**   **THRUL PAI**   **GYU**
that   unaware,   delusion   cause
      ignoring

Thus unawareness is the cause of delusion.

དེ་ལ་ཧད་ཀྱི་བརྒྱལ་བ་ལས༔ 49

DE LA   **HAD KYI**   **GYAL WA**   **LAE**
with that   sudden,   fainting   by, with
         instantly

After that comes sudden fainting followed by

དངངས་སྐྲག་ཤེས་པ་ཟ་ཟིར་འགྱུས༔ 50

NANG TRAG   **SHE PA**   **ZA ZIR**   **GYU**
fear   mind,   confused,   moving,
      thoughts   bewildered   agitated

Fearful thoughts and blurring agitation.

The Evocation of Samantabhadra

དེ་ལས་བདག་གཞན་དགྲར་འཛིན་སྐྱེས༔   51

DE	LA	DAG	ZHEN	DRAR	ZIN	KYE
that	from	self	other	as enemy, enmity	hold	arise, gives birth to

This gives rise to the active belief that self and others are enemies.

བག་ཆགས་རིམ་གྱིས་བརྟས་པ་ལས༔   52

BAG CHAG	RIM GYI	TAE PA	LAE
habits, tendencies	gradually	intensify, develop	from, due to

Habits and propensities gradually intensify and

འཁོར་བ་ལུགས་སུ་འཇུག་པ་བྱུང༔   53

KHOR WA	LUG	SU	JUG PA	JUNG
samsara	way	as	enter	arise, occurs

In this way samsara comes into formation.

Deluded beings begin when awareness of the source does not arise. With no recollection at all there is blankness and thus unawareness is the cause of delusion. After that comes sudden fainting followed by fearful thoughts and blurring agitation. This gives rise to the active belief that self and others are enemies. Habits and propensities gradually intensify and in this way samsara comes into formation.

དེ་ལས་ཉོན་མོངས་དུག་ལྔ་རྒྱས༔   54

DE	LAE	NYONG MONG	DUG	NGA	GYE
that	from	afflictions	poisons	five*	develop

(*stupidity, desire, aversion, pride, jealousy)

With this, the five afflicting poisons increase and

དུག་ལྔའི་ལས་ལ་རྒྱུན་ཆད་མེད༔   55

DUG	NGAI	LAE	LA	GYUN CHED ME
poisons	five's	activity	at	ceaselessly

There is ceaseless activity arising from these five poisons.

དེ་ཕྱིར་སེམས་ཅན་འཁྲུལ་བའི་གཞི༔   56

DE CHIR	SEM CHEN	THRUL WAI	ZHI
for that reason	sentient beings	delusion	source, ground

In this way the source of the delusion of sentient beings

དན་མེད་མ་རིག་ཡིན་པའི་ཕྱིར༔ 57

DREN ME MA RIG YIN PAI CHIR
recollection without ignorance is therefore
(i.e. unconscious)

Is ignorance without recollection.

སངས་རྒྱས་ང་ཡི་སྨོན་ལམ་གྱིས༔ 58

SANG GYE NGA YI MON LAM GYI
buddha I of evocation by

Therefore, I the Buddha make this evocation so that

ཁམས་གསུམ་སེམས་ཅན་ཐམས་ཅད་ཀྱིས༔ 58

KHAM SUM SEM CHEN THAM CHE KYI
realms three sentient beings all by

All sentient beings in the three realms

ཀུན་གྱིས་རིག་པ་དོ་ཤེས་ཤོག༔ 60

KUN GYI RIG PA NGO SHE SHO
all by awareness face see may!
 awaken to

May awaken to their own awareness!

With this, the five afflicting poisons increase and there is ceaseless activity arising from these five poisons. In this way the source of the delusion of sentient beings is ignorance without recollection. Therefore I, the Buddha, make this evocation so that all sentient beings in the three realms may awaken to their own awareness!

IGNORING AND DELUSION

ལྷན་ཅིག་སྐྱེས་པའི་མ་རིག་པ༔ 61

LHAN CHIG KYE PAI MA RIG PA
co-emergent, born ignoring
connate

With co-emergent ignoring

ཤེས་པ་དན་མེད་ཐོམ་མེ་བ༔ 62

SHE PA DREN ME THOM ME WA
mind without recollection blank

The mind is without recollection and blank.

The Evocation of Samantabhadra 261

ཀུན་ཏུ་བརྟགས་པའི་མ་རིག་པ༔ 63

KUN TU   **TAG PAI**   **MA RIG PA**
everything   naming*   ignoring
(* imagining and applying concepts, labels, signs and getting involved)
With the ignorance of identifying entities,

བདག་གཞན་གཉིས་སུ་འཛིན་པ་ཡིན༔ 64

DAG   **ZHEN**   **NYI**   **SU**   **DZIN PA**   **YIN**
self   other   two   as   keep, believe   is
Self and other are taken to be separate and distinct.

ལྷན་སྐྱེས་ཀུན་བརྟགས་མ་རིག་གཉིས༔ 65

LHAN KYE   **KUN TAG**   **MA RIG**   **NYI**
co-emergent   conceptual   ignoring   two, both
These two aspects of ignoring, co-emergent and identifying,

སེམས་ཅན་ཀུན་གྱི་འཁྲུལ་གཞི་ཡིན༔ 66

SEM CHEN   **KUN GYI**   **TRUL**   **ZHI**   **YIN**
sentient beings   all   of   delusion   source, basis   is
Are the source of the delusion of all sentient beings.

སངས་རྒྱས་ང་ཡི་སྨོན་ལམ་གྱིས༔ 67

SANG GYE   **NGA**   **YI**   **MON LAM**   **GYI**
buddha   I   of   evocation   by
I, the Buddha, make this evocation so that

འཁོར་བའི་སེམས་ཅན་ཐམས་ཅད་ཀྱི༔ 68

KHOR WAI   **SEM CHEN**   **THAM CHE**   **KYI**
samsara   sentient beings   all   of
All beings in samsara will

དྲན་མེད་འཐིབ་པའི་མུན་པ་སངས༔ 69

DREN ME   **THIB PAI**   **MUN PA**   **SANG**
non-recollection   thick, impenetrable   darkness   remove, purify
Remove the dense darkness of non-recollection,

གཉིས་སུ་འཛིན་པའི་ཤེས་པ་དྭངས༔ 70

NYI   **SU**   **DZIN PAI**   **SHE PA**   **DANG**
two   as   holding   mind   clear
Clarify the confusion of believing in duality, and

རིག་པ་རང་ངོ་ཤེས་པར་ཤོག༔ 71

RIG PA **RANG NGO** **SHE PAR** **SHO**
awareness own face, see, may!
 essence awaken to

Awaken to awareness as their true being!

With co-emergent ignoring the mind is without recollection and blank. With the ignorance of identifying entities, self and other are taken to be separate and distinct. These two aspects of ignoring, co-emergent and identifying, are the source of the delusion of all sentient beings. I, the Buddha, make this evocation so that all beings in samsara will remove the dense darkness of non-recollection, clarify the confusion of believing in duality, and awaken to awareness as their true being!

IGNORING RIPENS AS THE EXPERIENCE OF THE SIX REALMS

1. General and Human

གཉིས་འཛིན་བློ་ནི་ཐེ་ཚོམ་སྟེ༔ 72

NYI DZIN **LO NI** **THE TSOM** **TE**
dualistic intellect doubt, insecurity, thus
  uncertainty

Dualistic intelligence gives rise to uncertainty

ཞེན་པ་ཕྲ་མོ་སྐྱེས་པ་ལས༔ 73

ZHEN PA **THRA MO** **KYE PA** **LAE**
attachment, subtle creates then
longing

Arousing subtle longings

བག་ཆགས་འཐུག་པོ་རིམ་གྱིས་བརྟས༔ 74

BAG CHAG **THUG PO** **RIM GYI** **TAE**
habits, karmic heavy, gradually develop,
tendencies thick, coarse intensify

Which gradually intensify into dense habitual tendencies.

The Evocation of Samantabhadra

ཟས་ནོར་གོས་དང་གནས་དང་གྲོགས༔ 75

ZAE	NOR	GOE	DANG	NAE	DANG	DROG
food	wealth	clothing	and	dwelling	and	friends,
(i.e. the human realm)				places		companions

Food, wealth, clothing, dwellings, companions,

འདོད་ཡོན་ལྔ་དང་བྱམས་པའི་གཉེན༔ 76

DOE YON	NGA	DANG	JAM PAI	NYEN
desirable sense objects	five	and	loving	relatives

Objects desired by the five senses and beloved relations –

ཡིད་འོང་ཆགས་པའི་འདོད་པས་གདུངས༔ 77

YI ONG	CHAG PAI	DO PAE	DUNG
attractive, pleasurable	attachment	desire	torment

All these delights torment those who wish to have them.

དེ་དག་འཇིག་རྟེན་འཁྲུལ་བ་སྟེ༔ 78

DE DAG	JIG TEN	TRUL WA	TE
these	world	confusion, delusion	hence

All these worldly forms are generated by delusion.

གཟུང་འཛིན་ལས་ལ་ཟད་མཐའ་མེད༔ 79

ZUNG	DZIN	LAE	LA	ZAE THA	ME
graspable object	grasping subject	activities	to	end, limit inexhaustible	without

There is no end to activity arising from the interplay of graspable objects and grasping subjects.

Dualistic intelligence gives rise to uncertainty arousing subtle longings which gradually intensify into dense habitual tendencies. Food, wealth, clothing, dwellings, companions, objects desired by the five senses, and beloved relations – all these delights torment those who wish to have them. All these worldly forms are generated by delusion. There is no end to activity arising from the interplay of graspable objects and grasping subjects.

2. Hungry Ghosts

ཞེན་པའི་འབྲས་བུ་སྨིན་པའི་ཚེ༔ 80

ZHEN PAI   **DRAE BU**   **MIN PAI**   **TSE**
attachment   *fruit, result*   *ripened*   *when*

When the result of longing and clinging ripens,

ཀམ་ཆགས་གདུངས་བས་ཡི་དྭགས་སུ༔ 81

KAM CHAG   **DUNG WAE**   **YI DAG**   **SU**
craving   *tormented*   *hungry ghost*   *as*

There is birth as a craving tormented hungry ghost

སྐྱེས་ནས་བཀྲེས་སྐོམ་ཡ་རེ་ང༔ 82

KYE   **NAE**   **TRE**   **KOM**   **YA RE NGA**
born   *then*   *hunger*   *thirst*   *terrible, overwhelming*

Overwhelmed by hunger and thirst.

སངས་རྒྱས་ང་ཡི་སྨོན་ལམ་གྱིས༔ 83

SANG GYE   **NGA YI**   **MON LAM**   **GYI**
buddha   *my*   *evocation*   *by*

I, the Buddha, make this evocation so that

འདོད་ཆགས་ཞེན་པའི་སེམས་ཅན་རྣམས༔ 84

DOD   **CHAG**   **ZHEN PAI**   **SEM CHEN**   **NAM**
desire   *attachment*   *longing*   *sentient beings*   *all*

All sentient beings subject to desire, attachment and longing,

འདོད་པའི་གདུང་བ་ཕྱིར་མ་སྤངས༔ 85

DOD PAE   **DUNG WA**   **CHIR**   **MA**   **PANG**
by desire   *tormented, craving*   *back away*   *not*   *send, discard*

Neither discard the pangs of desire

འདོད་ཆགས་ཞེན་པ་ཚུར་མ་བླངས༔ 86

DOD   **CHAG**   **ZHEN PA**   **TSUR**   **MA**   **LANG**
desire   *attachment*   *longing*   *here, towards*   *not*   *take up, adopt*

Nor invite in desire, attachment and longing.

ཤེས་པ་རང་སོར་གློད་པ་ཡིས༔ 87

SHE PA	RANG SOR	LOD PA	YI
mind, mental activity	own mode, as it is, own place	relax, ease	by

With the mind released just as it is

རིག་པ་རང་སོ་ཟིན་གྱུར་ནས༔ 88

RIG PA	RANG SO	ZIN GYUR	NAE
awareness	self-restoring, self-refreshing	maintain, abide in own mode	then

Awareness settles refreshed in its own place.

ཀུན་རྟོག་ཡེ་ཤེས་ཐོབ་པར་ཤོག༔ 89

KUN TOG	YE SHE	THOB PAR	SHO
discerning	pristine knowing, illumination	gain, awaken to	may!

Then may all awaken to discerning illumination!

When the result of longing and clinging ripens, there is birth as a craving tormented hungry ghost overwhelmed by hunger and thirst. I, the Buddha, make this evocation so that all sentient beings subject to desire, attachment and longing, neither discard the pangs of desire nor invite in desire, attachment and longing. With the mind released just as it is awareness settles refreshed in its own place. Then may all awaken to discerning illumination!

3. Hells

ཕྱི་རོལ་ཡུལ་གྱི་སྣང་བ་ལ༔ 90

CHI ROL	YUL	GYI	NANG WA	LA
outside, external	object	of	appearance	to

With the appearance of objects taken to be external

འཇིགས་སྐྲག་ཤེས་པ་ཕྲ་མོ་འགྱུས༔ 91

JIG TRAG	SHE PA	TRA MO	GYU
fear	mind, thoughts	subtle, trembling	moves, agitation

There is agitation in the subtle mental formations experiencing fear.

སྣང་བའི་བག་ཆགས་བརྟས་པ་ལས༔ 92

DANG WAI   **BAG CHAG**   **TAE PA**   **LAE**
aversion   *habit, karma*   *intensifies*   *then*

This intensifies into the habitual tendency of aversion,

དགྲར་འཛིན་བརྡེག་གསོད་རགས་པ་སྐྱེས༔ 93

DRAR DZIN   **DEG**   **SOD**   **RAG PA**   **KYE**
enmity, believing   *beat,*   *kill*   *rough*   *arise*
others to be enemies   *violence*

Giving rise to violent wishes to beat and kill those taken to be enemies.

ཞེ་སྡང་འབྲས་བུ་སྨིན་པའི་ཚེ༔ 94

ZHE DANG   **DRAE BU**   **MIN PAI**   **TSE**
anger   *fruit*   *ripens*   *when*

When the result of anger ripens

དམྱལ་བའི་བཙོ་བསྲེག་སྡུག་རེ་བསྔལ༔ 95

NYAL WAI   **TSO**   **SEG**   **DUG RE NGAL**
hells   *boiled*   *burned*   *agony*

There is the agony of being boiled and burned in the hells.

With the appearance of objects taken to be external there is agitation in the subtle mental formations experiencing fear. This intensifies into the habitual tendency of aversion, giving rise to violent wishes to beat and kill those taken to be enemies. When the result of anger ripens there is the agony of being boiled and burned in the hells.

སངས་རྒྱས་ང་ཡི་སྨོན་ལམ་གྱིས༔ 96

SANG GYE   **NGA YI**   **MON LAM**   **GYI**
buddha   *my*   *evocation*   *by*

I, the Buddha, make this evocation so that

འགྲོ་དྲུག་སེམས་ཅན་ཐམས་ཅད་ཀྱིས༔ 97

DRO   **DRUG**   **SEM CHEN**   **THAM CHE KYI**
realms   *six*   *sentient beings*   *all*   *of*
of movement

All sentient beings moving in the six realms, will,

ཞེ་སྡང་དྲག་པོ་སྐྱེས་པའི་ཚེ༔ 98

ZHE DANG   **DRAG PO**   **KYE PAI**   **TSE**
anger   *intense, fierce*   *arises*   *when*

When intense anger arises

The Evocation of Samantabhadra

སྤང་བླང་མི་བྱ་རང་སོར་བཞག༔ 99

PANG	LANG	MI	JA	RANG SOR	ZHAG
abandoning, rejecting	adopting	not	do	own mode, place	abide in

Let the arising rest in its own place without adopting or rejecting.

རིག་པ་རང་སོ་ཟིན་གྱུར་ནས༔ 100

RIG PA	RANG SO	ZIN GYUR	NAE
awareness	as it is, self-restores	maintain, abide	then

Awareness settles relaxed in its own place.

གསལ་བའི་ཡེ་ཤེས་ཐོབ་པར་ཤོག༔ 101

SAL WAI	YE SHE	THOB PAR	SHO
clarity (i.e. mirror-like)	pristine knowing	gain, awaken to	may!

Then may all awaken to the clarifying illumination!

I, the Buddha, make this evocation so that all sentient beings moving in the six realms, will, when intense anger arises, let the arising rest in its own place without adopting or rejecting. Awareness settles refreshed in its own place. Then may all awaken to the clarifying illumination!

4. Gods

རང་སེམས་ཁེངས་པར་གྱུར་པ་ལས༔ 102

RANG	SEM	KHENG PAR	GYUR PA	LAE
own	mind	proud, conceited, inflated with pride	becomes	then

When the mind is swollen with pride

གཞན་ལ་འགྲན་སེམས་སྐྱེད་པའི་བློ༔ 103

ZHEN	LA	DRAN SEM	ME PAI	LO
others	to	competitive	contemptuous	intellect, attitude

One's intellect becomes competitive and contemptuous towards others.

ང་རྒྱལ་དྲེགས་པའི་སེམས་སྐྱེས་པས༔ 104

NGA GYAL	DREG PAI SEM	KYE	PAE
pride, arrogance	haughtiness	arises	by

Due to the arising of fierce pride

བདག་གཞན་འཐབ་རྩོད་སྡུག་བསྔལ་སྤྱོདཿ 105

DAG ZHAN THAB TSO DU NGAL CHO
self other conflict, quarrelling suffering experience

One experiences the suffering of quarrelling with others.

ལས་དེའི་འབྲས་བུ་སྨིན་པའི་ཚེཿ 106

LAE DE DRAE BU MIN PAI TSE
activity that fruit ripens when

When the result of this activity ripens

འཕོ་ལྟུང་མྱོང་བའི་ལྷ་རུ་སྐྱེསཿ 107

PHO   TUNG   NYONG WAI LHA RU KYE
cast out, falling   experience   god as born
die   down

One is born as a god and experiences ejection and downfall.

When the mind is swollen with pride one's intellect becomes competitive and contemptuous towards others. Due to the arising of fierce pride one experiences the suffering of quarrelling with others. When the result of this activity ripens one is born as a god and experiences ejection and downfall.

སངས་རྒྱས་ང་ཡི་སྨོན་ལམ་གྱིསཿ 108

SANG GYE NGA YI   MON LAM   GYI
buddha   my   evocation   by

I, the Buddha, make this evocation so that

ཁེངས་སེམས་སྐྱེས་པའི་སེམས་ཅན་རྣམསཿ 109

KHENG SEM   KYE PAI   SEM CHEN   NAM
conceited attitude   arisen   sentient beings all

All sentient beings who become conceited

དེ་ཚེ་ཤེས་པ་རང་སར་གློདཿ 110

DE   TSE   SHE PA   RANG SAR   LOE
that time   mind, mental   own   place relax, ease,
*   formation   not interfere*

Will at that time release their mental formations where they are.

རིག་པ་རང་སོ་ཟིན་གྱུར་ནསཿ 111

RIG PA   RANG SO   ZIN GYUR NAE
awareness   own mode,   abide   then
*   as it is*

Awareness settles refreshed in its own place, then

The Evocation of Samantabhadra

མཉམ་ཉིད་ཡེ་ཤེས་ཐོབ་པར་ཤོག༔ 112

NYAM NYI	YE SHE	THOB PAR	SHO
equanimity, equality	pristine knowing, illumination	gain, awakening to	may!

May they all awaken to the unbiased illumination!

I, the Buddha, make this evocation so that all sentient beings who become conceited will at that time release their mental formations where they are. Awareness settles refreshed in its own place, then may all awaken to the unbiased illumination!

5. Demigods

གཉིས་འཛིན་བརྟས་པའི་བག་ཆགས་ཀྱིས༔ 113

NYI	DZIN	TAE PAI	BAG CHAG	KYI
two	hold	intensifying	habit	by
belief in duality				

Due to intensification of the tendency to dualise

བདག་བསྟོད་གཞན་སྨོད་རྒྱག་རྡུའི་ལས༔ 114

DAG	TOE	ZHEN	MOE	ZUG NGUE	LAE
self	praise, glorify	others	disparage, belittle	affliction, painful disturbance	activity

There is the agitation of praising oneself and denigrating others.

འཐབ་རྩོད་འགྲན་སེམས་བརྟས་པ་ལས༔ 115

THAB TSOE	DREN SEM	TAE PA	LAE
fighting, quarrelsome	rivalry, competitiveness	intensifies	from this

From this comes increasingly quarrelsome rivalry.

གསོད་གཅོད་ལྷ་མིན་གནས་སུ་སྐྱེས༔ 116

SOE	CHOE	LHA MIN	NAE	SU	KYE
killed	cut up, mutilated	asura, demi-god	place	in	born

Due to this there is birth as a jealous god enduring mutilation and killing

འབྲས་བུ་དམྱལ་བའི་གནས་སུ་ལྷུང་༔ 117

DRAE BU	NYAL WAI	NAE SU	LHUNG
result	hell	place in	fall, plummet

With the result that one plummets into hell.

Due to intensification of the tendency to dualise there is the agitation of praising oneself and denigrating others. From this comes increasingly quarrelsome rivalry. Due to this there is birth as a jealous god enduring mutilation and killing, with the result that one plummets into hell.

སངས་རྒྱས་ང་ཡི་སྨོན་ལམ་གྱིས༔   118
SANG GYE   NGA YI   MON LAM   GYI
buddha   my   evocation   by
I, the Buddha, make this evocation so that

འགྲན་སེམས་འཐབ་རྩོད་སྐྱེས་པ་ལ༔   119
DRAN SEM   THAB TSO   KYE PA   LA
rivalry   fighting   born   to
Those born to rivalry and fighting

འགྲར་འཛིན་མི་བྱ་རང་སར་གློད༔   120
DRAR DZIN   MI   JA   RANG SAR   LOE
enmity   not do   own place   ease
Will cease from enmity and release these mental formations where they are.

ཤེས་པ་རང་སོ་ཟིན་གྱུར་ནས༔   121
SHE PA   RANG SO   ZIN GYUR   NAE
awareness   own mode   abide   then
Awareness settles refreshed as it is.

འཕྲིན་ལས་ཐོགས་མེད་ཡེ་ཤེས་ཤོག༔   122
THRIN LAE THOG ME   YE SHE   SHO
activity   unobstructed   pristine knowing,   may!
(all-accomplishing)   illumination
May they all awaken to illumination's unimpeded activity!

I, the Buddha, make this evocation so that those born to rivalry and fighting will cease from enmity and release these mental formations where they are. Awareness settles refreshed as it is. May all awaken to illumination's unimpeded activity!

The Evocation of Samantabhadra

6. Animals

དྲན་མེད་བཏང་སྙོམས་ཡེངས་པ་དང་༔ 123

DREN ME — unconscious, without recollection
TANG NYOM — without discernment, apathy
YENG PA — wavering, distracted
DANG — and

Due to non-recollection, apathy, distraction and

འཐིབས་དང་རྨུགས་དང་བརྗེད་ངས་དང་༔ 124

THIB — dull, foggy
DANG — and
MUG — torpor
DANG — and
JED NGAE — forgetfulness
DANG — and

Dullness, torpor, forgetfulness and

བརྒྱལ་དང་ལེ་ལོ་གཏི་མུག་གིས༔ 125

GYAL — fainting, fading
DANG — and
LE LO — lazy
TI MUG — assumption, confusion, stupidity
GI — by

Fainting, laziness and stupidity

འབྲས་བུ་སྐྱབས་མེད་བྱོལ་སོང་འཁྱམས༔ 126

DRAE BU — result, consequence
KYAB ME — unprotected
JOL SONG — animal
KHYAM — wander

There is the result of wandering as an animal without protection.

སངས་རྒྱས་ང་ཡི་སྨོན་ལམ་གྱིས༔ 127

SANG GYE — buddha
NGA YI — my
MON LAM — evocation
GYI — by

I, the Buddha, make this evocation so that

གཏི་མུག་བྱིང་བའི་སྨུན་པ་ལ༔ 128

TI MUG — stupidity, assumption
JING WAI — sinking
MUN PA — darkness
LA — towards, in

For those who sink in the darkness of stupidity

དྲན་པ་གསལ་བའི་མདངས་ཤར་ནས༔ 129

DRAN PA — recollection
SAL WAI — clarity
DANG — bright, radiant
SHAR — arise
NAE — then

The bright clarity of recollection will arise.

རྟོག་མེད་ཡེ་ཤེས་ཐོབ་པར་ཤོག༔

TOG	ME	YE SHE	THOB PAR	SHO
concept	without	pristine knowing,	gain,	may!
	(all-encompassing space)	illumination	awaken to	

130

May they awaken to the illumination unreliant on thoughts!

Due to non-recollection, apathy, distraction and dullness, torpor, forgetfulness and fainting, laziness and stupidity there is the result of wandering as an animal without protection. I, the Buddha, make this evocation so that for those who sink in the darkness of stupidity the bright clarity of recollection will arise. May all awaken to the illumination unreliant on thoughts!

SUMMARY

ཁམས་གསུམ་སེམས་ཅན་ཐམས་ཅད་ཀུན༔

KHAM	SUM	SEM CHEN	THAM CHE	KUN
realms	three	sentient beings	all	all

131

Each and every sentient being in the three realms

ཀུན་གཞི་སངས་རྒྱས་ང་དང་མཉམ༔

KUN ZHI	SANG GYE	NGA	DANG	NYAM
ground of all	buddha	I	and	equal, same

132

Has equally the same source as me, the Buddha.

དྲན་མེད་འཁྲུལ་བའི་གཞི་རུ་སོང༔

DREN ME	TRUL WAI	ZHI	RU	SONG
no recollection	deluded	basis, source	as	become

133

Yet for them this became the source of non-recollection and delusion and

ད་ལྟ་དོན་མེད་ལས་ལ་སྤྱོད༔

DAN TA	DON	ME	LAE	LA CHO
now	meaning, point, value	without	action	do, perform

134

Now they are busy with pointless activity.

ལས་དྲུག་རྨི་ལམ་འཁྲུལ་པ་འདྲ༔

LAE	DRUG	MI LAM	TRUL PA	DRA
actions	six*	dream	delusion	like
(* leading to birth in the six realms)				

135

Their activities of the six poisons are like a deluding dream.

The Evocation of Samantabhadra

Each and every sentient being in the three realms has equally the same source as me, the Buddha. Yet for them this became the source of non-recollection and illusion and now they are busy with pointless activity. Their activities of the six poisons are like a deluding dream.

ང་ནི་སངས་རྒྱས་ཐོག་མ་ཡིན༔ 136

NGA NI SANG GYE THOG MA YIN
I buddha primordial, am
first, original

I am the primordial buddha.

འགྲོ་དྲུག་སྤྲུལ་པས་འདུལ་བའི་ཕྱིར༔ 137

DRO DRUG TRUL PAE DUL WAI CHIR
beings six realms emanations educate in order to

In order to educate beings in the six realms with my emanations

ཀུན་ཏུ་བཟང་པོའི་སྨོན་ལམ་གྱིས༔ 138

KUN TU ZANG POI MON LAM GYI
Samantabhadra's evocation by

By this evocation of Samantabhadra,

སེམས་ཅན་ཐམས་ཅད་མ་ལུས་པ༔ 139

SEM CHEN THAM CHE MA LUE PA
sentient beings all without exception

May all sentient beings without exception

ཆོས་ཀྱི་དབྱིངས་སུ་འཚང་རྒྱ་ཤོག༔ 140

CHOE KYI YING SU TSANG GYA SHO
dharmadhatu, in awaken may!
all-encompassing space,
infinite hospitality

Awaken to perfect enlightenment in all-encompassing space!

I am the primordial Buddha. In order to educate beings in the six realms with my emanations by this evocation of myself, Samantabhadra, may all sentient beings without exception awaken to perfect enlightenment in all-encompassing space!

PRACTICE INSTRUCTION

ཨ་ཧོཿཕྱིན་ཆད་རྣལ་འབྱོར་སྟོབས་ཅན་གྱིསཿ 141

A HO	CHIN CHE	NAL JOR	TOB CHEN	GYI
expressive	in the future	yogi	powerful	by

A Ho! From now on, when a powerful yogi

འཁྲུལ་མེད་རིག་པ་རང་གསལ་ནསཿ 142

THRUL	ME	RIG PA	RANG	SAL	NAE
delusion	without	awareness	own	clarity	then, from

With the intrinsic clarity of awareness free of delusion

སྨོན་ལམ་སྟོབས་ཆེན་འདི་བཏབ་པསཿ 143

MON LAM	TOB CHEN	DI	TAB	PAE
evocation	powerful	this	recites	by

Recites this powerful evocation,

འདི་ཐོས་སེམས་ཅན་ཐམས་ཅད་ཀུནཿ 144

DI	THOE	SEM CHEN	THAM CHE	KUN
this	hear	sentient beings	all	all

All sentient beings who hear it

སྐྱེ་བ་གསུམ་ནས་མངོན་འཚང་རྒྱཿ 145

KYE WA	SUM	NAE	NGON	SANG GYA
life-times	three	then	full	buddhahood

Will be fully awakened in three lifetimes.

A Ho! From now on, when a powerful yogi with the intrinsic clarity of awareness free of delusion recites this powerful evocation, all sentient beings who hear it will be fully awakened in three lifetimes!

ཉི་ཟླ་གཟའ་ཡིས་ཟིན་པའམཿ 146

NYI	DA	ZA	YI	ZIN PA	AM
sun	moon	Rahu eclipse	by	held	or

If when the sun or moon is eclipsed in Rahu's grasp,

སྒྲ་དང་ས་གཡོས་བྱུང་བའམཿ 147

DRA	DANG	SA YOE	JUNG WA	AM
sound	and	earthquake	occurs	or

Or there are unusual sounds or earthquakes,

The Evocation of Samantabhadra

ཉི་མ་ཟློག་འགྱུར་ལོ་འཕོ་དུས༔ 148

NYI MA   DOG GYUR   LO PHO   DUE
sun   solstice   new year   time

Or at the solstice or at the turn of the year,

རང་ཉིད་ཀུན་ཏུ་བཟང་པོར་བསྐྱེད༔ 149

RANG NYID   KUN TU ZANG POR   KYE
yourself   Samantabhadra   imagine

Yogis visualise themselves as Samantabhadra and

ཀུན་གྱིས་ཐོབ་པར་འདི་བརྗོད་ན༔ 150

KUN   GYI   THOE PAR   DI   JOD   NA
all   by   hear   this   recite   if

Recite the evocation so that all can hear,

ཁམས་གསུམ་སེམས་ཅན་ཐམས་ཅད་ལ༔ 151

KHAM   SUM   SEM CHEN   THAM CHE   LA
realm   three   sentient beings   all   to

Then for all sentient beings in the three worlds

རྣལ་འབྱོར་དེ་ཡི་སྨོན་ལམ་གྱིས༔ 152

NAL JOR   DE   YI   MON LAM   GYI
yogi   these   of   evocation   by

The recitation of this evocation by yogis

སྡུག་བསྔལ་རིམ་གྱིས་གྲོལ་ནས་ཀྱང་༔ 153

DU NGAL   RIM GYI   DROL NAE   KYANG
suffering   gradually   relieve   also

Will bring gradual relief from suffering

མཐར་ཐུག་སངས་རྒྱས་ཐོབ་པར་ཤོག༔ 154

THAR THUG   SANG GYE   THOB PAR   SHO
finally   buddha   gain,   may!
*   awaken to*

And they will finally awaken to buddhahood!

If, when the sun or moon is eclipsed in Rahu's grasp, or there are unusual sounds or earthquakes, or at the solstice, or at the turn of the year, yogis visualise themselves as Samantabhadra and recite the evocation so that all can hear, then for all sentient beings in the three worlds the recitation of this evocation by yogis will bring gradual relief from suffering and they will finally awaken to buddhahood!

ཅེས་གསུངས་སོ༔ རྫོགས་པ་ཆེན་པོ་ཀུན་བཟང་དགོངས་པ་ཟང་ཐལ་དུ་བསྟན་པའི་རྒྱུད་ལས༔ སྨོན་ལམ་སྟོབས་པོ་ཆེ་བཏབ་པས་སེམས་ཅན་ཐམས་ཅད་འཚང་མི་རྒྱ་བའི་དབང་མེད་པར་བསྟན་པའི་ལེའུ་ཁོལ་དུ་ཕྱུང་བའོ།

Thus it is said. From THE DZOGCHEN TANTRA WHICH SHOWS THE DIRECT AWARENESS OF SAMANTABHADRA, this is extracted from the chapter which teaches that by reciting this powerful evocation it is impossible that all sentient beings will not attain enlightenment.

Translated by James Low in September 2017, Revised May 2018

As with all translations from Tibetan at this time, this version is provisional and further refinement of English equivalents to the many technical terms in Tibetan will evolve in time.

ཡུམ་དོན་དོ་སྒྲོད་པ་ནི།

UNCOVERING THE PRESENCE OF THE MOTHER OF ALL THE BUDDHAS

A Treasure Text of
Gonpo Wangyal

གང་ཟག་དབང་རྣོ་དད་འདུན་ཅན་རྣམས་ཀྱི་རྟོགས་ཆེན་གྱི་དགོངས་པ་ཉམས་སུ་ལེན་པར་འདོད་པ་རྣམས་ཡིད་འོང་དབེན་པའི་གནས་སུ༔ རང་གཞན་སེམས་ཅན་ཐམས་ཅད་བློ་ཡིས་བླང་སྟེ༔ དཀའ་ཐུབ་འགྱོར་གྱི་ལུས་རྟེན་ཐོབ༔ ཚེ་འདི་མི་རྟག་པ་བསྒོམ་པ་གཙོ་བོར་བྱས༔ འཁོར་བ་ལ་བློ་ལྡོག་སྟེ་སེམས་ཅན་གྱི་དོན་བྱའི་སྨོན་པའི་དང་ནས༔ སྒོ་གསུམ་རང་བབས་སུ་བཞག་སྟེ༔ ཕྱིའི་དོ་རི་བྲག་ཐམས་ཅད་དང་༔ ནང་ཆུད་ཀྱི་སེམས་ཅན་ཐམས་ཅད༔ རང་གི་སེམས་ཀྱིས་མིང་བཏགས་པ་ཙམ་མ་གཏོགས་མེད་པར་ཐག་བཅད༔ སེམས་དེ་ཡང་གཟུགས་དང་ཁ་དོག་དབྱིབས་ཐམས་ཅད༔ བྱུང་གནས་འགྲོ་གསུམ་གྱི་སྐྱོན་ཡང

279

ཡང་བཅད༔ ཀུན་ཏུ་བཏགས་པའི་དོ་བོ་ཡོད་པ་དེ་ཕྱི་ནང་རང་ལུས་མགོ་ནས་ཀྦྷང་པའི་བར་བཙལ་བས་མ་རྙེད་ནས༔ སྟོང་ཞིང་བདག་མེད་པར་ཡང་ཡང་བཏགས༔ སྟོང་པ་བདག་མེད་དེ་ལ་ཡིན་མིན་གྱི་བློ་སྣ་ཚོགས་གར་བས་བློ་དེ་ཡང་གཟུང་འཛིན་ཐམས་ཅད་དང་བྲལ་བ་ཡིན་པས༔ སྦྱོར་བསྡུ་དང་བྲེས་མི་གཅོད་པར་རང་བབས་སུ་བཞག་པས༔ གོ་མཁན་ཤེས་མཁན་ཚོར་མཁན་གྱི་རིག་པ་ཞིག་འདུག་པ་དེ་རིག་པའི་རང་མདངས་ཤར་བ་ཡིན་དེའི་རང་ལ་དུས་རྒྱུན་དུ་གནད་དུ་བསྐྱུན་པ་གལ་ཆེའོ། བདེ་སྐྱིད་ཀྱི་ཉམས་ཅི་བྱུང་ཡང་རིག་པའི་རང་མདངས་ཤར་བ་ཡིན་པར་ཐག་བཅད༔ བཟོ་བཅོས་གང་ཡང་མི་བྱེད་པར་ཉམས་ཀྱི་སྡུག་བསྡལ་ཡིད་སེམས་དང་རིག་པའི་ཡེ་ཤེས་གཉིས་མེད་དུ་བསྒྱོལ་བས་རིག་པ་ཁོ་ན་ལ་གཙོ་བོར་འདུག་པ་ཤེས་པ་གལ་ཆེ༔ དེ་ཡང་མ་བཅོས་ཡེ་གནས་ཀྱི་རིག་པ་ཡེ་ཤེས་ཀྱི་རང་བཞིན་དུ་རྟེན་ནེ་བ༔ ཡེངས་མེད་ཡུལ་མེད་འཛིན་མེད་དུས་ལ་ཧྲིག་གེ་བ་འཁོར་འདས་ཀྱི་རྟོག་ཚོགས་ཐམས་ཅད་ཡེ་གདོད་མའི་གཞི་ལ་རྟོགས་པ༔ དེ་དགོས་ཐམས་ཅད་དང་བྲལ་བའི་རིག་པ་མངོན་སུམ་དུ་མཐོང༔ དོན་ལ་རྟོག་ཚོགས་གར་འདང་རིག་པའི་རང་མདངས་ཁོ་ན་ལས་མེད་པར་ཐག་ཆོད་དགོས༔ སྣང་ཚད་རང་སྣང་གསལ་སྣང་འགགས་མེད་དུ༔ གོད་ནས་གོད་འཕེལ་དུ་རིག་པ་འཕོ་འགྱུར་མེད་པ་ཀུན་ལ་ཁྱབ་བདལ་དུ་རྟོགས་འདུག་པ་ནི་བཙོད་མེད་དོན་གྱི་བློ་འདས་ཆོས་ཟད་བློས་མེད་ཆེན་པོ་ལྷུན་གྲུབ་ཡུག་རྒྱ་ཆེན་པོ་ཀུན་བཟང་ཐུགས་ཀྱི་དགོངས་པ་མངོན་དུ་འགྱུར༔ བར་དོར་དབྱིངས་སུ་གྲོལ༔ སེམས་ཅན་ཐམས་ཅད་ཀྱི་དོན་བྱེད་ནུས་པའི་བདག་ཉིད་ཅན་ཡིན་ནོ༔ དེ་ལྟར་ཉམས་སུ་ལེན་པ་གལ་ཆེ༔ ཡུམ་དོན་ཏོ་སྦྱོང་ཞི་སོང༔

BRIGHT, ACUTE PEOPLE WITH STRONG FAITH who wish to practise the immediacy of dzogchen, should stay in a peaceful, isolated place and reflect on their own situation and that of all sentient beings.

At the moment, we find ourselves having the freedoms and opportunities that support practice, so it is vital that we meditate on the impermanence of this life situation. Developing revulsion for samsara and abiding in the attitude of wanting to benefit sentient beings, we let our body, speech and mind be as they are without doing anything artificial.

The entire outer container consisting of the earth, stones, mountains, rocks and so on, together with its inhabitants, all sentient beings, are only names and definitions put by your mind. Examine this until it is truly clear. Regarding your mind, you must again and again establish whether it has any form, colour or size, and whether it comes from anywhere, stays anywhere or goes anywhere. When, due to relying on reificatory identification, you think that you have found some real essence, then search outside and inside, examine your own body from head to toe until you are sure that nothing can be found.

Again and again establish clearly that there is only emptiness devoid of inherent self-identity. Regarding this emptiness devoid of inherent self-identity, many different thoughts about the existence or non-existence of entities arise, yet these distinguishing concepts are themselves inherently free of the duality of subjects who identify and objects which are identified. Therefore, without awaiting future thoughts or going after past ones, let the mind flow freely. With this, the awareness of the one who understands, thinks or perceives is the arising of the intrinsic radiance of awareness itself. It is vital to always abide in this presence.

Whatever feelings come, be they happy or troublesome, they are the arising of the intrinsic radiance of awareness. Practise so that this becomes clear to you.

Then, without the least effort or artificiality, whatever experiences arise will be liberated in the non-duality encompassing all of our habitual ideation, conceptualisation, object-engaged mental activity and the pristine illumination of awareness. It is vital to directly awaken to presence as this awareness. This is the most important point.

Furthermore, pristine illumination awareness, unartificial, primordially open and at ease, is, of itself, naked, unwavering, free of objects to rely on and the tendency to rely. It is clear, bright, the original unchanging ground and sphere of all the multitude of concepts that constitute samsara and nirvana. Be present with the immediacy of your own awareness free of all hopes and doubts!

It is vital to directly see that all the many different thoughts which arise are nothing other than the intrinsic radiance of awareness. With the ceaseless flow of specific appearances as not other than one's own experience, the appearance of clarity will improve and develop, and unchanging omnipresent awareness will become one's way of being. With this one abides present in the inexpressible truth of the inconceivable great non-meditation of the end of all things, the spontaneous mahamudra, the heart of Samantabhadra. In the bardo you will be liberated in infinite hospitality. You will truly have the power to work for the benefit of all beings. It is vital to practise in this way.

This concludes "Uncovering the Presence of the Mother of all the Buddhas".

From Gonpo Wangyal's treasure,
"Pure Vision Opening The Door To Liberation"

Translated by C R Lama and James Low, 1975
Revised by James Low, 2018

མཁའ་འགྲོ་རྡོ་རྗེ་དཔལ་སྒྲོན་མའི་ཞལ་གདམས་མན་ངག་ཟིན་བྲིས་བཞུགས།།

THE RECORD OF THE HEART-FELT ADVICE OF THE DAKINI, INDESTRUCTIBLE GLORIOUS LAMP

BY *AYU KHANDRO*

ཧཱུྂ༔ ཀ་དག་སྟོང་པ་ཆེན་པོའི་དབྱིངས་ཉིད་ལས། སྣ་ཚོགས་སྐུ་འཕྲུལ་གཟུགས་ཀྱི་སྐུར་སྟོན་པས། རྣག་འཛུག་བདེ་ཆེན་བདུད་རྩིས་ཡོངས་སྨིན་མ། མཁའ་འགྲོ་གཙོ་མོ་དཔལ་གྱི་སྒྲོན་མར་འདུད།།

ཧཱུྂ༔ སྙིང་པོ་འཁོར་བ་དང་ཞི་བ་ཐུང་འདས་ཐམས་ཅད་རྩ་བ་ནི་རང་གི་སེམས་ལ་ཐུག་ཡོད།[1] སེམས་དེ་ཡང་བཏགས་ན་བདེན་པར་གྲུབ་པ་ཅི་ཞིག་ཀྱང་མེད།[2] སྐྱེ་འགྲོ་སེམས་ཅན་ཐམས་ཅད་གཞི་བདེ་བར་གཤེགས་པའི་སྙིང་པོས་མ་ཁྱབ་པ་གཅིག་ཀྱང་མེད།[3] དོན་ཀྱང་མ་རིག་རྟོག་པའི་ལས་རླུང་གཡོས་པའི་རྐྱེན་གྱིས་ཀུན་ཀྱང་གཅིག་འཛིན་གྱི་དབར་འཁྲུལ་པར་གྱུར་ཅིང་འཁོར་བ་མཐར་མེད་དུ་འཁྱམས་དགོས་པ་འདི་བྱུང་བ་ཡིན།[4]

སེམས་ཀྱི་གནས་ཀྱི་གནས་ལུགས་སེམས་ཉིད་དམ། ཡེ་གཞི་སྟིང་པོ་བྱང་ཆུབ་ཀྱི་སེམས་དེའི་ཐོག་མར་བཟང་ངན་གྱི་རྒྱ་གདགས་ཀྱུང་མ་བསྐྱེད་པས་རང་བྱུང་། ལམ་གྱིས་བསྒོམ་དུ་མེད་པས་རང་གྲོལ། འབྲས་བུ་བསྒྲུབ་ཏུ་མེད་པས་ཡེ་རྫོགས། ཚིག་གིས་བརྗོད་དུ་མེད་པས་མཚོན་མ་ལས་འདས་པ། བསམ་པས་དཔྱད་དུ་མེད་པས་བློ་འདས་ཆེན་པོ། མཐར་བརྒྱད་བྲལ་བ་ཐམས་ཅད་ལས་ཡོངས་སུ་འདས་པའི་རིག་སྟོང་ཆེན་པོ་སྟེ། འོད་གསལ་གཉུག་མའི་དང་དུ་ཅི་བདེར་བཞག་པས་རང་སར་གྲོལ་བ་ཡིན༡

འོན་ཀྱང་སྣ་ཚོགས་རྟོག་པའི་སྣ་མས་སྟེ་ལམ་བཞིན་དུ་འཁོར་བའི་གྱོང་དུ་ཁྲིད་ཅིང་། རང་དོང་བསླུས་ན་བདེན་པས་སྟོང་པའི་ཕྱིར་སངས་རྒྱས་ཞེས་ལ་དེ་ཡང་རང་གི་གཤིས་ཀྱི་ཡིན་ལུགས་ཙམ་ལས་གཞན་པ་ཅི་ཞིག་ཀྱང་འཚོལ་དུ་མེད། གལ་གཤིས་ཀྱི་གནས་ལུགས་དེ་ཀ་བྱུང་བའི་ཆོས་གང་གིས་ཀྱང་བསྒྱུར་དུ་མི་གཏུབ། གནས་ལུགས་ཡིན་ཕྱོག་དེར་རང་བབས་སུ་བཞག་ན་དེ་ལས་མི་གཡོ་བ་འབྱུང་༢

དེ་ལ་གཉེན་པོ་བསྟེན་ན་གོལ་སྒྲིབ་ཀྱི་གཉེར་འགྱུར་བས་གཉེན་པོ་གང་ཞིག་ཀྱང་མི་འཚོལ། བཟང་ངན་གྱི་རྟོག་པ་ཅི་སྐྱེས་ནའང་མ་བཅོས་མ་བསླད་པར་རང་སར་ལྷན་ནེར་བཞག་ཅིང་གསལ་ཚམ་རིག་ཚམ་པའི་དང་དེ་ཀའི་རྒྱུན་བསྐྱངས་ན་རྟོག་ཚོགས་རང་དོར་གྲོལ་ཐུབ་པ་ཞིག་ཡོང་། བསྒོམ་དུ་མེད་པའི་དེ་བཞིན་ཉིད་ལ་བསྟེན་གོམས་རྒྱུན་བསྐྱངས་ལས་ཉིན་མོངས་པ་རིམ་གྱིས་འགྲི། དེ་བཞིན་ཉིད་ཀྱི་རྒྱུན་སྐྱོང་སྲངས་ཀྱང་། ཇི་ལྟར་སྨྲ་བསྟན་གྱི་རྒྱུད་རན་པོར་བསྐུལ་དགོས་པ་ལྟར་ཐབ་སྐྱོད་རན་པོའི་དང་ནས་མ་ཡེངས་དྲན་པའི་དང་བསྐྱངས་དགོས་པ་ཡིན། དཔྱད་པའི་སྒོམ་པ་གཉིས་ཀྱང་འཆང་མི་རྒྱབས་རིག་པ་རྗེན་གཅེར་དུ་འབྱུང་དེ་སྐྱ་ཅིག་རྟོགས་པའི་ཡེ་ཤེས་དེ་ཀའི་དང་གདངས་བསྒྱུར་དགོས་པ་འདི་ཉི་ཛམས་ལེན་མི་སྲོག་ཙ་ལྔ་བུ་ཡིན༣

ཆོས་ཐམས་ཅད་སྟོང་པ་ཡིན་དུ་ཁས་ལེན་མཁན་དང་ཤོད་མཁན་དུ་མ་ཞིག་ཡོད་མོད། དབང་དུས་སུ་བསྟན་པའི་ལྷན་སྐྱེས་རིག་སྟོང་དེ་ཉིད་ལྟའི་ཤེས་པ་ཡོད་དཔྱད་ལས་འདས་པ། གཏེར་

གོལ་སྐྱོན་ཅིག་མའི་རོག ། མ་བཅོམ་ཅིག་བཞག་རྟོགས་པ་ཆེན་པོ་འདི་རང་ཡིན་ལ། ༴

དེ་ཡང་སྟོང་པས་རྒྱས་འདེབས་པའི་ལུགས་ཀྱང་མིན་ལ། དབྱིངས་སུ་རིག་པ་གཏོད་པའི་འཛིན་པ་འང་མིན་པོ། ༶

གང་ཤར་རིག་པ་སྐྱོང་ཐོག་ཏུ་ལ་བཟླ་བ་འདི་ཉི་མ་ན་དྭགས་ཀུན་གྱི་སྙིང་པོ་དུ་ཞེས་པར་མཛོད་ཅིག ། ༡༠ ཅེས་གསུངས་སོ།།

[སྤྱན་འདྲེ་

༡ཕྱི་ ༢ནང་སྟོང་པ་རང་བཞིན་མེད་ ༣རིག་པའི་གནས་ལུགས་ ༤མི་རིག་པའི་འཁྲུལ་ལུགས་དངོས་གཞི་ ༥གཞི་གནས་ལུགས་སྐྱོང་ ༦མ་རིག་ཤེལ་ཕྱིར་ལམ་ཅིག་དགོས་ ༧ལམ་གྱི་སྒྲོན་མེ་བའི་ཁྱད་ ༨ཕྱིའི་འབྲས་བུ་ ༩འབྲས་བུའི་སྦྱོན་ ༡༠སྙིང་ཚིག]

From the primordial purity of infinite hospitality free of artifice
By showing diverse illusory forms she is completely euphoric
With the elixir of the great joy of non-duality.
We bow to the supreme dakini Glorious Lamp.

ARRIVE AT THE CLARITY that all that constitutes the realms of becoming, known as samsara, and the peace of liberation, known as nirvana, has just one root – one's own mind.[1] If this mind is examined it is found to be without any inherent existence.[2]

There is not one single sentient being anywhere whose ground or basis is not the buddha nature or heart of all the sugatas.[3] However, due to the circumstances of the movement of the karmic wind arising from the mental activity generated by ignorance, these beings are all enveloped by the net of dualism and so have to wander endlessly in endless samsara.[4]

The actual situation of the mind, the mind itself, or the truth (sNying Po) of the primordial ground or basis, bodhicitta, the mind as it is, is from the very beginning uninfluenced in any way by the causal force of discriminating between good and bad, and thus is self-present. It is free of any meditation which belongs to a path and thus is self-liberating. It is free of the accomplishments of the result and thus is complete from the very beginning. It is free of communication by language and thus is beyond the realms of signs. It is not accessible to measurement by thought and thus is the great freedom from the intellect. It is completely beyond all the elaborations of the eight* limiting positions and thus is the great inseparability of awareness and emptiness. Whatever occurs, it remains happily in the state of unchanging original clarity and thus is self-liberating in its own place.[5]

However, due to the illusion of diverse thoughts in the manner of a dream, sentient beings are led to all the sites of existence in samsara. When you have seen your own origin, by the truth of that, due to emptiness, the way of being of how you are is what is known as 'buddha' and you won't go searching for anything else. Indeed the manner of abiding of the ground cannot be altered by the activity of any phenomena. The manner of abiding just is, and with it there is no interruption of the spontaneous flow and thus there is no wavering from it.[6]

Having confidence in this ally, when mistakes and confusion occur you will not go looking for other allies. And when good or bad thoughts of whatever kind arise, without artificiality or adulteration, remain shining in your own place. By continuously keeping to just that state of clarity and awareness you will experience the self-liberation of whatever occurs. By developing the continuous practice of the non-meditation of thusness, the afflictions will gradually diminish. However, although we practice to always abide in thusness, just as a sweet sound requires the string to be just right, if you find you are tuned too tightly or too loosely then you must maintain the state of undistracted recollection.

It is not useful to hold to any kind of analytic contemplation, therefore let awareness be naked and uncovered. The very state of the original knowing of that instant actualising is to be experienced in its fullness. This is the life blood of practice.[7]

There are many who accept and explain that all phenomena are empty. But simultaneous awareness and emptiness that is shown at the time of initiation is your own current presence which is beyond being judged as existing. Your nature is instant naked liberation. Unartificial, instantly at ease infinite completion (*dzogchen*) – this is it.[8]

Furthermore there is no other way of opening with emptiness. You can turn towards awareness of infinite hospitality, or not.[9]

At the time of enjoying everything in awareness this instruction essence of all arose in my mind.[10]

Ayu Khandro

GUIDE TO THE TOPICS

1 to 4 is the Introduction.
    1   outer and 2 inner. Both are empty with no inherent self-nature.
    3   the manner of being of presence.
    4   the confused manner of ignorance.

5 to 9 is the Main Part.
    5   the nature of the base/ground/source.
    6   the need for a path in order to remove ignorance.
    7   an explanation to clear the faults of the path.
    8   the general result.
    9   faults regarding the result.
    10   heart statement.

*   beginning and ending, nihilism and eternalism, coming and going, unity and diversity

Translated by James Low, 1983 and revised 2018

LINKS TO THE ORIGINAL TEXTS AND TEACHINGS ON THEM

James Low taught in the past extensively on these four texts of this last chapter, Sweet Simplicity. Audio and video recordings of these teachings are made available either on James Low's website or on his Vimeo channel.

Additionally most of these texts are translated in several other languages which can be viewed and downloaded for free for personal use.

The Dhammapada: An edition, containing versions of the text in Pali, Sanskrit and Tibetan with Hindi and English translations, was prepared by C R Lama and published in 1985. It has been scanned in 2018 and made freely available: simplybeing.co.uk/dhammapada/.

You can find all these links as well as the original texts on James Low's website www. simplybeing.co.uk. An overview of all links can be found on the following address: www.wandel-verlag.de/finding-freedom-dlds

We wish to thank all those people who enthusiastically and sedulously made this available in collaborative effort. May it be useful.

Khordong Commentary Series

I   Martin J. Boord. *A Bolt Of Lightning From The Blue, The vast commentary on Vajrakīla that clearly defines the essential points.* edition khordong. Berlin, 2002. reprint: Wandel Verlag. Berlin, 2010

II   James Low. *Being Right Here, Commentary on The Mirror of Clear Meaning by Nuden Dorje.* Snow Lion. New York & Colorado, 2004

II.dt   – *Hier und Jetzt Sein. Ein Kommentar zu „Don Sal Melong" – „Der Spiegel der klaren Bedeutung", ein Dzogchen-Schatztext von Nuden Dorje.* Überarbeitete Neuauflage, edition khordong, Wandel Verlag. Berlin, 2018

II.pl   – *Być tu i teraz.* wydawnictwo A. Kraków, 2005

II.it   – *Esserci, Un commento a »Lo specchio del chiaro significato.«* Ubaldini Editore. Roma, 2005

II.fr   – *Le Miroir au Sens Limpide.* Éditions Almora. 2009

II.es   – *Aquí y ahora.* Ediciones Dharma. España, 2011

II.es   – *Estar Cá Presente Um Texto Do Tesouro Dzogchen De Nuden Dorje Intitulado O Espelho Do Significado Claro.* partly and digital only. Portuguese, 2017

III   James Low. *Being Guru Rinpoche, Commentary on Nuden Dorje's Terma: The Vidyadhara Guru Sadhana.* Trafford. Canada, 2006

III.pl   – *Być Guru Rinpocze.* Wydawnictwo Norbu. 2006

III.dt   – *Eins mit Guru Rinpoche.* edition khordong. Berlin, 2007. reprint: edition khordong, Wandel Verlag. Berlin, 2012

III.fr   – *Dans le Mandala de Padmasambhava.* Editions Khordong.France. Lyon, 2008

III.es   – *Ser Guru Rimpoché.* Ediciones Dharma, España, 2013

IV   Tulku Tsultrim Zangpo (Tulku Tsurlo). *The Five Nails – A Commentary on the Northern Treasures Accumulation Praxis.* edition khordong, Wandel Verlag. Berlin, 2011

IV.dt   – *Die Fünf Nägel – Ein Kommentar zu den Vorbereitenden Übungen der Nördlichen Schätze.* edition khordong, Wandel Verlag. Berlin, 2011

Further titles

V   Rig-'dzin rdo-rje (Martin J. Boord). *A Roll of Thunder from the Void, Vajrakīla Texts of the Northern Treasures Tradition, Volume Two.* edition khordong, Wandel Verlag. Berlin, 2010

VI   Chimed Rigdzin Rinpoche, James Low. *Radiant Aspiration, The Butterlamp Prayer: Lamp of Aspiration.* Simply Being. London, 2011

VI.dt   – *Lichter der Weisheit, Das Butterlampen-Wunschgebet von Chhimed Rigdzin Rinpoche. Mit einem Kommentar von James Low.* edition khordong, Wandel Verlag. Berlin, 2014

VI.pl   – *Ą Świetliste Dążenie.* kuntuzangpo.net, 2013

VI.es   – *La Aspiración Radiante.* Ediciones Dharma. España, 2017

VII.tib   Tulku Tsultrim Zangpo (Tulku Tsurlo). *Boundless Vision. A Byangter Manual on Dzogchen Training. An Outline Commentary on the Boundless Vision of Universal Goodness (Kun bZang dGongs Pa Zang Thal).* Tibetischer Text. edition khordong, Wandel Verlag. Berlin, 2012

VIII   Rig-'dzin rdo-rje (Martin J. Boord). *Illuminating Sunshine, Buddhist funeral rituals of Avalokiteśvara.* edition khordong, Wandel Verlag. Berlin, 2012

IX.dt   James Low. *Zuhause im Spiel der Wirklichkeit, Ein Kommentar zum Dzogchen Schatztext »Unmittelbares Aufzeigen der Buddhaschaft jenseits aller Klassifizierung« von Nuden Dorje.* edition khordong, Wandel Verlag. Berlin, 2012

X   Rig-'dzin rdo-rje (Martin J. Boord). *Gathering the Elements, Vajrakīla Texts of the Northern Treasures Tradition, Volume One.* edition khordong, Wandel Verlag. Berlin, 2013

XI   Rigzin Pema Tinley / Khenpo Chowang. *The Path of Secret Mantra: Teachings of the Northern Treasures Five Nails. Pema Tinley's guide to vajrayāna practice.* edition khordong, Wandel Verlag. Berlin, 2014

XII   Rig-'dzin rdo-rje (Martin J. Boord). *A Blaze of Fire in the Dark, Homa rituals of Vajrakīla. Vajrakīla Texts of the Northern Treasures Tradition, Volume Three.* edition khordong, Wandel Verlag. Berlin, 2015

XIII   – *A Cloudburst of Blessings, The water initiation and other rites of empowerment for the practice of the Northern Treasures Vajrakīla, Vajrakīla Texts of the Northern Treasures Tradition, Volume Four.* edition khordong, Wandel Verlag. 2017

XIV   James Low. *Finding Freedom. Texts from the Theravadin, Mahayana and Dzogchen Buddhist traditions.* Introduced and translated by James Low with the guidance of Chimed Rigdzin Rinpoche. edition khordong, Wandel Verlag. Berlin, 2019

Other titles

Die Geheimen Dakini-Lehren, Padmasambhavas mündliche Unterweisungen der Prinzessin Tsogyal, Ein Juwel der Tibetischen Weisheitsliteratur. Überarbeitete Neuausgabe. edition khordong, Wandel Verlag. Berlin, 2011

Tulku Thondup. *Die verborgenen Schätze Tibets, Eine Erklärung der Termatradition der Nyingmaschule des Buddhismus.* Überarbeitete Neuausgabe. edition khordong, Wandel Verlag. Berlin, 2013

The Seven Chapters of Prayer, as taught by Padma Sambhava of Urgyen, known in Tibetan as Le'u bDun Ma. Translated by Chhimed Rigdzin Rinpoche & James Low. With an introduction by James Low. Practice texts. edition khordong. Berlin, 2008. reprint: Wandel Verlag. Berlin, 2010

Das Gebet in sieben Kapiteln gelehrt von Padmasambhava (Le'u bDun Ma), editiert von Chhimed Rigdzin Rinpoche. Übersetzt aus dem tibetischen von Chhimed Rigdzin Rinpoche & James Low. Übertragung ins Deutsche von Jomo Gudrun & Camel Chhimed Wangpo. Praxistext. edition khordong. Berlin, 2008. Nachdruck: Wandel Verlag. Berlin, 2010

Die Fünf Nägel, Die vorbereitenden Übungen der Nördlichen Schätze. Überarbeiteter und ergänzter Praxistext. edition khordong, Wandel Verlag. Berlin, 2013

James Low. *Aus dem Handgepäck eines Tibetischen Yogi – Grundlegende Texte der Dzogchen-Tradition.* Überarbeitete Neuausgabe. edition khordong, WV. Berlin, 2013

Keith Dowman. *Der Flug des Garuda, Fünf Dzogchen-Texte aus dem tibetischen Buddhismus.* Erweiterte & überarbeitete Neuausgabe. edition khordong, Wandel Verlag. Berlin, 2015

Dudjom Rinpoche. *Die Klausur auf dem Berge, Dzogchen-Lehren und Kommentare.* Erweiterte & überarbeitete Neuausgabe. edition khordong, Wandel Verlag. 2016

James Low. *Gesammelte Schriften von Chimed Rigdzin Rinpoche (C R Lama), Zusammengestellt und herausgegeben von James Low.* edition khordong, Wandel Verlag. Berlin, 2016

Dudjom Lingpa. *Buddhaschaft ohne Meditation, Eine visionäre Beschreibung, bekannt als »Verfeinerung der eigenen Wahrnehmung« (Nang-jang).* edition khordong, Wandel Verlag. Berlin, 2018

Chögyam Trungpa. *Das Herz des Buddha. Buddhistische Lebenspraxis im modernen Alltagsleben.* Herausgegeben von Judith L. Lief. edition khordong, Wandel Verlag. Berlin, 2018

In preparation

JAMES LOW. *Freiheit Erlangen. Texte aus den buddhistischen Traditionen des Theravada, Mahayana und Dzogchen.* Herausgegeben und übersetzt von James Low.

PADMASAMBHAVA UND JAMGÖN MIPHAM. *Die Girlande der Sichtweisen. Eine Anleitung zu Sicht, Meditation und Resultat der Neun Fahrzeuge.*

JAMGÖN MIPHAM. *Strahlende Essenz – Ein Leitfaden für das Guhyagarbha-Tantra.*

The Five Nails, the accumulation praxis of the Northern Treasures. Practice text. Re-edited and supplimented.

Vajrakila Texts of the Northern Treasures Tradition
by Rig-'dzin rdo-rje (Martin J. Boord)

Volume 5: *An Overwhelming Hurricane*
Averting disaster and turning back obstacles for the benefit of a wider world. *forthcoming*

Volume 6: *A Fortress of Solid Rock*
Completing the accumulation of the essential life force and consolidating all the elements of the tradition in order to remain firm in one's *samādhi. forthcoming*

BPC-105WN

ISBN 978-3-942380-27-0